IMAGES
of America

BENTONVILLE

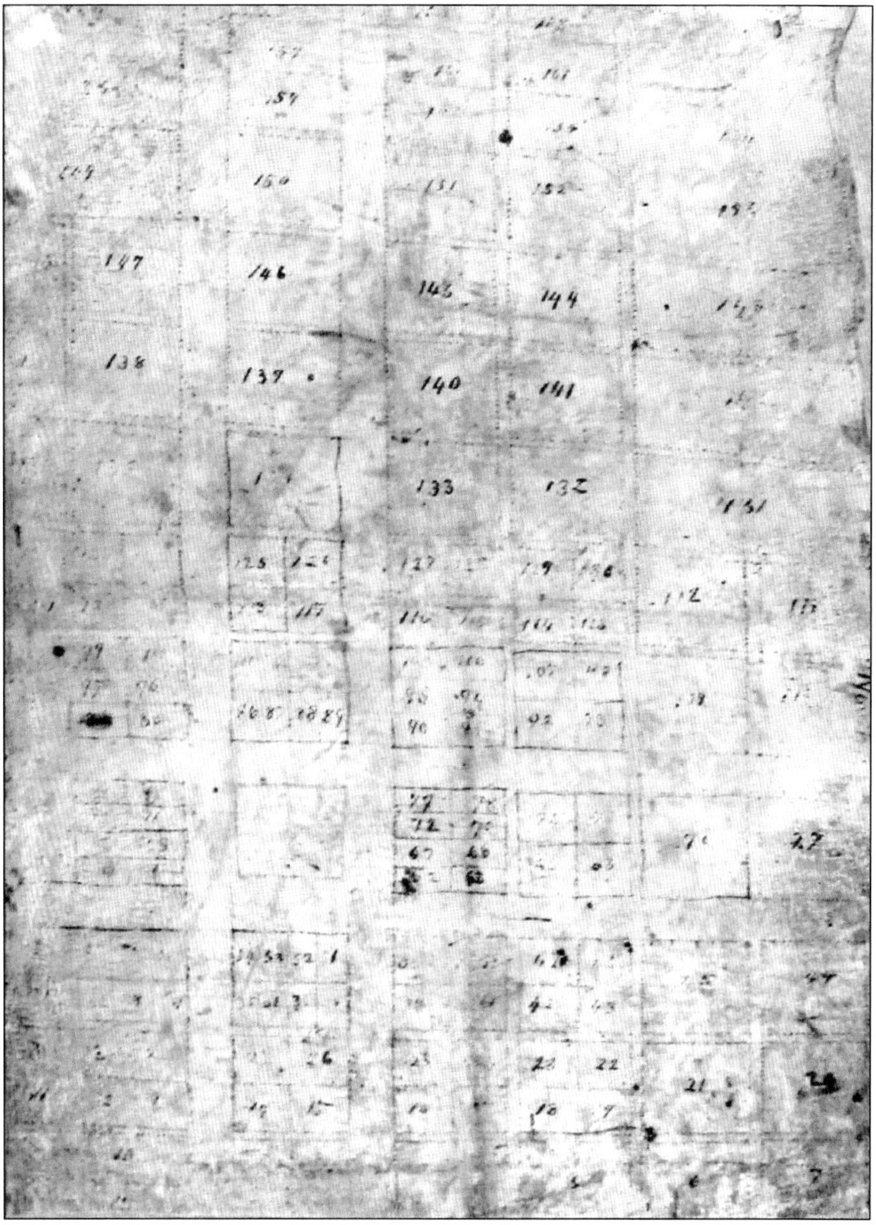

The First Bentonville Map. John B. Dickson was the Benton County clerk when the oldest plat map of Bentonville was drawn with quill pen and ink on a sheepskin document. In the plat drawing, the town square appears as the blank square block in the second row from the bottom and left of center. The original 166 town lots were marked off with 165 square feet for residential lots and 82.5 square feet for commercial lots. (Courtesy of Rogers Historical Museum.)

On the Cover: Trades Day was a popular sales promotion held at the downtown square in the late 1920s. During the week, shoppers who made purchases were given coupons for a drawing held every Saturday. The idea of being lucky enough to win attracted large crowds to the square, since winners had to be present to collect a prize. In the background, looking west, is a vintage view of the town square. (Courtesy of the author.)

IMAGES
of America

BENTONVILLE

Monte Harris

ARCADIA
PUBLISHING

ISBN 978-0-7385-8724-0

Published by Arcadia Publishing
Charleston, South Carolina

Printed in the United States of America

Library of Congress Control Number: 2010935201

For all general information, please contact Arcadia Publishing:
Telephone 843-853-2070
Fax 843-853-0044
E-mail sales@arcadiapublishing.com
For customer service and orders:
Toll-Free 1-888-313-2665

Visit us on the Internet at www.arcadiapublishing.com

This book is dedicated to all the past citizens who worked diligently to build Bentonville and to the citizens of today who are working to preserve the best of the past for future generations

Contents

ACKNOWLEDGMENTS

The photographs and information in this book could not have been completed without the help of many knowledgeable and kind people.

In particular, I would like to thank Dr. Gaye Bland, director of the Rogers Historical Museum, for her confidence in this project. I greatly appreciate her willingness to share technical guidance and advice regarding quality reproduction of historical photographs.

Thanks to Marie Demeroukas, photograph archivist/librarian, and Allyn Lord, director of the Shiloh Museum of Ozark History, for their help and guidance in locating Bentonville images.

I enjoyed the time spent with fellow Bentonville natives, who always were willing to share memories and answer questions. If they did not know the answer, they would suggest someone who did. The majority of these individuals are directly related to the earliest Bentonville citizens, so their family histories and experiences literally parallel the story of Bentonville.

I am especially grateful to Mary Marquess and Lorene Boling, who graciously shared their heirloom photographs and recounted Bentonville memories, which helped set the time line of this book. Peggy Banks also contributed valuable information with her recollections of a lifetime in Bentonville. I greatly appreciate Patty Pearce Payne for allowing the inclusion of several old Bentonville photographs from her family's collection. Many thanks to Gary Black for his contribution of time and historical photographs included in this book. Thanks to Cindy Flint Walters, Sharon A. Bell, and the First Presbyterian Church for their generosity in sharing church archive photographs. I want to acknowledge the Jefferson family, who allowed me to research their family history and include images of early citizens who helped build Bentonville. Larry Horton, Linda Norman, Gloria Coffelt Moore, Cathy Coffelt Palmer, and Tomi Lundy always were willing to help answer questions and identify photographs.

I particularly want to thank Marilyn Collins, author of Images of America: *Rogers*, who first recommended this book project to me.

Last, but not least, I am grateful to Amy Perryman of Arcadia Publishing for providing unwavering guidance and kind counsel as I worked my way through this project.

INTRODUCTION

There was no town when the first wagon train arrived on the site now known as Bentonville. Back in those days, the area was known as Osage Prairie. Packing up all of one's possessions and moving to a completely undeveloped place was not a new idea, even during that time in history. Most of these early Bentonville people were second- and third-generation pioneers who migrated down the East Coast to Virginia and through North Carolina and Tennessee. Each generation had left their family home and moved farther west to follow their dream of presiding over their own domain. It was the same dream shared by every generation in America from then until now.

Many of the early families had the resources to send a small team to survey and identify the best sections of land. At that time, the land where Bentonville is situated today was unplowed grassy prairie with an abundance of springs and creeks around low hills and scattered stands of trees. After choosing the best sites—usually near a spring—the group returned to the East with good news, and the families began preparing for the move to Arkansas.

Naturally, the first families were able to choose the best land and exerted the greatest influence on the location of new towns. Next, the most experienced and skilled builders were selected and sent to construct the initial structures in order to have the place ready and comfortable for the arrival of the women and children. Finally, the surveyors platted the town into residential and commercial lots, and by 1837, the town of Bentonville was open for business.

As soon as commercial lots were available for sale, mercantile business was the next economic enterprise to open on the town square. Dr. Nicholas Spring and his partner, a Mr. Blythe, are credited with opening the first general store. George H. Jefferson opened a hotel and a livery at about the same time that the city and county government built the first courthouse. By the 1840s, stagecoach traffic brought passengers and mail-order goods into Bentonville, which expanded the business base enough for the addition of yet another hotel and more retail business.

The Dickson family greatly influenced the building of Bentonville. In fact, many Dickson family members not only helped build Bentonville but continued to live and serve in public office for many years. Descendants of the Dickson family appreciated the importance of local history and were responsible for saving one of the oldest structures, which stood until the 1950s. The old building was photographed by the newspaper before it was finally torn down. It was built in 1832 by Robert Dickson, who, along with his son Joseph, owned land in and around the town of Bentonville.

Maj. John B. Dickson owned the property that today is known as Compton's Gardens. Dickson was the first clerk of Benton County and was married to Charlotte Benton Temple, a cousin of Sen. Thomas Hart Benton. John and Charlotte's daughter, Jane Dickson, married J. W. Clark, and they owned and operated the historical Eagle Hotel in Bentonville.

George H. Jefferson and his family were among the early arrivals in Bentonville. He owned a hotel and furniture shop on the town square in 1842. The Jeffersons were members of the

Cumberland Presbyterian Church and, like the Dickson family, were involved in many business ventures, including real estate deals.

The Spring family opened the first store and played a major role in the development of retail business on the Bentonville square. William Spring's daughter was the wife of George P. Wallace, who was the first man to serve as Benton County judge. The first Benton County business was conducted in April 1837 in the home of Judge Wallace. The Wallace house apparently existed into modern times but was inadvertently destroyed during one of many development projects. Today, the old Wallace farm property encompasses most of Memorial Park and portions of Heritage Heights housing addition.

The Civil War caused a screeching halt to economic development and normal daily life in downtown Bentonville. In February 1862, it is said the citizens burned the Methodist church, the school, and the jail in order to deny the Union army the use of as many buildings as possible. Sadly almost all of Bentonville was destroyed by fire and violence before the Union forces moved on to Pea Ridge and the bloody battle of March 1862.

After the war, according to Civil War veterans, Bentonville was one of the first towns to extend a hand of reconciliation and welcome old soldiers from both sides in a series of organized reunions. It is said that Union veterans asked to be included and were warmly welcomed at the first old soldiers' reunion, which was organized by former Confederates in 1877. The event was so successful that an annual old soldiers' reunion was held in honor of both sides for many years.

As is often the case in times of crisis, the church groups were the first to gather the strength to begin rebuilding Bentonville after the Civil War. According to more than one local history source, it was the Presbyterians who led the first community renewal projects. The Presbyterians, certainly with the help of many other citizens, constructed a community building or meetinghouse that was used for church services by several denominations until each group could rebuild. At some point, a Sabbath school was organized, and on June 10, 1866, the decision was made to expand the use of the Sabbath school to a daily regular school.

In 2009, a little brick schoolhouse was rediscovered inside the walls of a more modern building. Preservation of this building is particularly important, because it provides physical evidence from a time in Bentonville history when much was lost and little is known.

Through the years, Bentonville citizens survived other catastrophes, such as a fire on the north side of the square in 1880, World Wars I and II, and all the economic challenges in between. The conservative nature of a hardworking community and a creative ability to make do with what one has seem to have been the recurring themes in Bentonville history.

Retail sales, real estate, law, and education have been the dominate building blocks of the town of Bentonville from the very beginning. Today, those are the same leading economic categories that drive the spirit of business, which in turn has produced a friendly small town with a high quality of life.

One

Early Bentonville 1837–1865

The town of Bentonville was established in the 1830s by people primarily from Tennessee. The land now known as Benton County was once part of Washington County. As the westward movement gained popularity, the U.S. government offered public domain land for sale, which added even more appeal to families ready to pack the wagons and follow their dreams.

Many of the best houses and commercial buildings in Bentonville were built with brick. Clay brick was the building material of choice, because Bentonville was located on the Osage Prairie, which had a limited number of trees in those days. There was, and still is, an abundance of red clay dirt in Benton County.

In 1841, John and William Walker received the contract for the first official two-story brick courthouse that was built in the town square. Soon John Braithwaite, an experienced brick mason, arrived from England and settled in Bentonville. Braithwaite built a beautiful farmhouse that still stands on land that once included a large apple orchard. Over the years, John's son and grandson continued the Braithwaite legacy with numerous eclectic cobblestone houses, as well as the 1949 brick First Baptist Church and the Thomas Jefferson Elementary School in 1960. Today, many developers still choose to build with brick, which complements and connects the Bentonville of yesterday with the Bentonville of tomorrow.

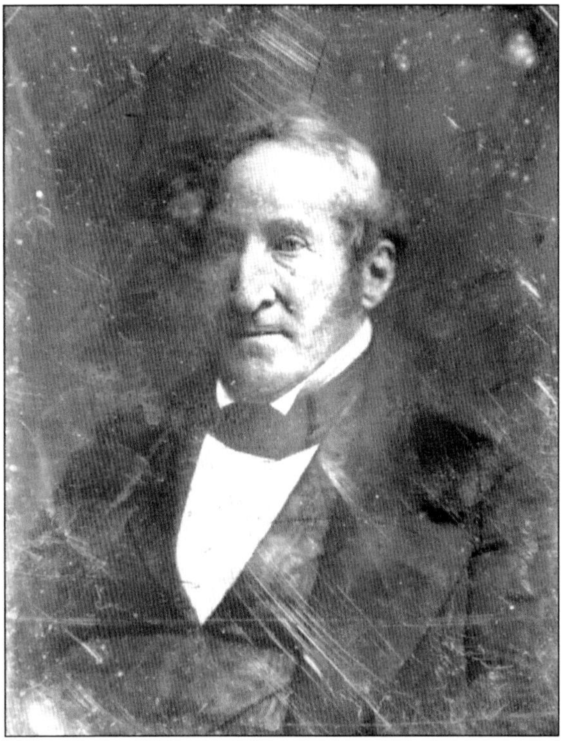

SEN. THOMAS HART BENTON, 1782–1858. Bentonville and the Benton County were both named in honor of Sen. Thomas Hart Benton, who was born in North Carolina, reared in Tennessee, and served as a U.S. senator from Missouri for 30 years. He was with Gen. Andrew Jackson in the War of 1812 and supported Jackson for president even though Benton once shot and wounded Jackson during an argument. It is said that Bentonville resident Charlotte Benton Temple Dickson (1800–1843) was a cousin to the senator. (Courtesy of the Library of Congress.)

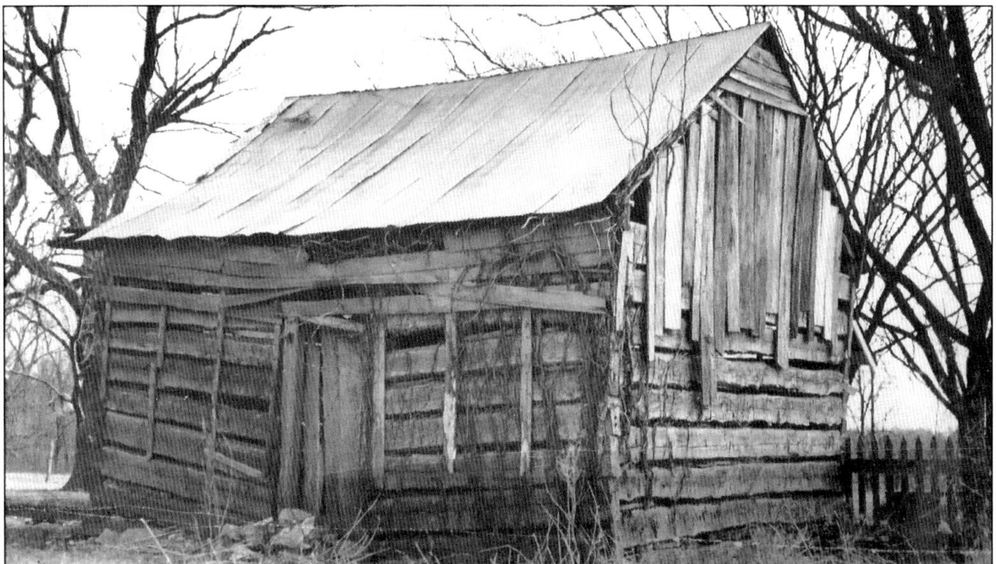

THE DICKSON CABIN, 1832. Robert Dickson (1773–1848) and his family were among the earliest settlers of Benton and Washington Counties. This small building was constructed in 1832 and was still standing when this image appeared in the *Benton County Democrat—1950, The Century of Progress* edition. It must be noted that the structure was over 100 years old when this picture was taken. It is not known if this was an unattached kitchen or part of the main house, but it certainly would have looked quite different when the Dicksons, a well-to-do Tennessee family, began their new life in Bentonville. (Courtesy of the author.)

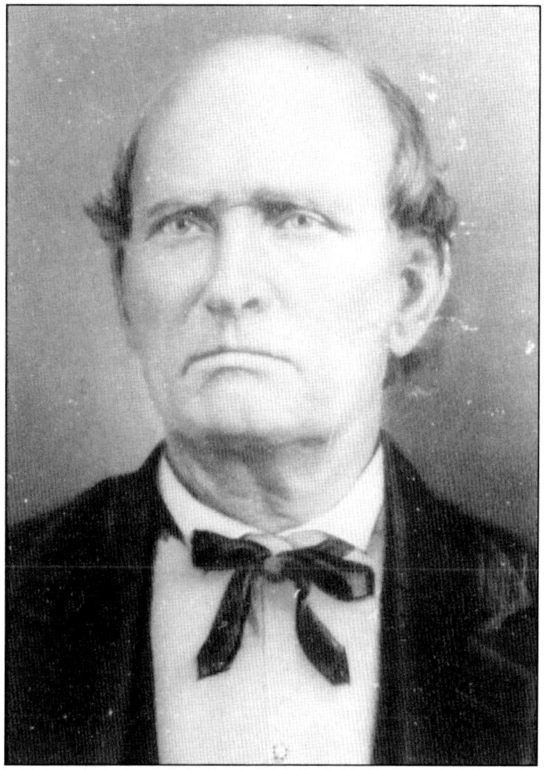

JUDGE ALFRED B. GREENWOOD. Judge Greenwood moved to Bentonville in 1838 and opened the first law office. Greenwood had traveled as far as Nashville, Tennessee, with a group of Cherokee during the forced removal that is now known as the Trail of Tears. For some unknown reason, Greenwood decided to return to Georgia, pack up his family, and move to Bentonville, where he began a long and successful career in law and politics. He died in 1889 and is buried in the Bentonville Cemetery. (Courtesy of Gary Black.)

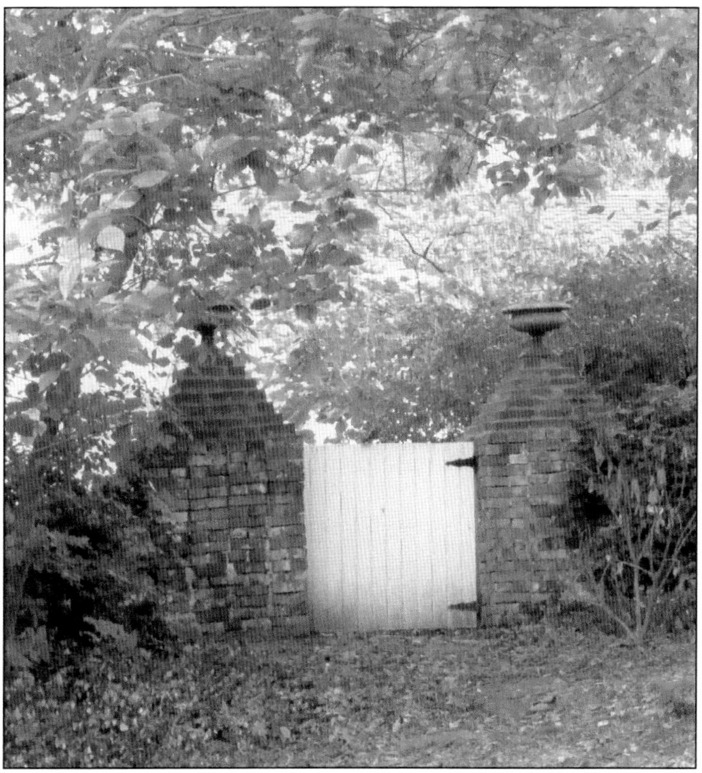

THE GREENWOOD GARDEN GATE. The fieldstone fence and old brick gate pillars can still be seen behind the modern Greenwood house today. The old gate pillars face an earlier roadway and indicate that the 1830s house may have faced in the opposite direction. The fence is constructed of small rocks picked from the field and placed in a long row during plowing and planting time. The fence marks off a field that borders the creek where the old Greenwood barn stood until June 1958. (Courtesy of the author.)

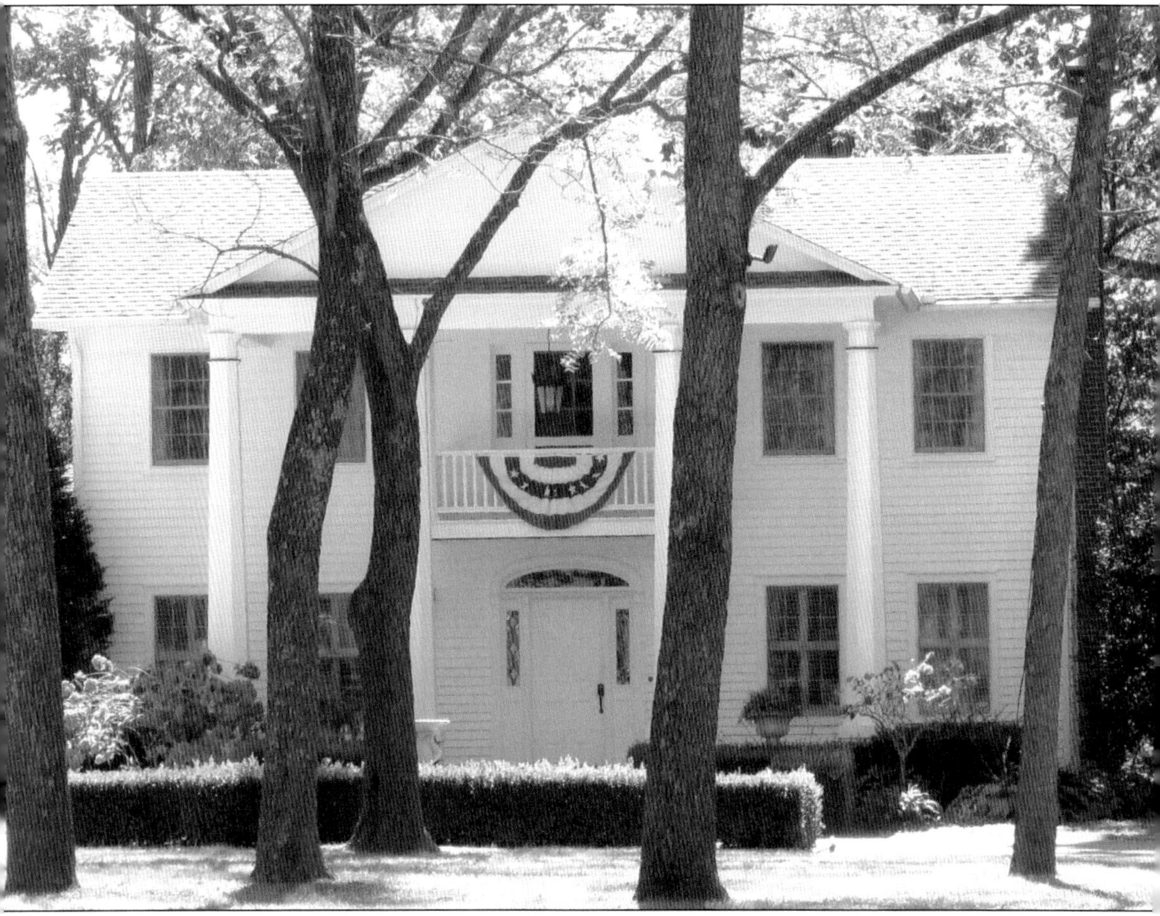

THE OLD JUDGE GREENWOOD PLACE. According to an old newspaper article, Judge Greenwood's original home was torn down in the 1920s. The house located on Greenwood's old property today was designed by Oklahoma City architect J. E. Stringham and built by the Traylor family, who lived there for many years. In more recent times, it was the home of Bud Walton, brother and business partner of Sam Walton. Today, the Colonial-style house, situated on a spacious lawn in a grove of heirloom oak trees, is one of Bentonville's prettiest places. (Courtesy of the author.)

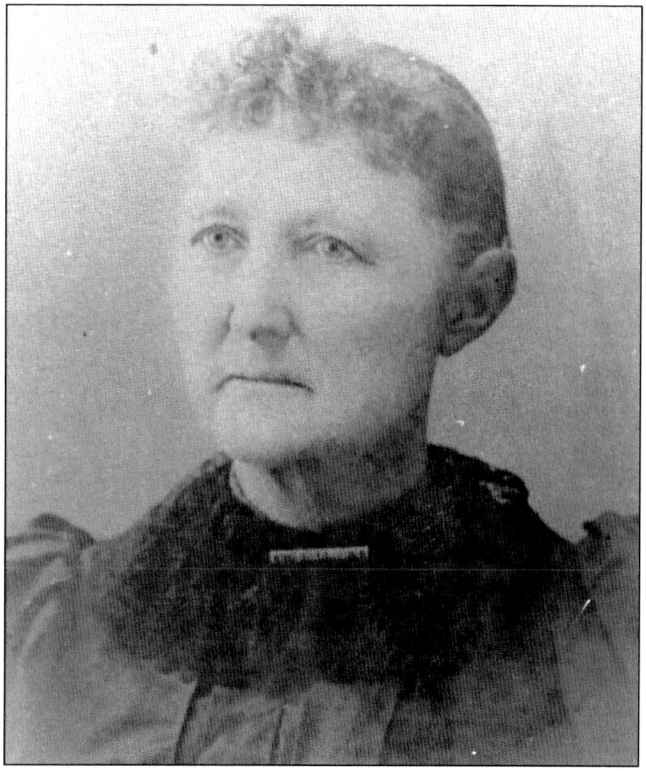

JUDGE GREENWOOD'S DAUGHTER. Sophia Greenwood was born in Georgia and was a baby when she moved to Bentonville with her father, Judge Alfred B. Greenwood, and family. Sophia grew up in Bentonville and married attorney John Black in 1855. They had six children who attended school in the old building on Northwest Second Street, which was rediscovered in the summer of 2010. The school, first known as the Bentonville Sabbath School, was later used as a regular school and is now undergoing careful preservation by the Peel-Compton Foundation. (Courtesy of Mary Marquess.)

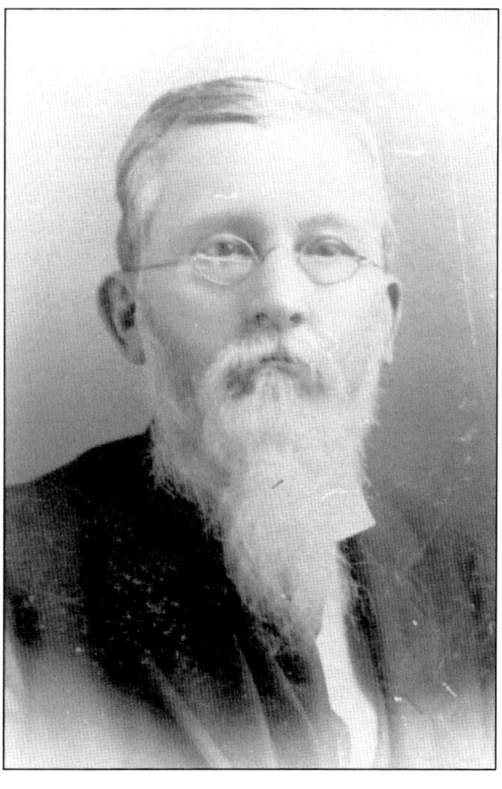

JUDGE GREENWOOD'S SON-IN-LAW. John Black was among the early Bentonville citizens who knew how important education was for the children and the future success of the town. He was a practicing attorney and served as school superintendent for the Bentonville Sabbath School, which was the first school organized in Bentonville after the Civil War. John Black served in several public offices, including Benton County attorney, county court clerk, and probate court recorder. He was described by his peers as a man of good character and much public spirit. (Courtesy of Mary Marquess.)

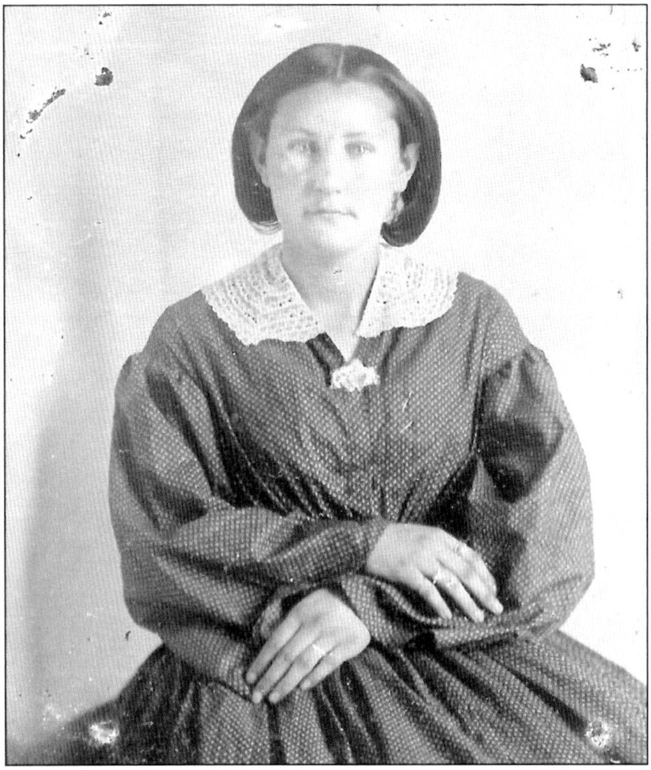

ELIZABETH H. JEFFERSON, 1841–1900. Elizabeth Harrison Jefferson was born in 1841 and was a young lady in pre–Civil War Bentonville society. Elizabeth's mother was a cousin to the Dickson family, and her father built a hotel on the town square in 1842. In those days, the hotel business accommodated stagecoach passenger service connecting Van Buren to St. Louis as well as a steady stream of wagon traffic from the east heading west. (Courtesy of Willa Lawson and the Jefferson family.)

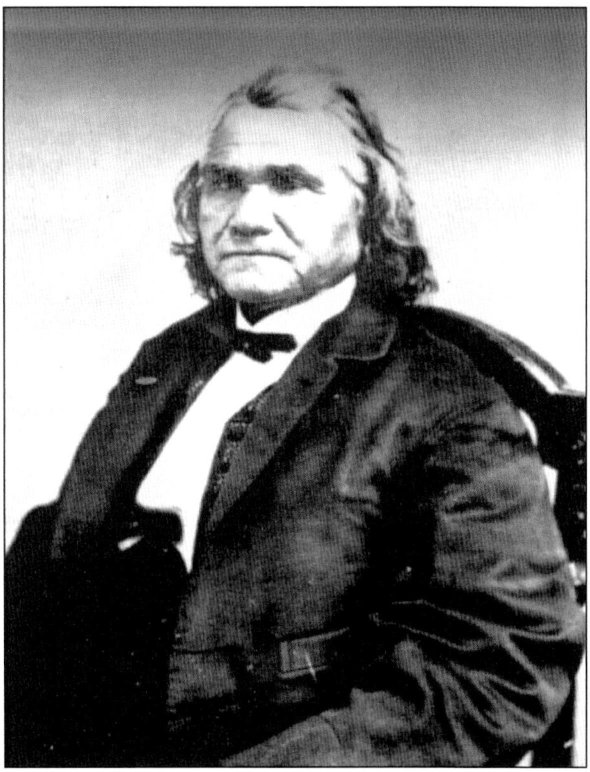

CHEROKEE STAND WATIE, 1806–1871. Stand Watie was tried for murder in 1842, when the Benton County Courthouse was located in the center of the town square. Stand Watie was deeply involved in the politics of the Cherokee Nation during the time of forced removal from the Cherokee homeland to Indian Territory. Several members of his family were killed, and when an attack was made on Watie, he turned himself into authorities and admitted killing the man. Watie not only had a team of five lawyers to defend his plea of self-defense, but he also won the sympathy of the Benton County jury, as it ruled that he was not guilty. (Courtesy of Wikipedia.)

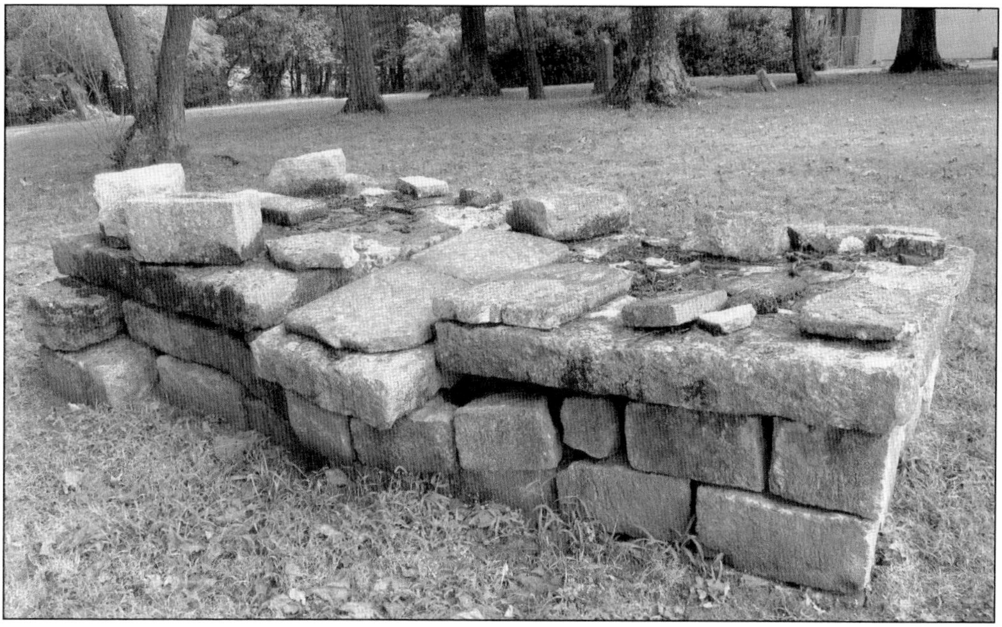

AARON SCHOOLFIELD'S GRAVE, 1843. The Schoolfield tombstone is constructed of hand-cut limestone, placed in a common way to protect graves from wild animals in the early days. This particular heavy stone cairn is 9 feet long and 3 feet wide. Aaron Schoolfield (1775–1843) could be called a true patriarch of Bentonville, as his granddaughter married George P. Wallace, who served as the first Benton County judge. Another of Aaron's granddaughters married Dr. Nicholas Spring, who opened Bentonville's first store. (Courtesy of the author.)

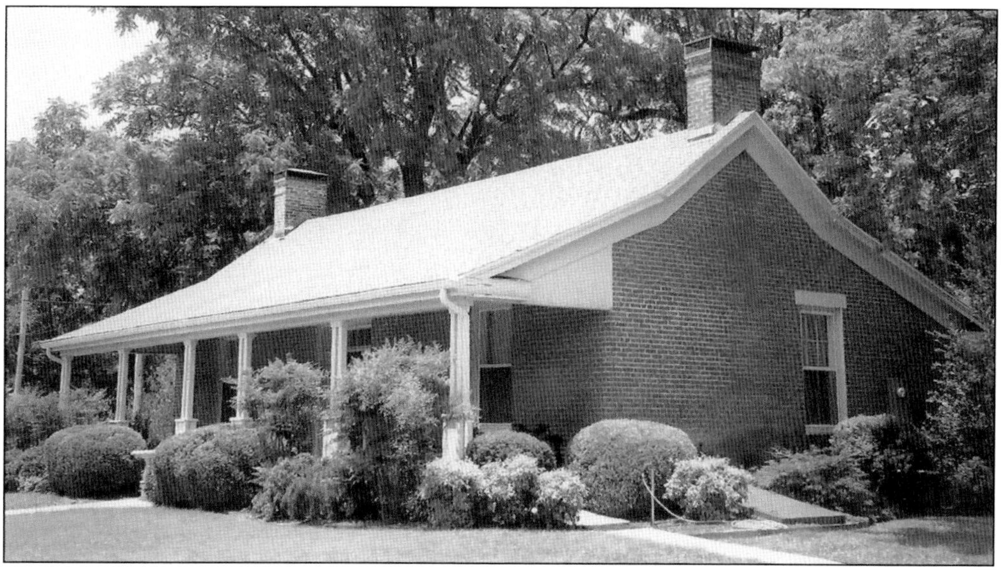

THE BRAITHWAITE HOUSE. John Braithwaite arrived in America from England around 1843. His first son was born in Arkansas in 1844. The Braithwaite House is a handmade brick structure that, fortunately, has been preserved as an example of a pre–Civil War Arkansas farmhouse. John Braithwaite was a brick mason, and it is believed he built several buildings in and around Bentonville. The family is best remembered for its apple orchards and the Arkansas black apple, which is still available in northwest Arkansas today. (Courtesy of the author.)

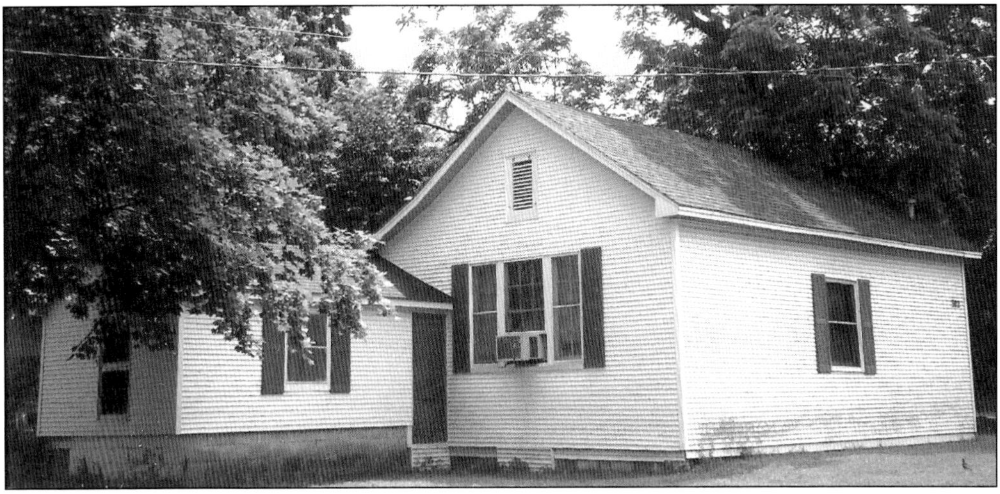

The Armstrong House. Today, few people recognize the little house pictured above as one of the last pre–Civil War structures left standing in Bentonville. Fortunately, the photograph below, taken of the building before the hand-cut wood trim was removed, led to the identification as partial remains of the old Armstrong House. The little building is located in the Armstrong Addition on Southeast Third Street. (Above, courtesy of the author; below, Patty Pearce Payne.)

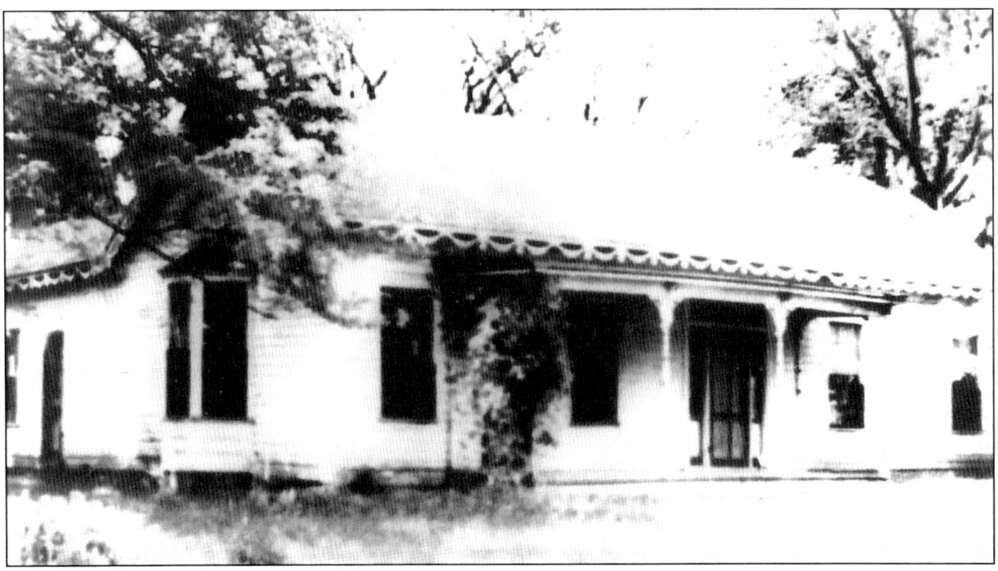

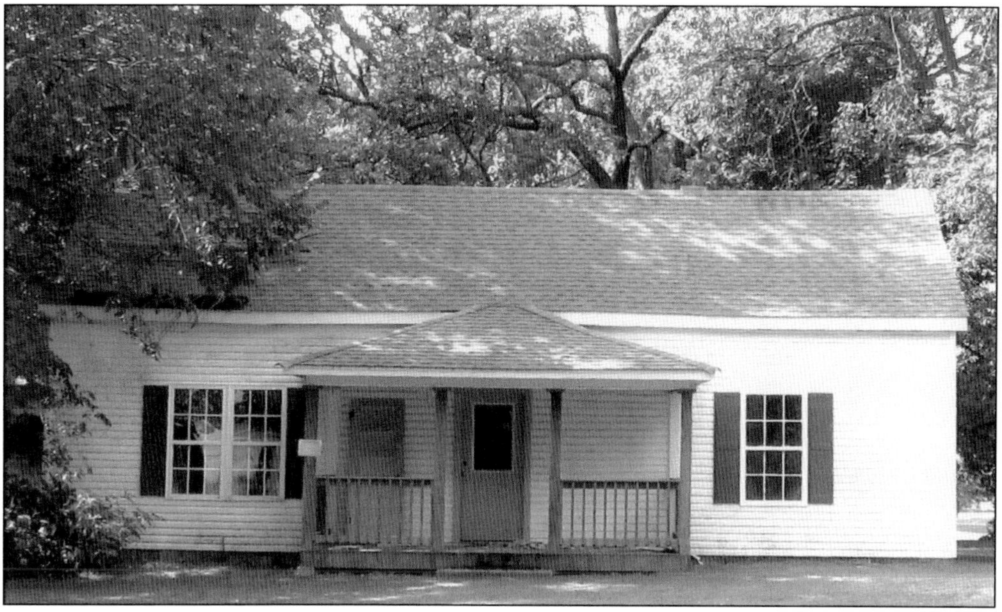

Old Pre–Civil War House. The Morris House is a great example of the small cottage-style home that was prevalent in old Bentonville before the Civil War. Early structures are very rare in Bentonville, because the town was practically destroyed by fire the day before the Battle of Pea Ridge in March 1862. The little house features a central hall and has Greek Revival architectural details. (Courtesy of the author.)

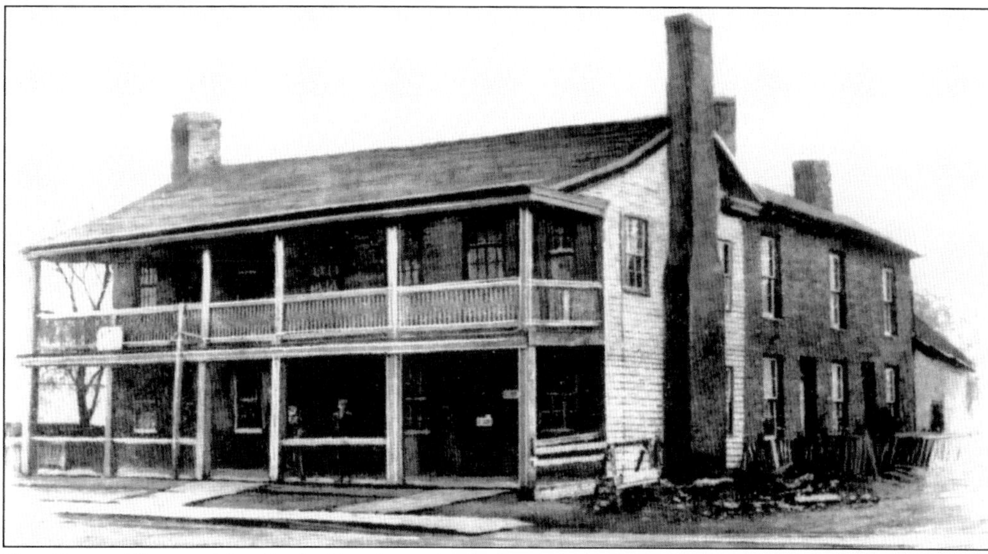

The Eagle Hotel. The Eagle Hotel was built around 1842 on the site where the Massey Hotel building stands today. The Clark family was living in and operating the hotel in 1862 when Union general Franz Sigel walked into the dining room and ordered his breakfast. He had to leave his meal unfinished when his staff reported that the Confederate army was marching into town. General Sigel returned many years later and was invited by town leaders to once again sit down and order breakfast at the same hotel. Sigel leisurely finished his breakfast and remarked on the wonderful welcome he had received on his second visit to Bentonville. (Courtesy of Pea Ridge National Military Park.)

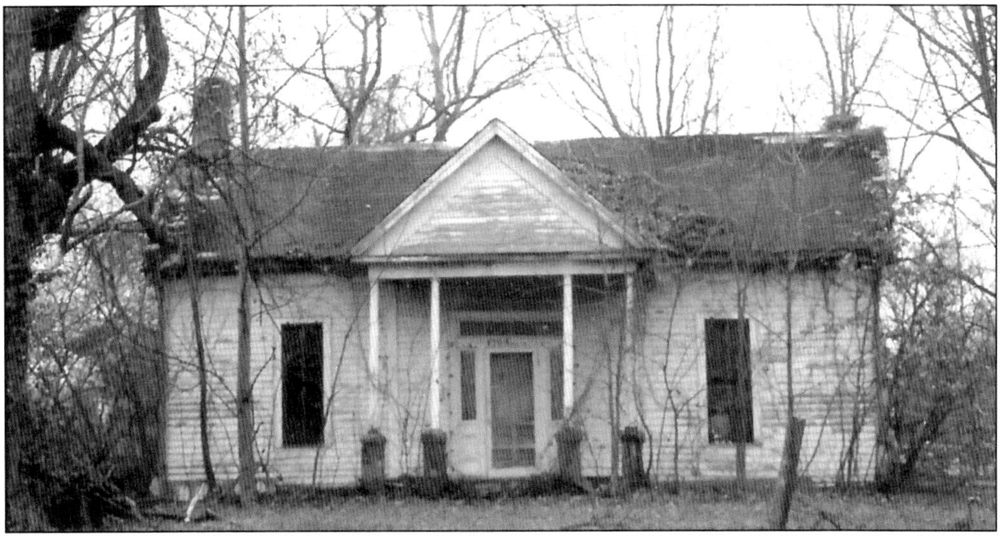

The Lost Cottage. This pre–Civil War cottage survived the fires of the Civil War and was listed on the National Register of Historic Places. The house was Greek Revival in design, with a central hall, and the front door was complete with the original sidelight windows. Unfortunately the little house was destroyed by fire on February 11, 2000, and Bentonville lost one of the town's historical architectural treasures. (Courtesy of the author.)

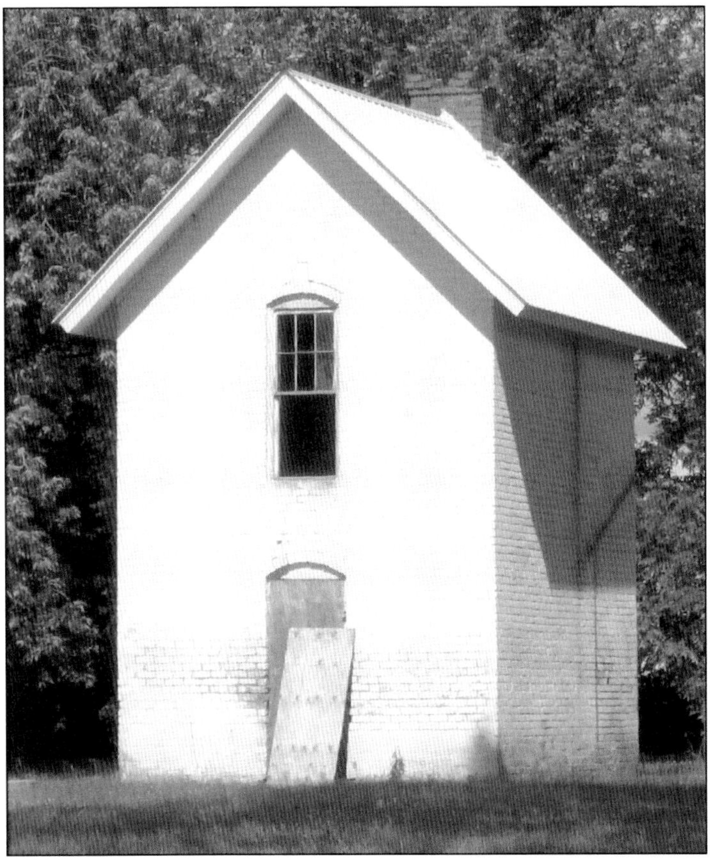

The Mystery Building. The history of this little brick building may never be known, since the main house was torn down before historical documentation could be completed. Located on J Street, the little brick building may have been a detached kitchen with a sleeping room upstairs for domestic servants. On the back of the building is a second-story door, indicating that there once was an exterior stairway. The building is reminiscent of structures common to pre–Civil War times because of its tall and narrow dimensions. Hopefully this little building will be preserved, and one day its secret history will be revealed. (Courtesy of the author.)

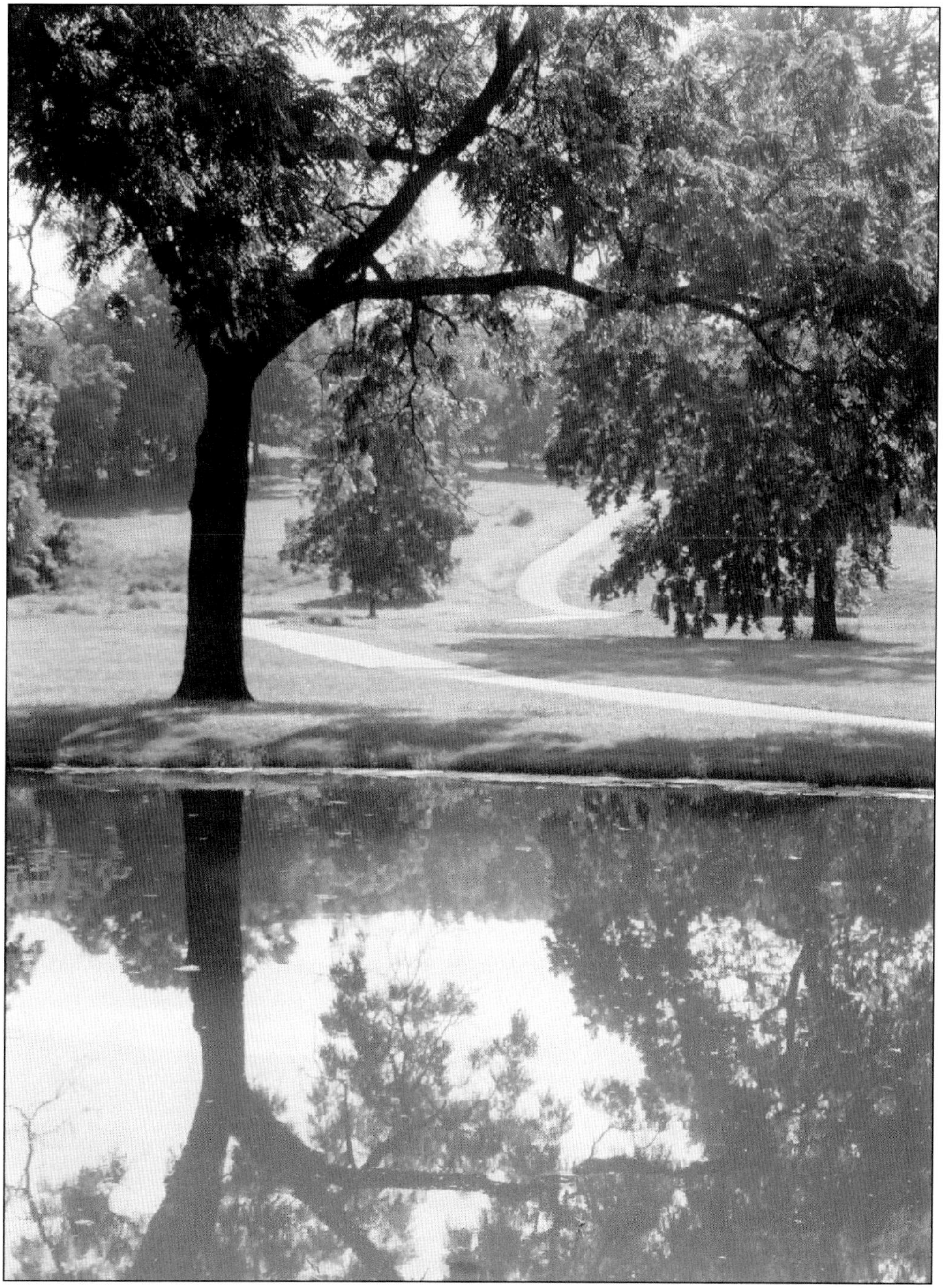

Spring Valley. This beautiful reflective pool of water is part of a larger system of springs that served as the source of drinking water in Bentonville for many years. It is said that this particular location was once considered the best place to build the town. The spring valley may have proved to be too low and damp for year-round healthy living because, in those early days, cholera was a continuous threat. The final decision was to build Bentonville on higher ground a short distance to the west. (Courtesy of the author.)

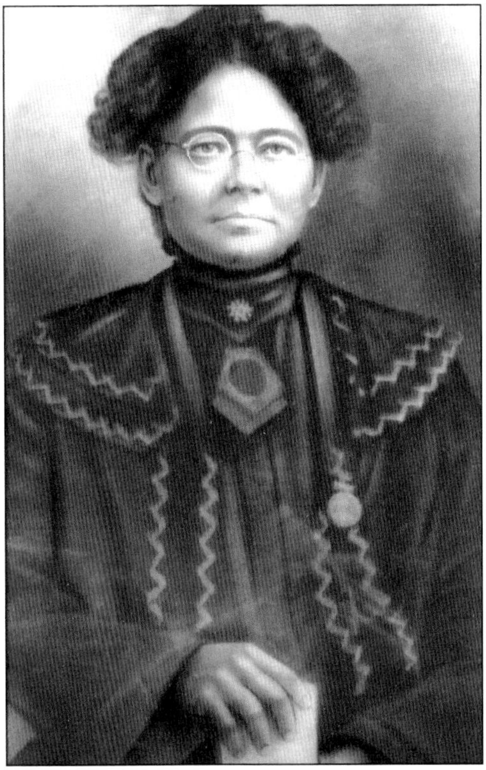

Betty Troutt, 1849–1936. Elizabeth Joslin Yates Troutt was known as Betty to her friends and family. Her Bentonville home was located next to St. Paul's Methodist Church. Betty's house was torn down. The church building still remains but is now a private residence. (Courtesy of Jo Hall.)

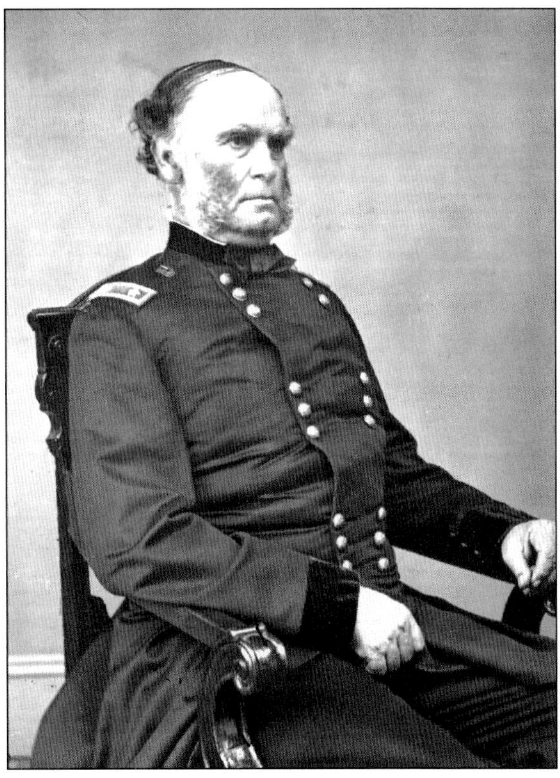

Union General Samuel Curtis, 1805–1866. Arkansas was no longer part of the United States when Union troops marched into Bentonville on February 18, 1862, at 20 minutes past noon. While hundreds of soldiers bivouacked around the town square and along the creek near Judge Greenwood's farm, the Confederate flag was removed from the courthouse and delivered to General Curtis in another camp some miles away. (Courtesy of Pea Ridge National Military Park.)

Confederate General Ben McCulloch, 1811–1862. Under the orders of Gen. Benjamin McCulloch and Gen. Sterling Price, Confederate soldiers marched into Bentonville as Union troops were in the process of packing up to evacuate the town square on a cold day in March 1862. This was the beginning of a bloody confrontation that escalated into the Battle of Pea Ridge, in which General McCulloch, a former Texas Ranger and veteran of the Mexican War, was shot and killed. (Courtesy of Pea Ridge National Military Park.)

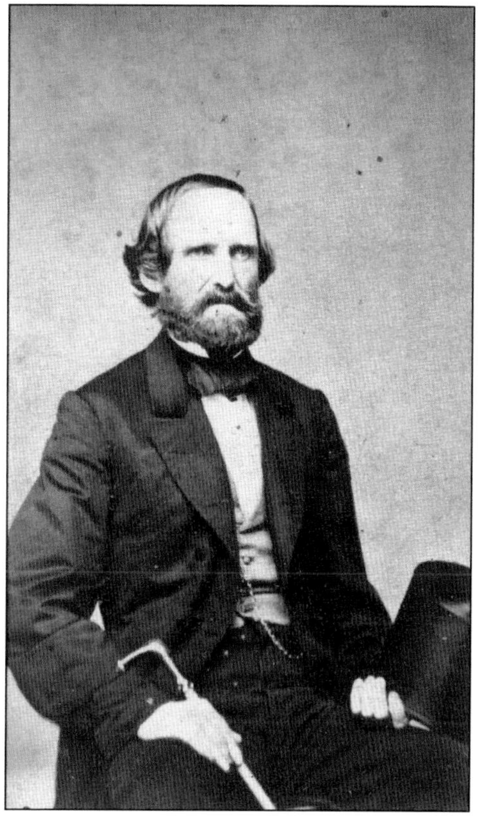

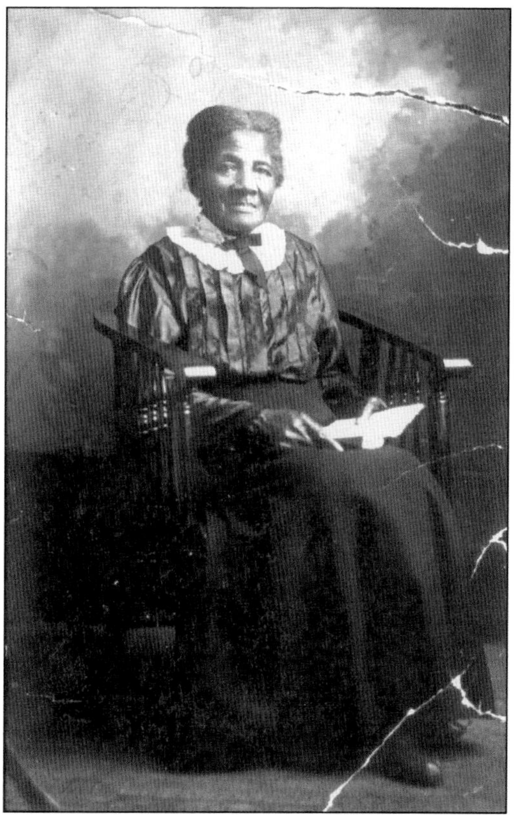

Clara Sanford, 1837–1927. Clara Elizabeth Sanford was born before the Civil War. She remembered leaving the war-torn Bentonville area with her children and traveling in a wagon to Frog Bayou (near Van Buren), where they stayed safe with family and friends until the war was over. When they returned home, they found everything had been burned. (Courtesy of Shiloh Museum of Ozark History/Elizabeth Robertson Collection.)

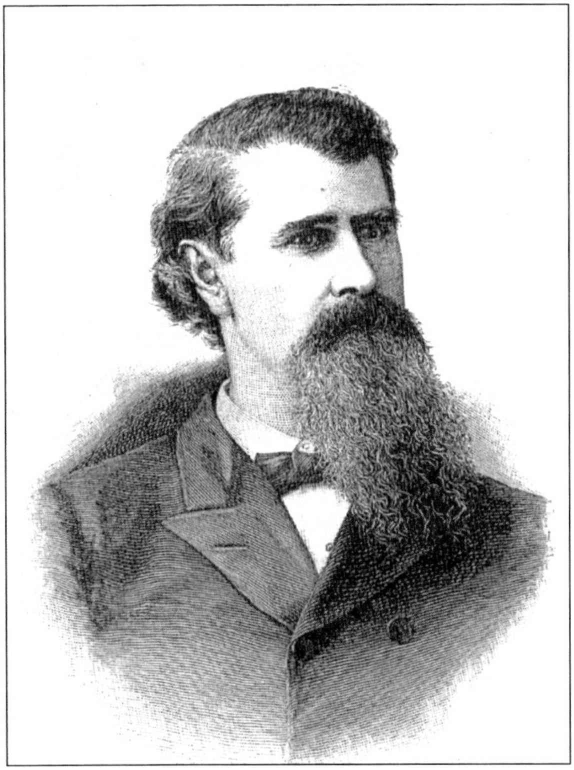

James H. Berry, 1841–1913. Sen. James H. Berry moved to Bentonville after the Civil War. He was a soldier with the Confederate army and suffered a severe injury during a battle in Mississippi. After the Civil War, he taught school and practiced law before being elected to the office of Arkansas governor. He then served as senator for 26 years and was a well-respected politician in Benton County. (Courtesy of the UDC James H. Berry Chapter.)

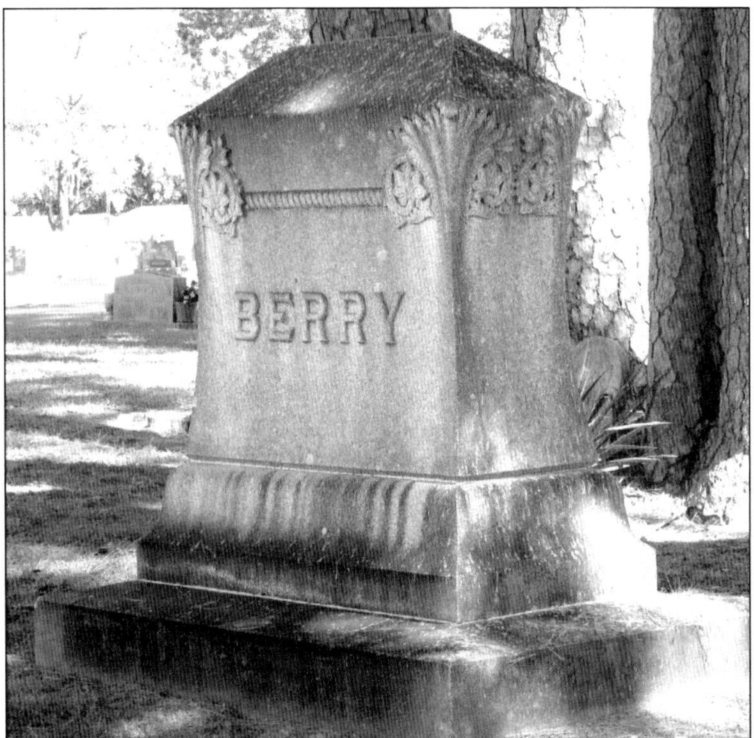

The Berry Family Monument. The Berry family was prominent in Bentonville for several reasons. James H. Berry was elected Arkansas governor and U.S. senator. His sister, Mary Berry, married Col. Sam Peel, who served as congressman. James, his wife, and their children are buried under the tall pines in the old part of the Bentonville Cemetery. (Courtesy of the author.)

Two

Starting Over after the Civil War 1866–1880

Bentonville and the rest of northwest Arkansas was virtually in ruins after the Civil War. Many of the citizens of Bentonville left town during the intense violence, but according to the census records, most Bentonville families returned to start over and rebuild their homes, farms, churches, and schools.

Toward the end of the war, the Bentonville Farm Colony was organized to help citizens begin to plant crops and band together against marauding outlaws. Many citizens submitted lengthy claim forms to the U.S. government to be reimbursed for losses sustained during the Civil War. The claims were thoroughly investigated, even going so far as interviewing neighbors, and if any evidence was found to indicate support of the Confederacy at any time, a request was denied. Some people had kept vouchers signed by Union soldiers that served to prove their claims of losses, such as store merchandise, livestock, bushels of apples, wheat, rye, corn, and many other items of value.

After homes were repaired and crops planted, the next project was to build a place where church groups could meet and school classes could be held. All of the church congregations worked together and shared the first facility constructed after the war.

A temporary painted wooden plank courthouse was built so that Benton County could resume business. A new official brick courthouse was completed in 1874, and the temporary building was moved to the Benton County Poor Farm to be used for living quarters.

For many years, there were reunions for the old soldiers, who shared their stories around campfires. The reunions helped families remember their lost loved ones and honor their brave actions—regardless of which side they had fought for. There were some who chose not to speak of that dark period of history because they did not want to relive the pain and suffering.

Today, there are many important lessons that can be learned from the Civil War period of American history. One can only imagine what it was like to have lived during that time. It is interesting to momentarily contemplate today, even with all the electronic gadgets, air-conditioned homes, snack foods, and comfortable automobiles, if one would be able to survive such difficult times.

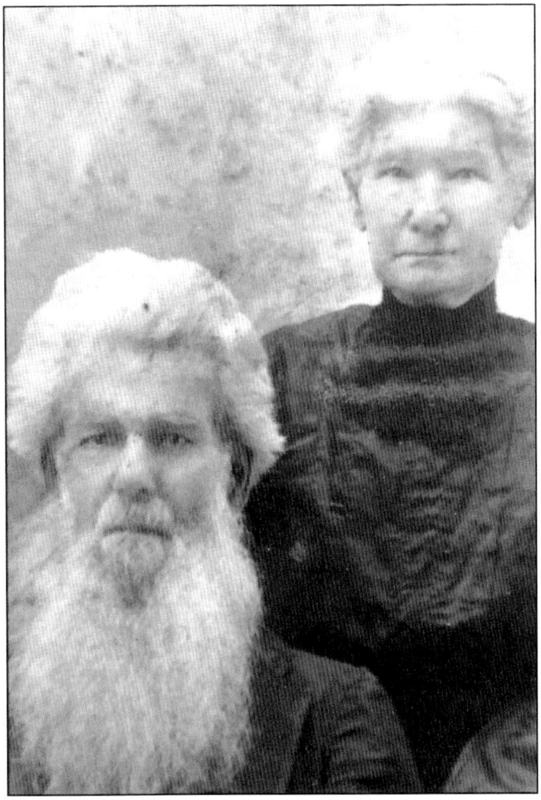

ABSALOM AND EMILY ALFREY. Absalom Alfrey was appointed leader of the Bentonville Farm Colony, organized by Union colonel M. LaRue Harrison to reestablish farming efforts after years of stagnation due to the Civil War. Absalom and his wife, Emily, lived on a farm near the modern Highway 72 East–Interstate 540 intersection. (Courtesy of Mary Marquess.)

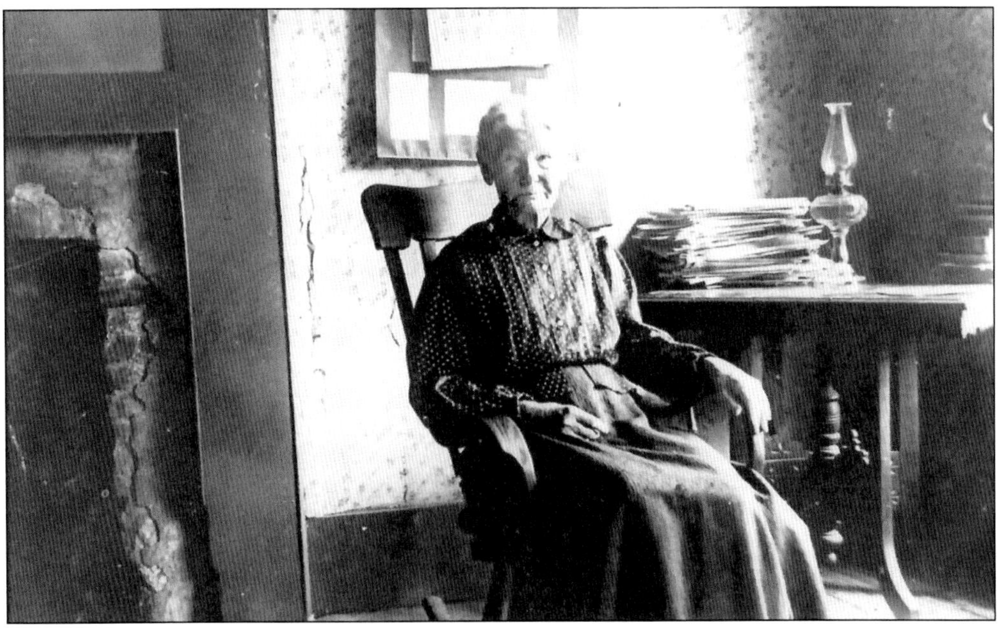

THE WIDOW EMILY ALFREY. Emily Alfrey was born in 1836, the same year that Arkansas became a state. She was a survivor of the Civil War. By the time she posed for this photograph, she was a widow, resting in her rocking chair with many familiar objects around her. (Courtesy of Linda Norman.)

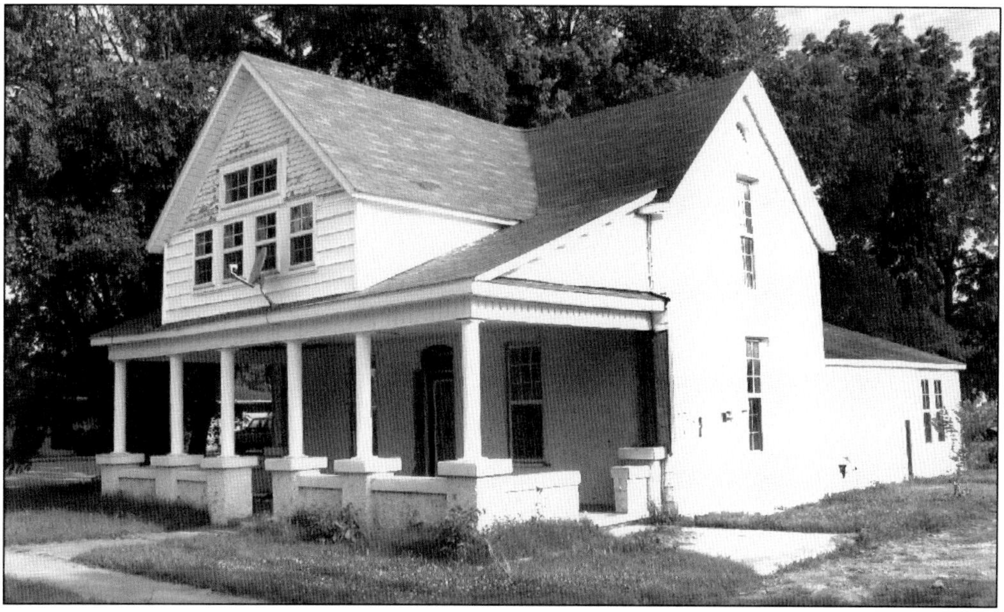

The Old House with a Secret. This ordinary house was renovated and updated many times through the years, covering and recovering the exterior walls with a thick coat of concrete stucco and vinyl siding. The house was scheduled for demolition in the summer of 2009, when old records revealed an important detail in the history of this property. Tucked away inside the walls of this house was an older structure that had been an important building in its day. (Courtesy of the author.)

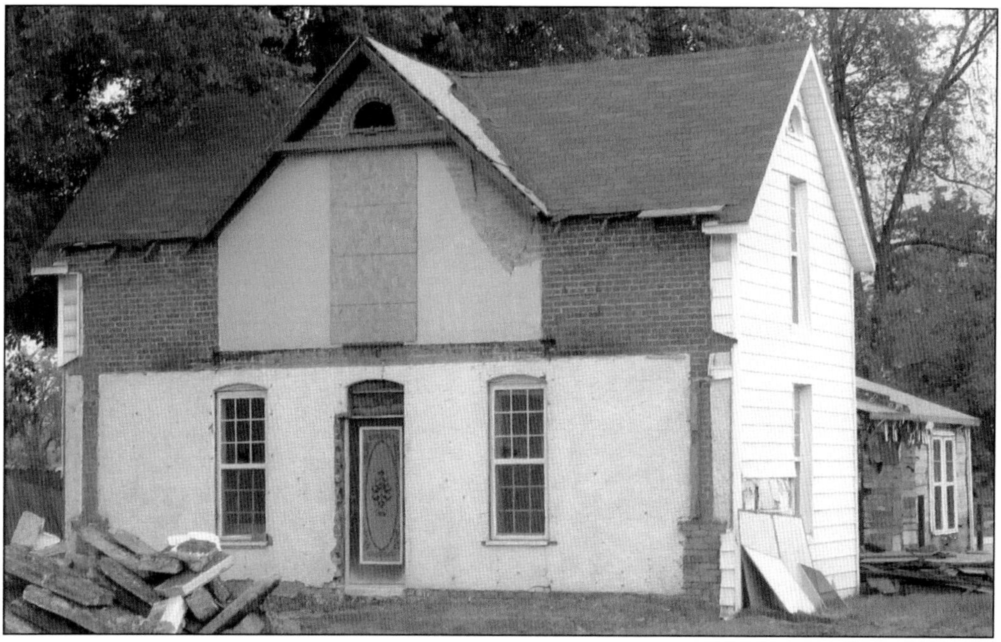

Inside the Old House Was an Even Older School. Through many renovations, an old brick structure had been encased within the more modern wall coverings of this structure. A 2009 parking lot project brought attention to the situation, which led the Peel-Compton Foundation to purchase the property and adopt a preservation plan. (Courtesy of the author.)

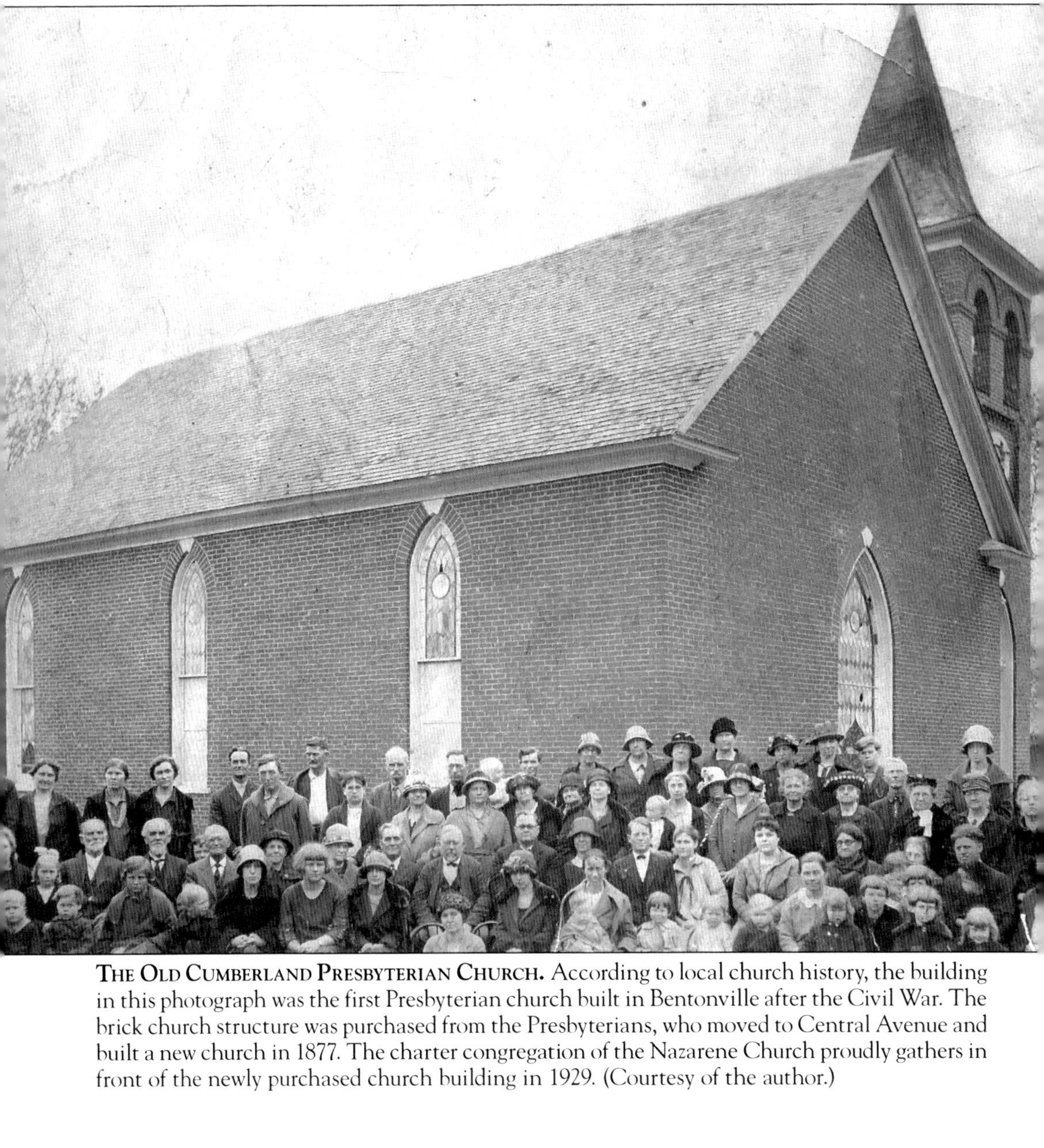

The Old Cumberland Presbyterian Church. According to local church history, the building in this photograph was the first Presbyterian church built in Bentonville after the Civil War. The brick church structure was purchased from the Presbyterians, who moved to Central Avenue and built a new church in 1877. The charter congregation of the Nazarene Church proudly gathers in front of the newly purchased church building in 1929. (Courtesy of the author.)

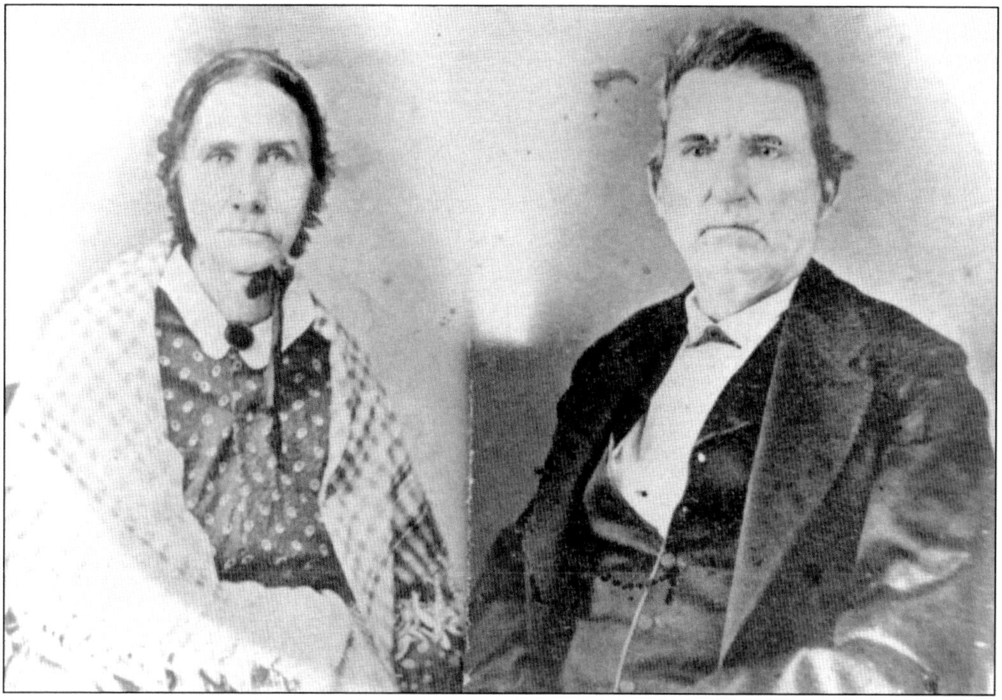

Chris and Margaret Miriah Woods Pace. Margaret Miriah and her husband, Christopher Pace, moved from Tennessee to the Bentonville area in 1835. They were the grandparents of Lon Pace, who built many of the impressive structures in downtown Bentonville, such as the old Benton County jail and the Benton County Bank building. Margaret Miriah and Christopher witnessed and survived the Civil War. (Courtesy of Rogers Historical Museum.)

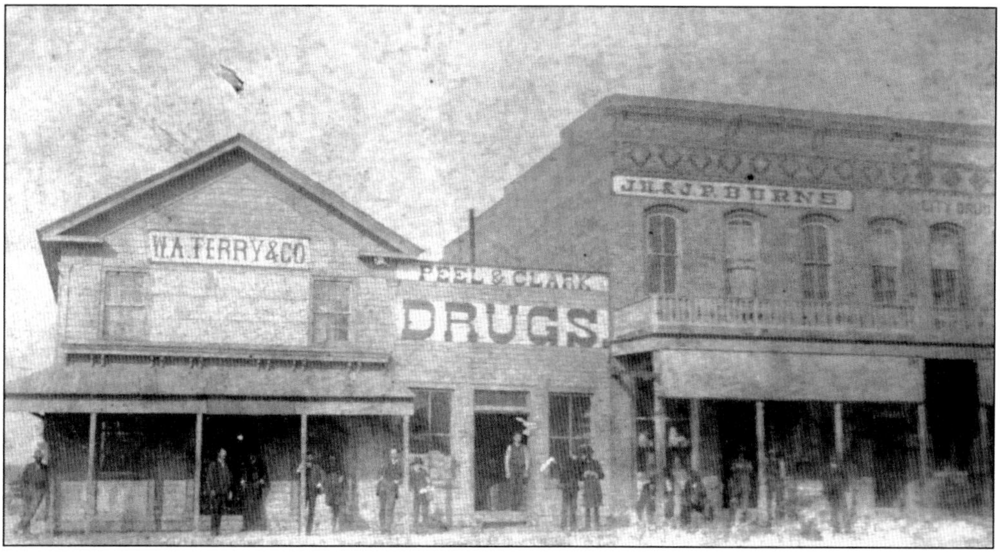

Post–Civil War Stores on the Square. W. A. Terry and Company erected their first building in the 1870s. It was on the same corner where the large three-story Terry Block building was established in 1888. The building was moved around the corner to the west and used for a few more years. The J. H. and J. P. Burns building to the right is the entrance to the Walmart Visitor Center today. (Courtesy of Patty Pearce Payne.)

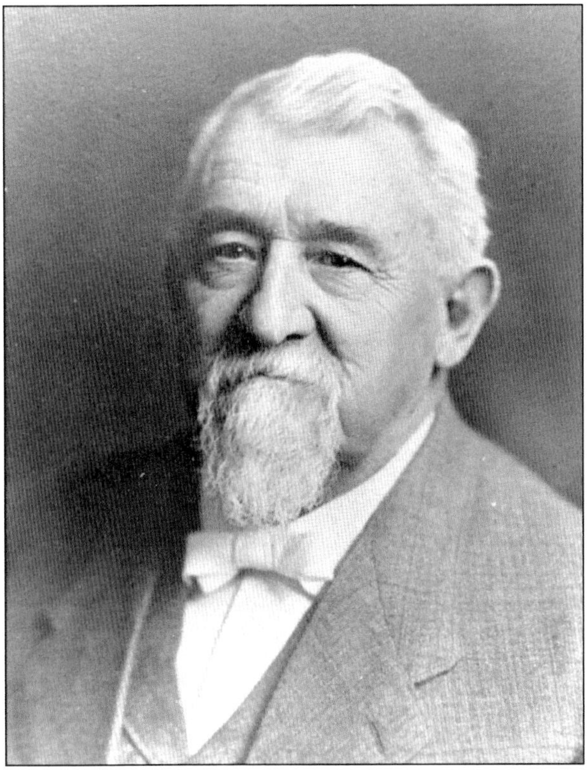

Col. Samuel Peel, 1831–1924. Col. Samuel Peel moved to Bentonville after the Civil War. A few years later, in 1875, he built his large home, known today as the Peel Mansion. The 1903 Benton County plat map shows a large apple orchard on the property. Peel's brother-in-law was Sen. James H. Berry. Sam Peel practiced law and served as a congressman. (Courtesy of Gary Black.)

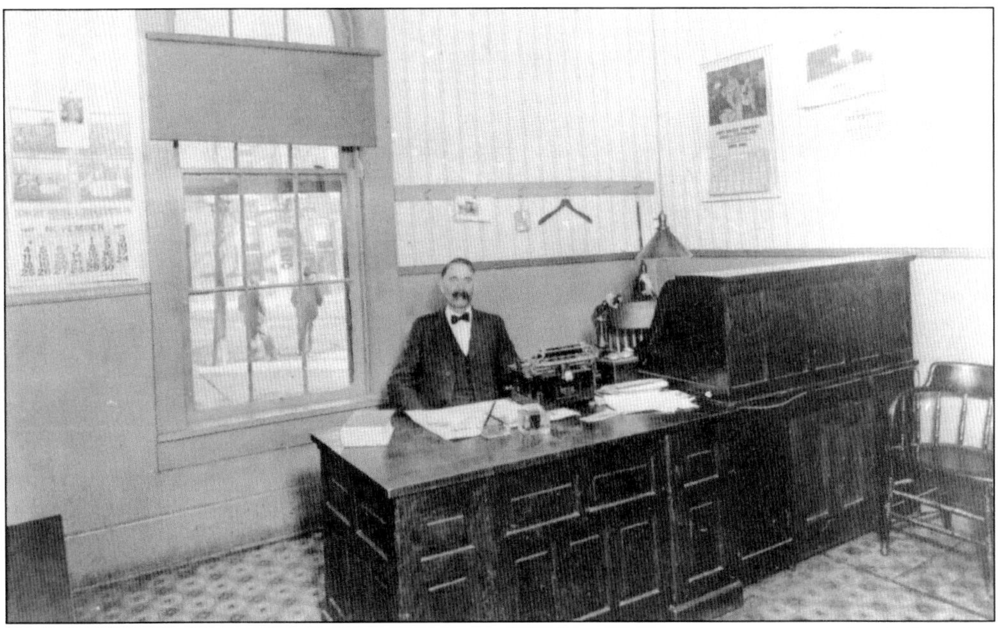

The Judge's Office in the Old Courthouse. Judge Leonard Norris sits at the desk in his office at the old Benton County Courthouse, which once stood on the northwest corner of the square. The old courthouse was built in 1874 and was used until 1928, when a new building was completed. The view out the window of everyday life on the street captured a magical moment in time. (Courtesy of Gary Black.)

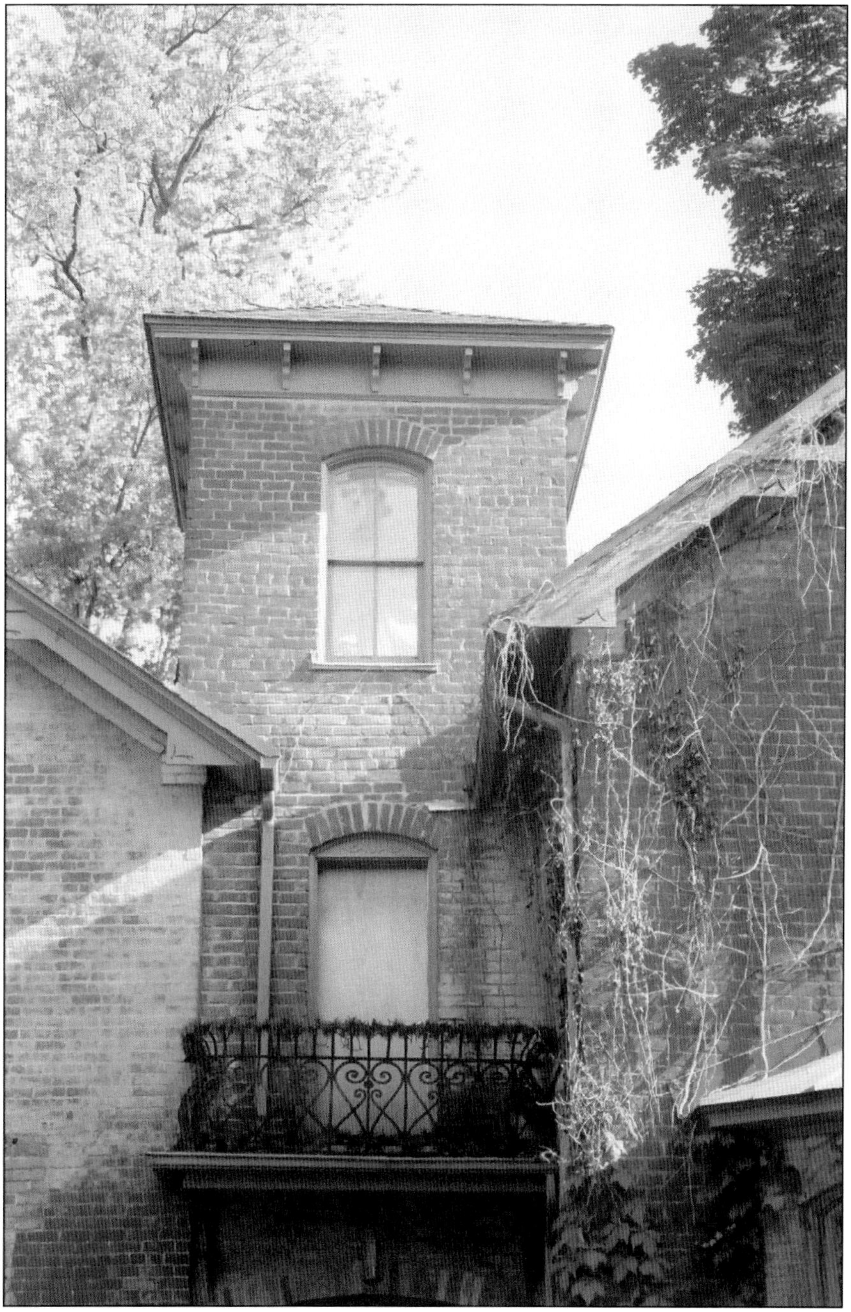

THE CRAIG-BRYAN HOUSE. The Craig-Bryan House on West Central Avenue was built in the 1870s, but it is believed that the central tower was added later. The wrought iron balcony is a true Bentonville historical artifact, as it was once part of the 1874 Benton County Courthouse on the northwest corner of the town square. When the courthouse was torn down in 1928, people were allowed to salvage usable materials, and that is how the wrought iron bailiff's balcony ended up on the Craig-Bryan House. In the old courthouse, the bailiff could step out onto the second-story balcony and call out the name of the next person scheduled to appear on the docket. (Courtesy of the author.)

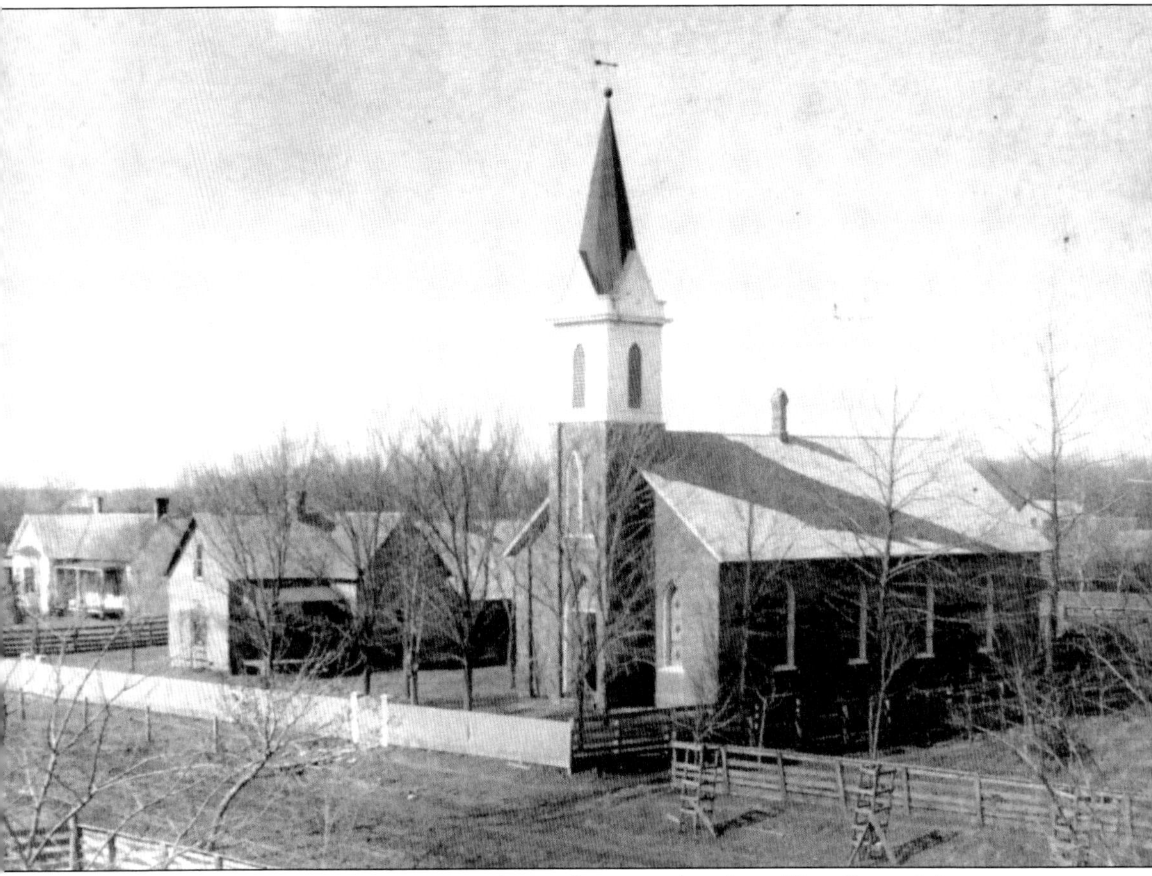

THE PRESBYTERIAN CHURCH, 1877. The Presbyterian church on West Central Avenue is a rare image of Bentonville in the days when fencing was important to protect yards and young trees from being stomped by livestock. This photograph was included in the Dr. Thomas Anderson Watson family album and was donated to the church by Watson's granddaughter Ruth Wharton. The Watsons were among the 35 members who reconstituted the church after the Civil War. To the left of the church is the manse, which is where the pastor lived. The manse was later moved to a nearby street and has been Ray Jefferson's home ever since. The church building no longer exists. (Courtesy of the First Presbyterian Church.)

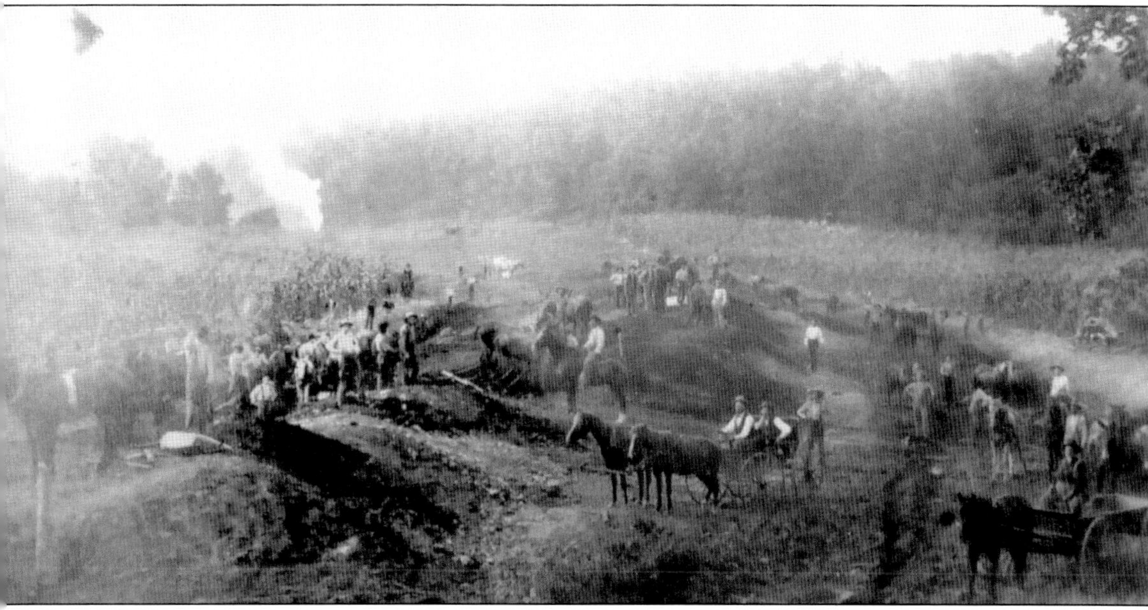

The Spring Family Farm. The William and Lucinda Spring family homestead was located in the area known now as Slaughter Pen Hollow. This photograph was taken in the 1890s and is the only known image that shows the natural lay of the land along the creek valley, which now has been totally reconstructed. Because the farm was situated along the main north-south road into Bentonville during the Civil War, records show the Spring family was visited from 1861 through 1864 by various Union army regiments, who confiscated more than $8,000 worth of wheat, corn, bacon, rye, mules, hogs, horses, and an iron-axle wagon. (Courtesy of Patty Pearce Payne.)

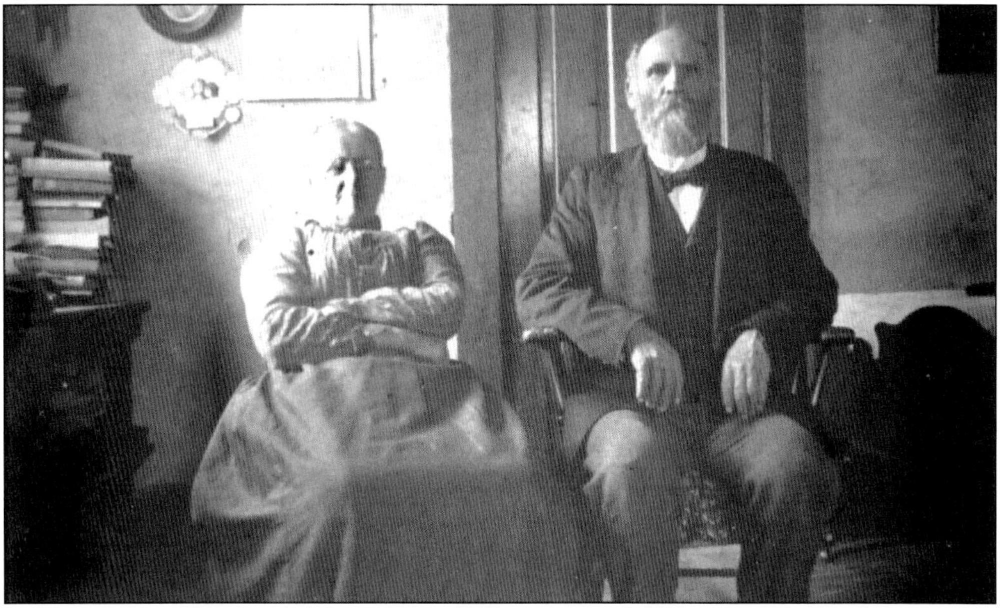

REV. PETER CARNAHAN. Peter Carnahan and Martha Jane Buchanan were married in June 1862, just after the Battle of Pea Ridge and right before Peter enlisted in the Confederate army. Peter helped Benton County clerk John R. Woods take the county records to Texas for safekeeping until the war was over. According to an article in the *Benton County Pioneer*, Peter Carnahan married more couples during his ministerial service than any other preacher in Benton County. (Courtesy of Shiloh Museum of Ozark History/Mildred Carnahan Collection.)

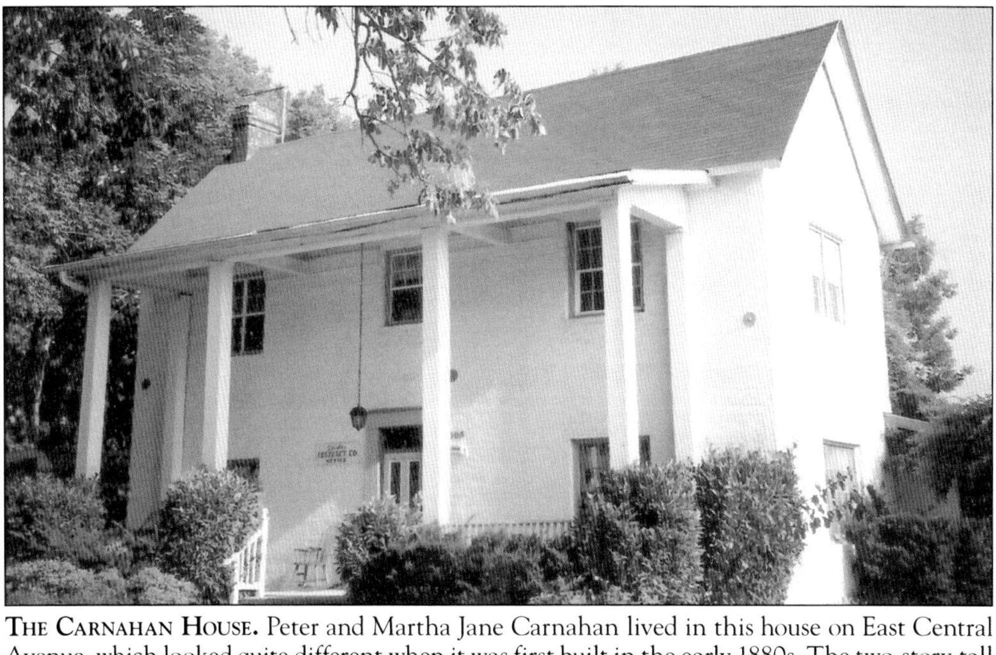

THE CARNAHAN HOUSE. Peter and Martha Jane Carnahan lived in this house on East Central Avenue, which looked quite different when it was first built in the early 1880s. The two-story-tall columns were added and the brick painted white many years later. The structure has at different times housed a restaurant, a real estate title company, and an interior decorator's studio. (Courtesy of Shiloh Museum of Ozark History.)

Three

The Building Boom 1881–1890

There had been plenty of talk about building a railroad through northwest Arkansas before the Civil War. But, of course, the war interrupted any plans to extend rail service beyond Pierce City, Missouri. There was, however, stagecoach traffic that began in the 1840s, when Dr. Thomas J. Pollard operated regular routes out of Fayetteville, Arkansas. If one could afford it, merchandise could be ordered by mail and shipped from large commercial centers such as New Orleans, Philadelphia, and St. Louis. A steamboat could carry the merchandise up the Arkansas River to Van Buren, where it would be transferred to wagons and hauled around the Boston Mountains, through Cane Hill, and on to Fayetteville and Bentonville.

By 1881, the mainline railroad through Rogers was complete, and a rail spur was under construction to Bentonville. More large commercial apple orchards were beginning to bear fruit, and the railroad offered another way to expand business opportunities. The lumber mills of northwest Arkansas were in operation again, and in Bentonville, as always, there was plenty of red clay available for brick making.

Ever since the collapse of the Arkansas banking system in the 1840s, many of the citizens of Bentonville had bitter feelings for commercial banks. It seemed safer to shelter one's wealth in land and the barter system, but the economy was beginning to look bright, and people seemed ready to do business with banks again. During this economic boom, the People's Bank and the Benton County Bank were built on the town square. Many of the brick buildings and houses still stand from that particular time, which attests to the economic success of Bentonville in those years.

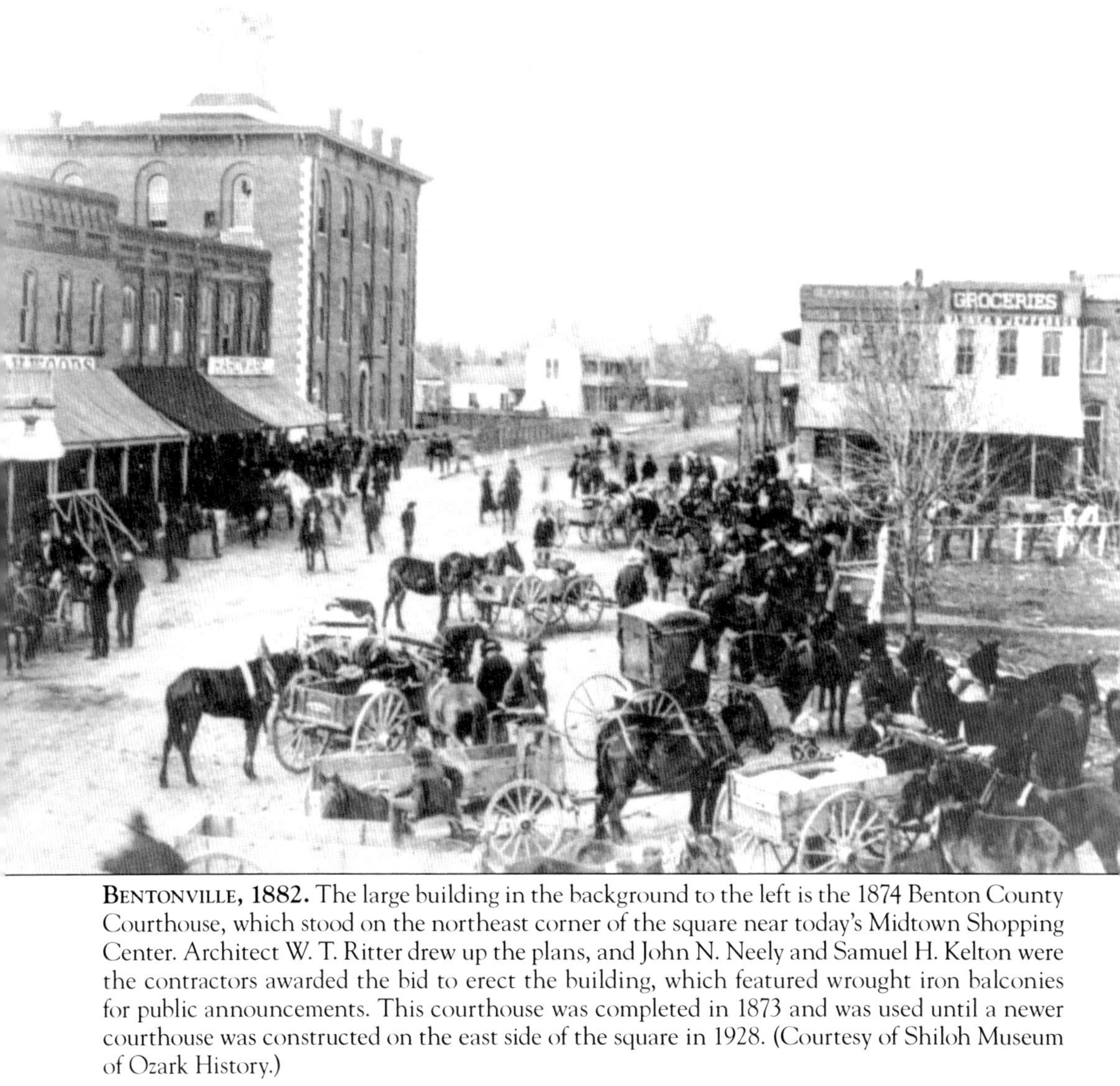

BENTONVILLE, 1882. The large building in the background to the left is the 1874 Benton County Courthouse, which stood on the northeast corner of the square near today's Midtown Shopping Center. Architect W. T. Ritter drew up the plans, and John N. Neely and Samuel H. Kelton were the contractors awarded the bid to erect the building, which featured wrought iron balconies for public announcements. This courthouse was completed in 1873 and was used until a newer courthouse was constructed on the east side of the square in 1928. (Courtesy of Shiloh Museum of Ozark History.)

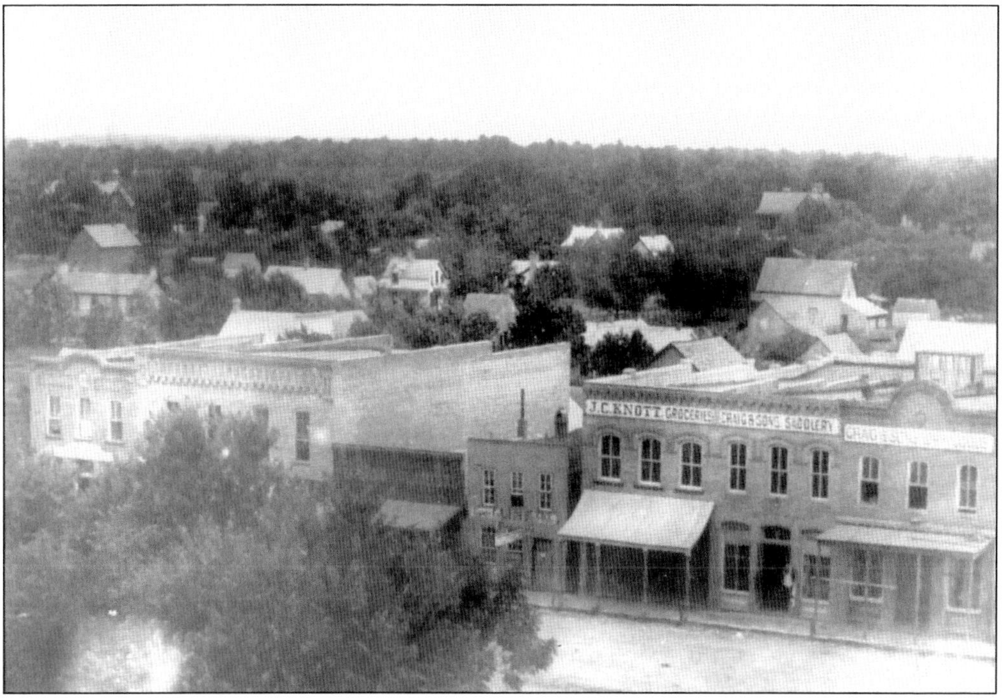

Early Views of the South Side of the Square. The top image shows the south side of the town square with two early buildings in the middle that no longer exist. Visible among the trees in the far left background is believed to be the roof and chimney of the 1887 Elliot House, which still stands at 303 Southeast Third Street. In the photograph below is the double storefront buildings that later replaced the two small buildings shown in the center of the top photograph. Those buildings housed Roy's Office Supply for many years, and today they are the location of the popular Table Mesa bistro. The tall glass front windows filled interiors with natural light and allowed space for window displays. (Both, courtesy of Patty Pearce Payne.)

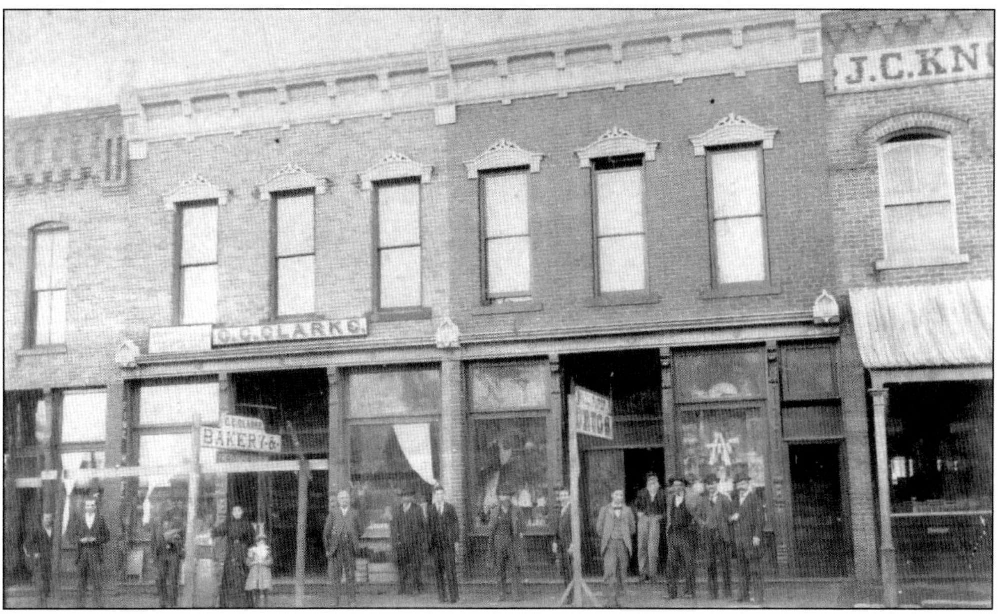

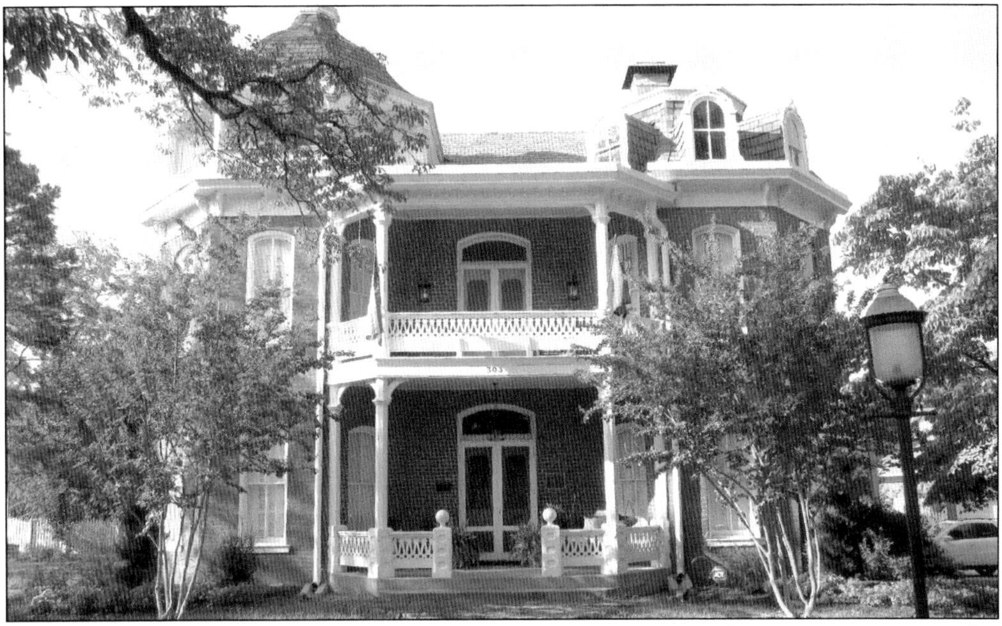

The Elliott House, 1887. The Honorable Samuel N. Elliott served as Benton County judge from 1876 to 1884. Judge Elliott had two sons who operated silver mines in New Mexico. It is said that profit from the silver mines help finance the building of this elegant Bentonville home. Jane Brack Elliott was an active member of the Presbyterian church, but Judge Elliott professed to be an independent freethinker in the realm of religion. (Courtesy of the author.)

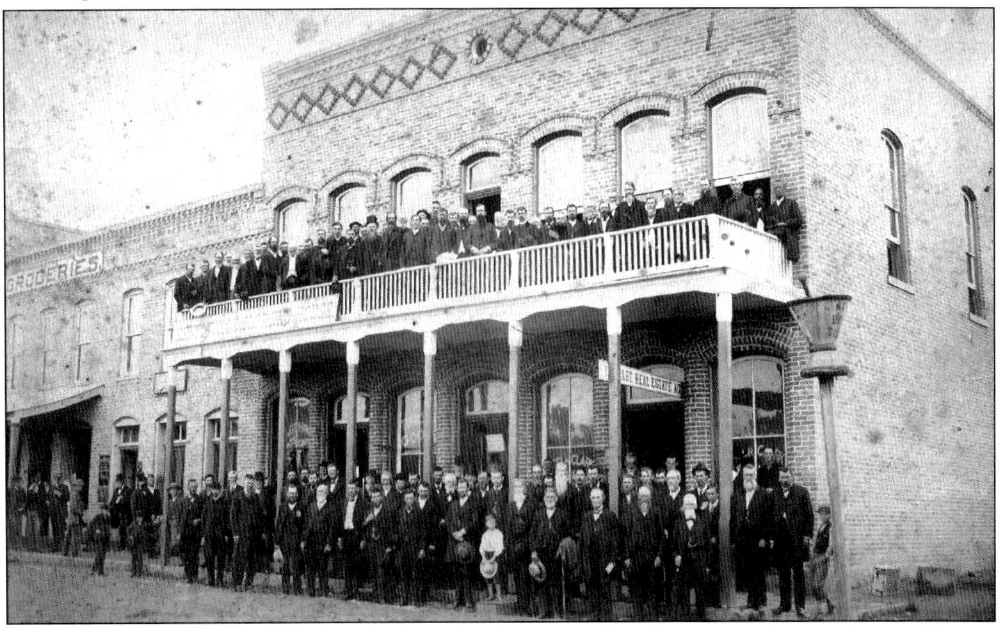

The Old Opera House. The Cumberland Presbyterian Church ministers' general assembly was held in 1885 in the opera house on the north side of the square, where the Arvest building is located today. The opera house was basically an auditorium used for traveling musicians, entertainers, and special events. The building was constructed after a fire destroyed almost all of the buildings on the north side of the square around 1880. (Courtesy of Gary Black.)

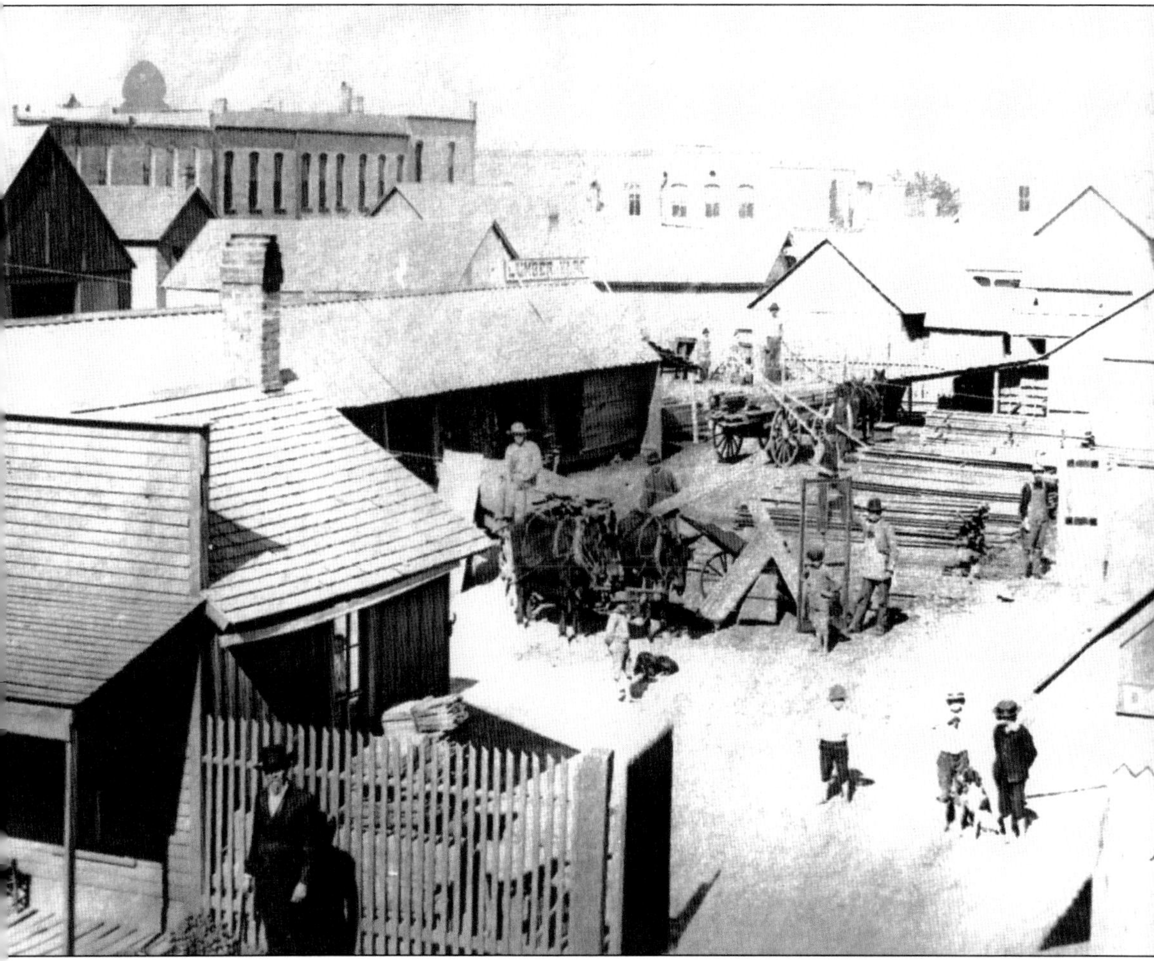

The Building Material Business. This lumberyard was located directly behind the present-day Massey building in downtown. This business supplied lumber for the building boom of the 1880s. The lumberyard covered most of the block from A Street to Main Street. The man standing in the foreground is identified as Dr. J. H. Hobbs. (Courtesy of Gary Black.)

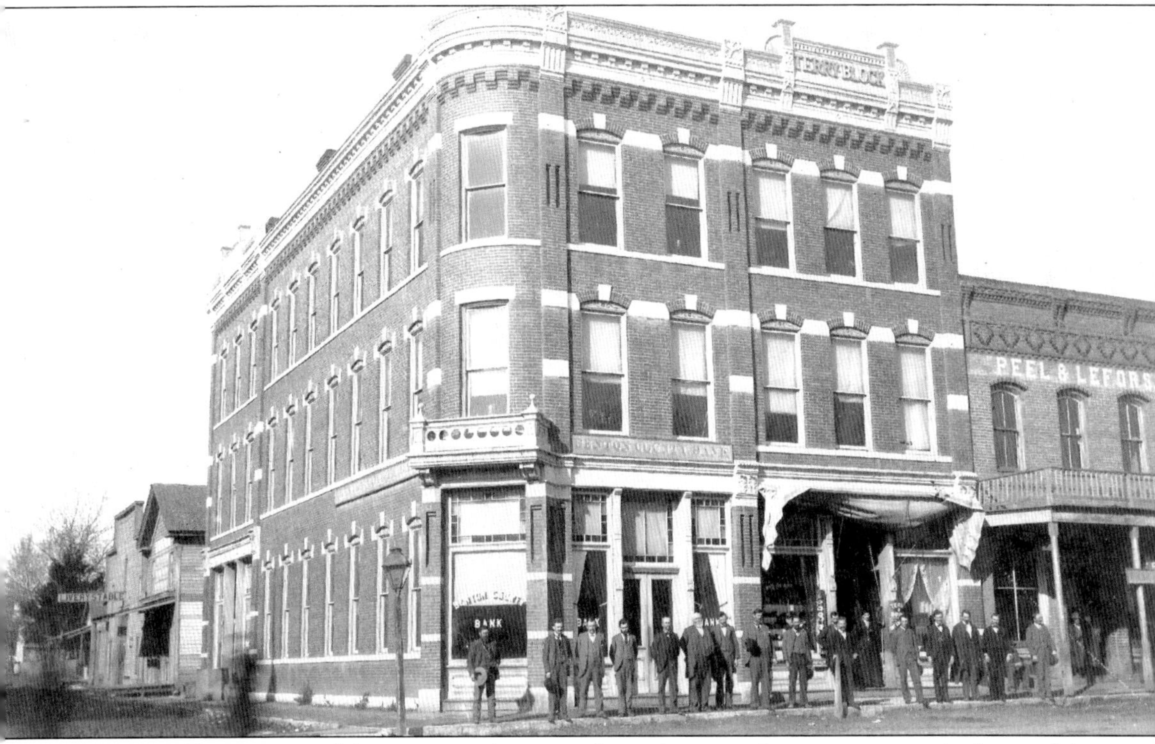

PROUD BENTONVILLE MERCHANTS. A group of merchants and investors poses in front of the beautiful Terry Block building soon after it opened for business. William A. Terry constructed his first mercantile building at this same location in 1874. That building was considered too good to be torn down and can be seen in this photograph around the corner, where it was moved to make room for the new three-story structure. William Terry was not only a merchant but also president of the Benton County Bank, which occupied the front corner of the building. (Courtesy of Patty Pearce Payne.)

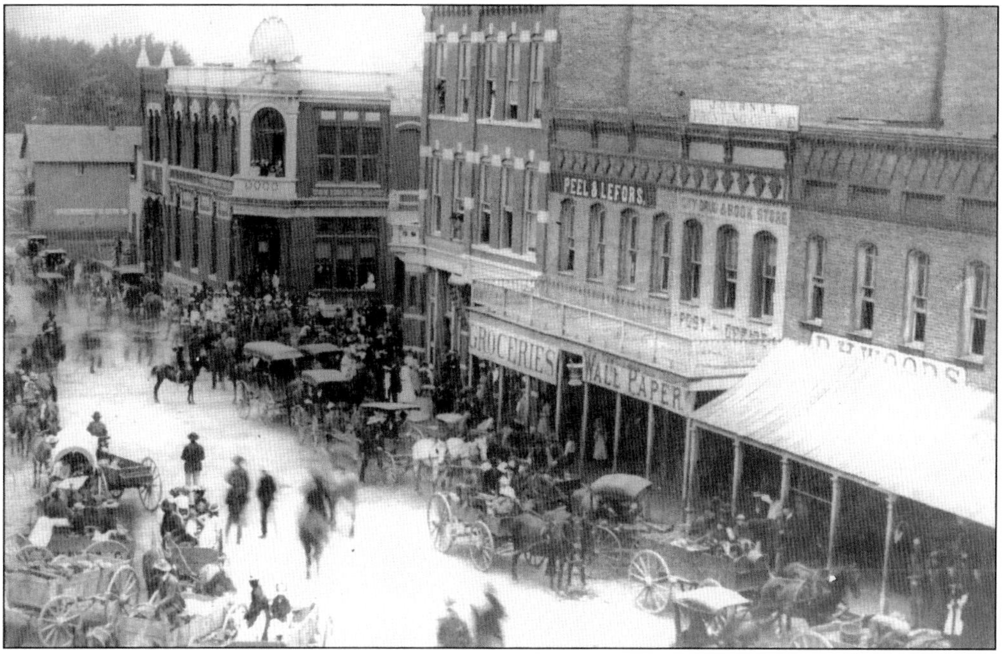

A Busy Day in Bentonville. There was heavy buggy traffic on this busy day in the 1890s. At the time, there were three or four businesses and a post office operating out of the building that today houses the Walmart Visitor Center on Main Street. The photograph was taken from the top of the Benton County Courthouse building, and the crowded street may have been in anticipation of a parade or celebration. (Courtesy of Gary Black.)

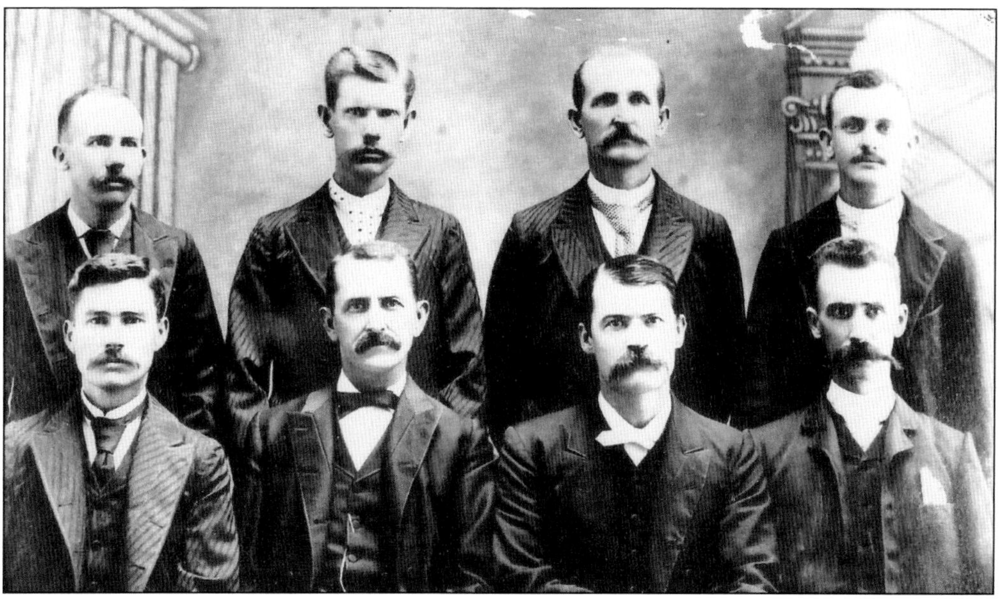

The Hungry Eight. Col. William Terry was not the only successful merchant in business on the Bentonville Square during the 1890s. This well-dressed group of gentlemen was nicknamed the "Hungry Eight," apparently because of their aggressive retail competition. From left to right are (first row) George Jackson, Col. William A. Terry, Bob Brasher, and Bennet Burks; (second row) Jim Lankford, Jim Alfrey, Alex Hall, and Asa Lankford. (Courtesy of Patty Pearce Payne.)

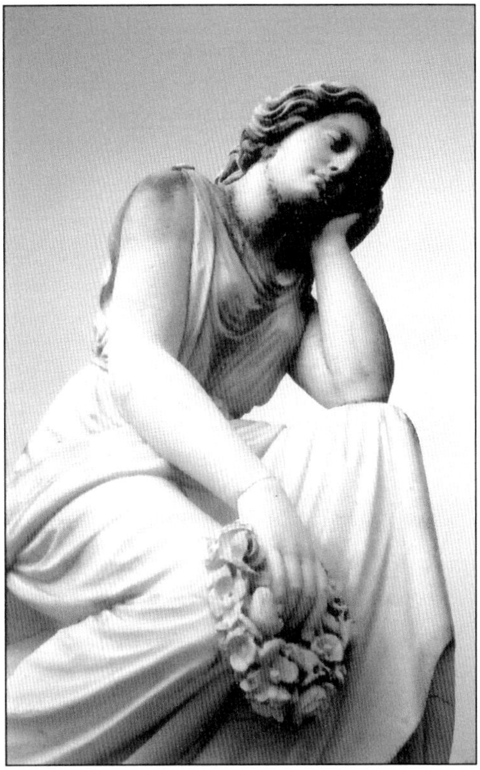

The Terry Memorial Statue. The Terry Memorial is not only a grave marker for the once influential Bentonville family but is also an exquisite outdoor sculpture. The lovely statue is finely carved white Carrera marble and depicts a Grecian-style lady frozen in grief and holding a wreath of flowers in her right hand. The statue is one of the most beautiful in northwest Arkansas. (Courtesy of the author.)

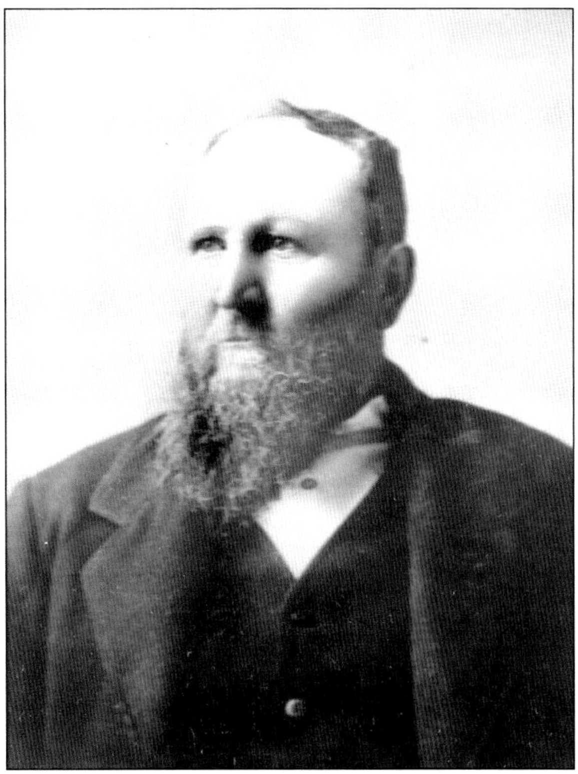

George Harrison Jefferson, 1834–1891. George Harrison Jefferson grew up in Bentonville, where his family owned a hotel and a furniture shop. In 1887, George was with a Bentonville posse led by U.S. Marshal Dan Maples that ventured into Indian Territory looking for wanted criminals. Maples was shot and killed as he and George returned to camp after conducting police business in Tahlequah. George exchanged gunfire with the fleeing assassin, but to no avail. Maples's body was brought back to Bentonville and buried in the Bentonville Cemetery. (Courtesy of James Jefferson.)

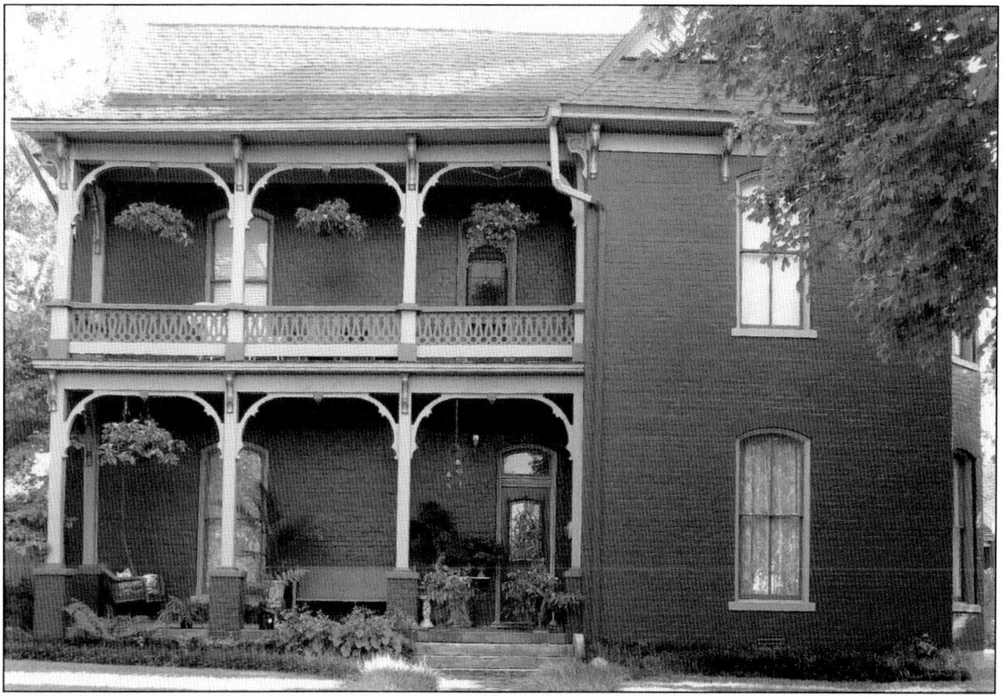

The James Atkins Rice House. Both James Rice and his brother Charles were successful attorneys in Bentonville. James built a large brick home that still stands on the south side of town. He married Lucy Winton from Pea Ridge, whose family owned the large Winton farm that later became part of the Pea Ridge National Military Park property. James was mayor of Bentonville for several years and also served two terms on the Arkansas state legislature. (Courtesy of the author.)

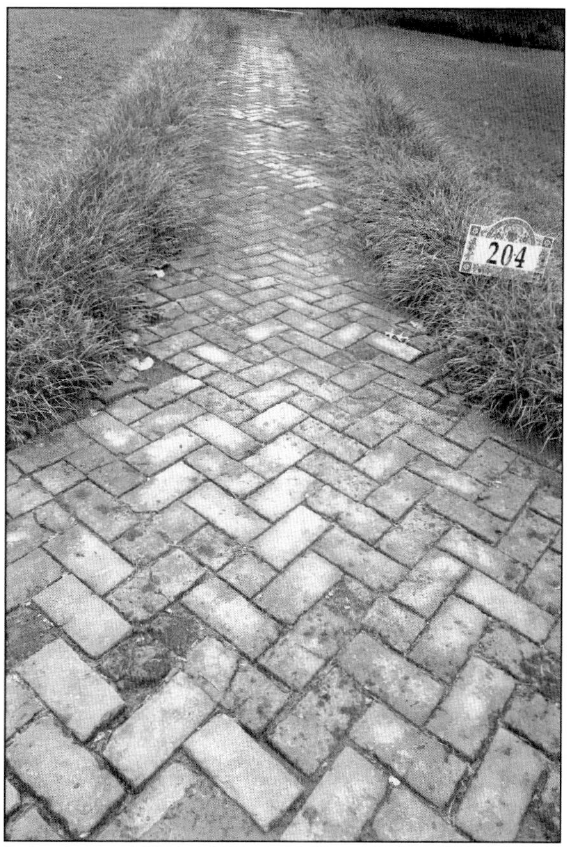

Old Brick Sidewalk. Many of the old sidewalks have been replaced, but this walkway in a herringbone design has been well preserved. The walk leads to the front door of the James A. Rice historical house. (Courtesy of the author.)

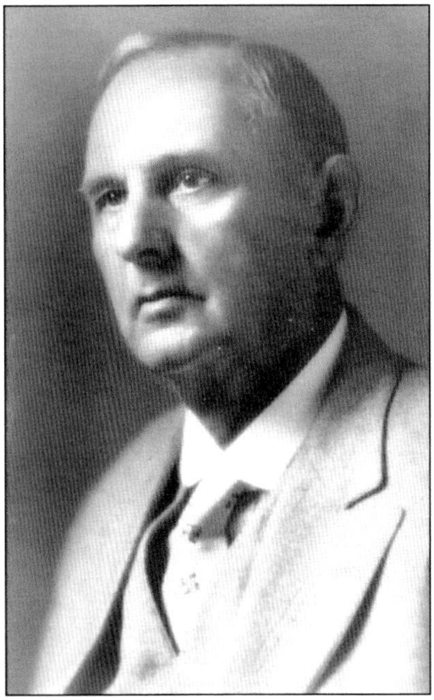

Charles M. Rice, 1859–1939. Charles Matlock Rice moved from Tennessee to Pea Ridge with his family and was a young man during the Civil War. The sons of the Rice family tended to either become doctors or lawyers, so after graduating from Ann Arbor University Law School, Charles Rice and his wife returned to Bentonville, where he practiced law for the rest of his life. (Courtesy of Mary Marquess.)

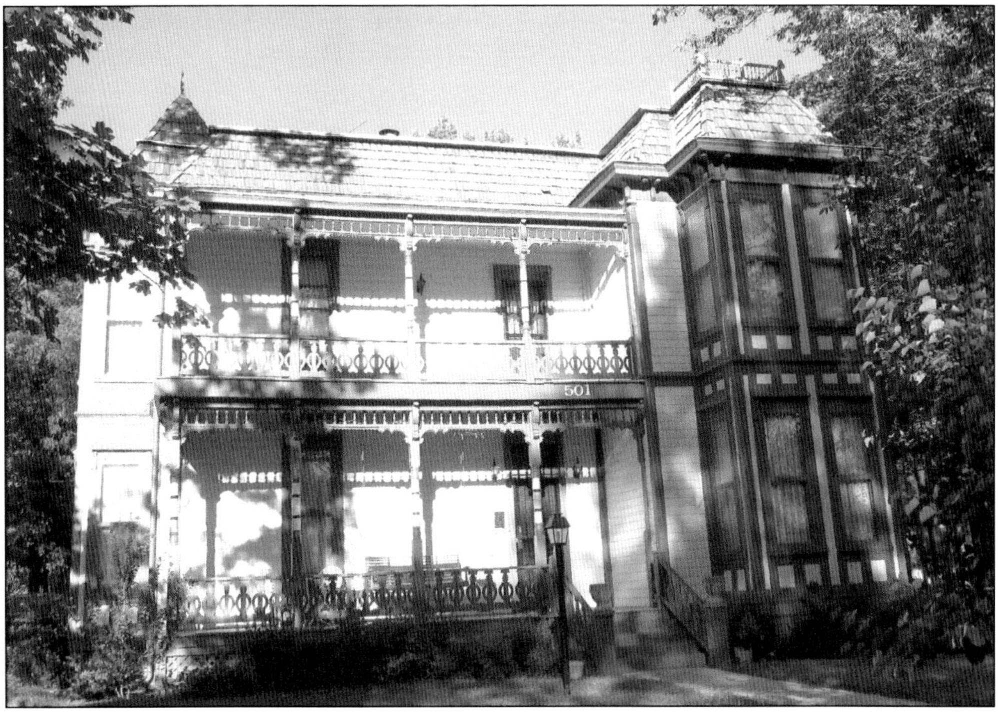

The Charles Matlock Rice House. One of the largest north Bentonville homes, this was built in the 1890s by William B. Deming. Deming was able to obtain virgin timber and well-trained workmen, so this house and many of the homes he built are still standing straight and strong today. Charles Rice and his wife, Mattie Anderson Regan Rice, raised five children in this comfortable home. Mattie hand carved some of the detailed woodwork inside the house, which has been carefully preserved. (Courtesy of the author.)

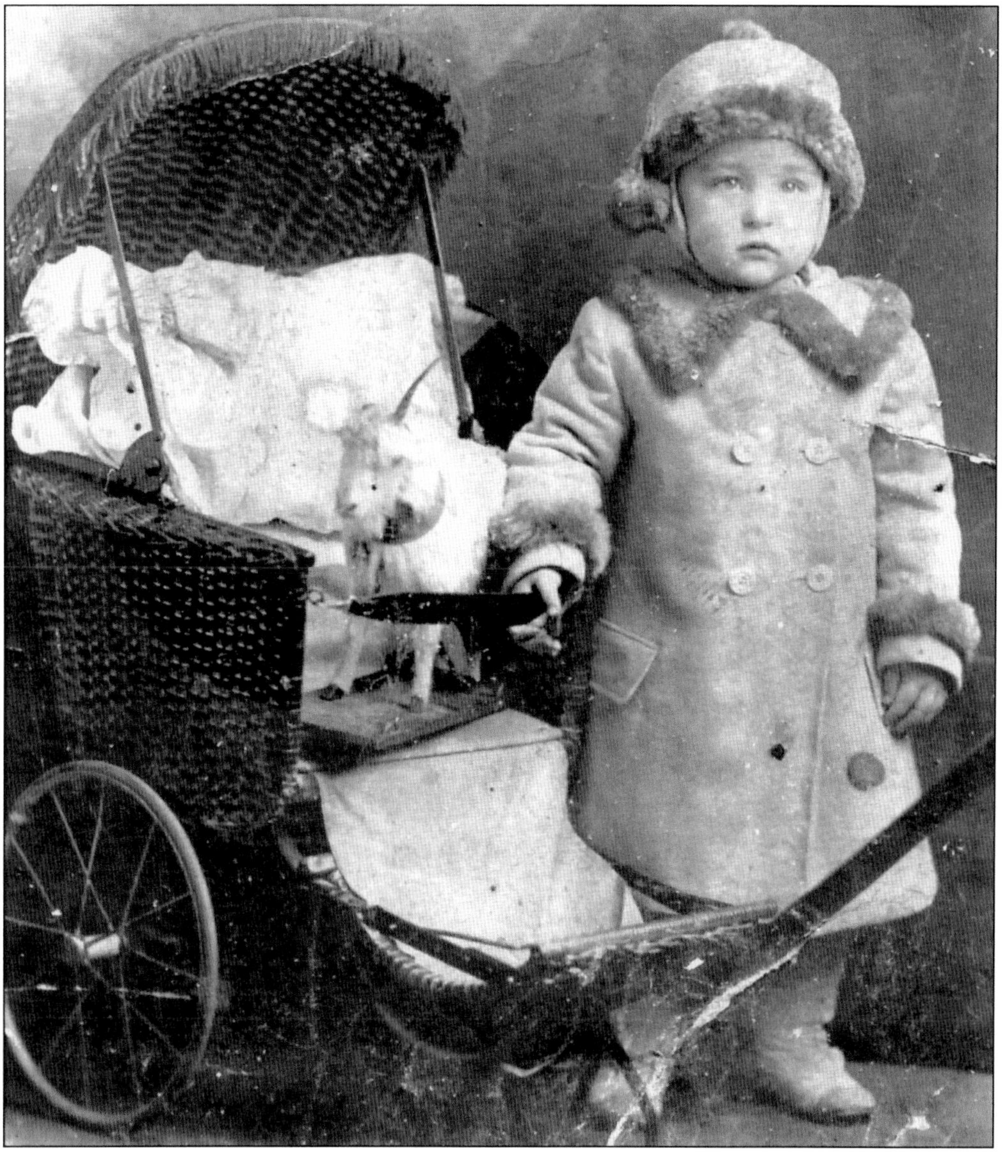

JEFFERSON RANDOLPH RICE. The son of Charles Matlock and Mattie Regan Rice, Jefferson was born in 1890, about the same time that the family moved into their new home on North Main Street in the Demings Addition. Jefferson attended the University of Arkansas, was a lieutenant in World War I, and returned home, where he served as mayor, city attorney, and municipal judge. He also followed the family tradition of his father and uncle as a practicing attorney. (Courtesy of Mary Marquess.)

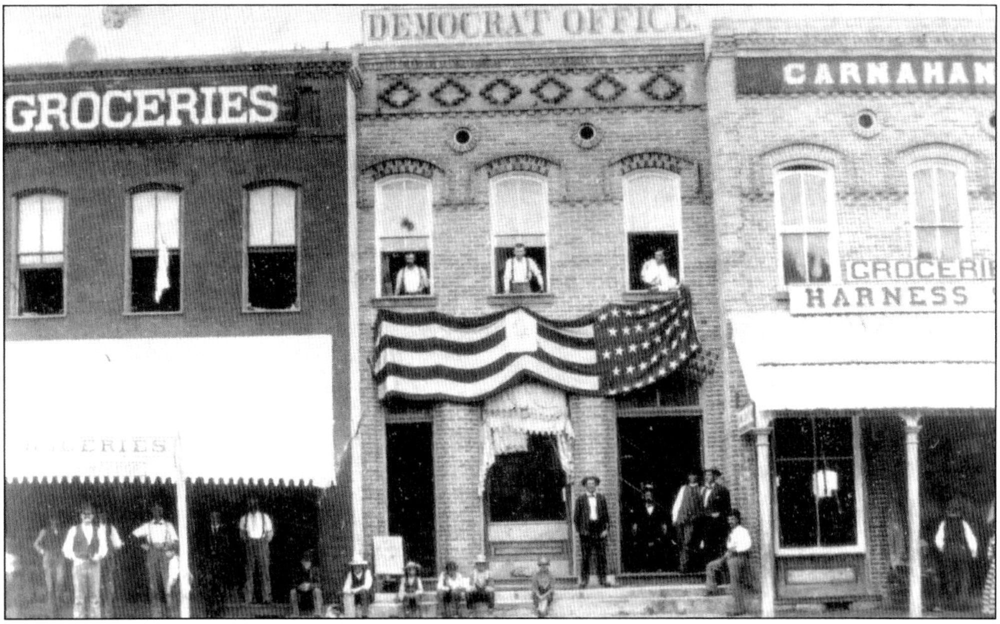

THE *BENTON COUNTY DEMOCRAT* NEWSPAPER. The *Benton County Democrat* newspaper office was draped with a political banner in support of Pres. Grover Cleveland, who was the son of a Presbyterian pastor and was born in New Jersey in 1837. Cleveland did not win the election, even though he received more popular votes. Benjamin Harrison won the most electoral votes and became the 23rd U.S. president. But in 1893, Cleveland returned to the Oval Office for a second, nonconsecutive term. The newspaper office was located on the north side of the square. (Courtesy of Rogers Historical Museum.)

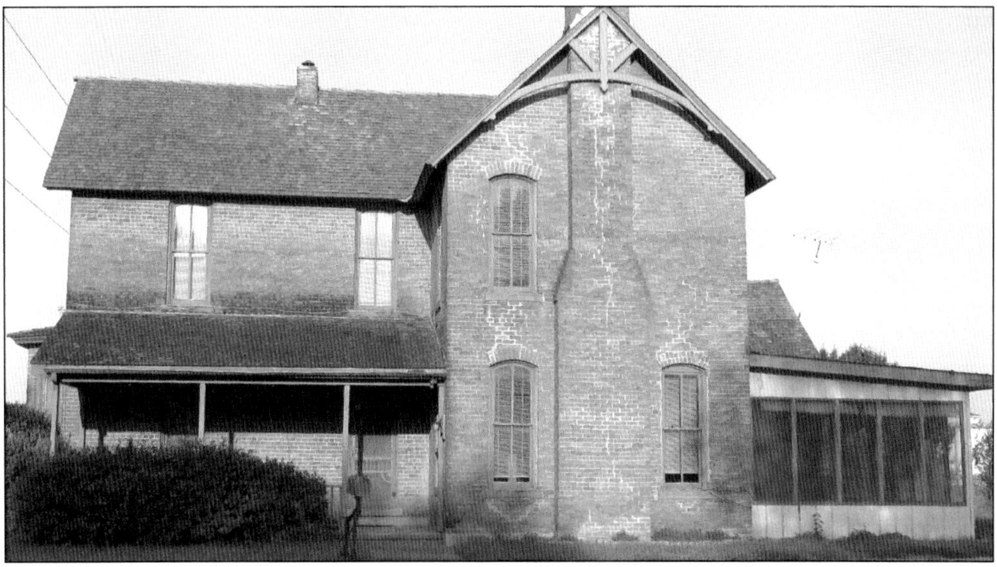

THE DICKSON HOUSE. J. Alvin Dickson was the grandson of early Bentonville pioneer John B. Dickson, who was the first county clerk and leader in many community ventures. J. Alvin married Lillie Woolsey and moved into this home in 1877. J. Alvin and his father-in-law, Henry Woolsey, were co-owners of a large nursery business that profited from the railroad spur situated on their land. (Courtesy of the author.)

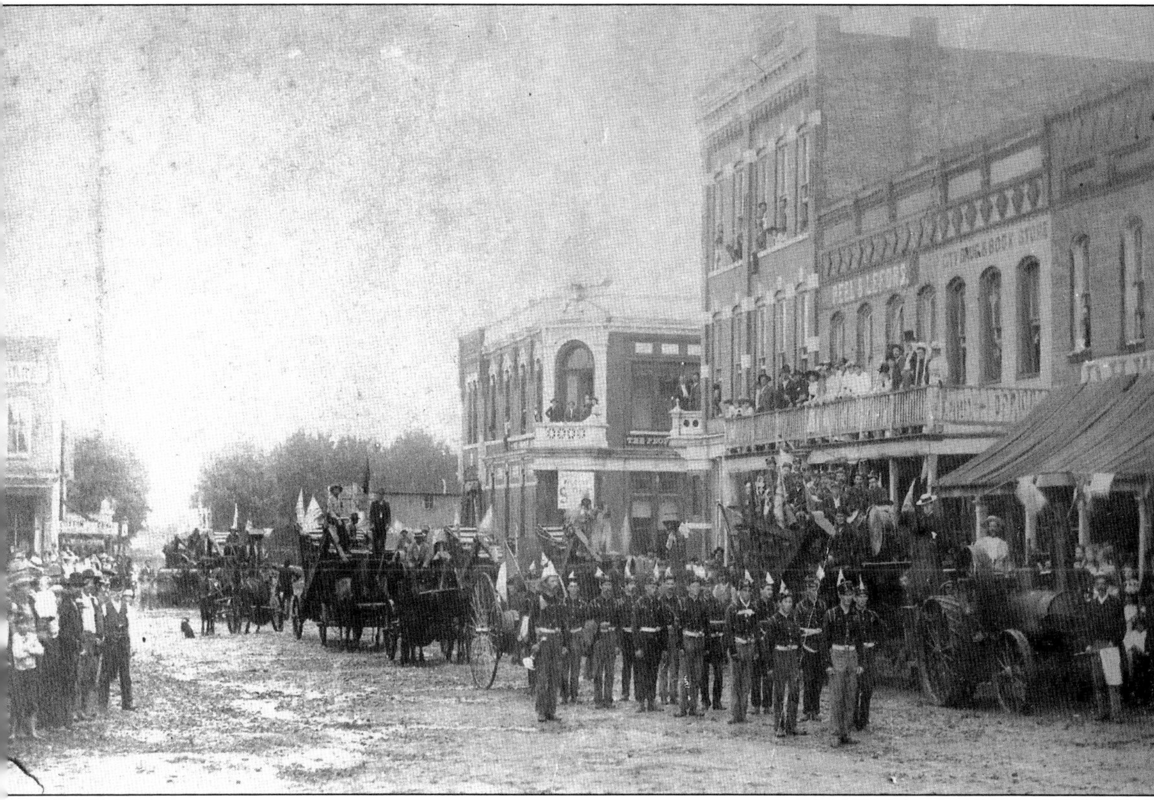

THE CONFEDERATE SOLDIERS REUNION, 1893. This reunion was hosted by the National United Confederate Veterans Association and brought 15,000 people from 15 states to Bentonville for the three-day event. The Stevenson's Hose Company is lined up in the foreground, and Alex Black's First Regimental Band is in a wagon pulled by a tractor. There are people viewing the festivities from every available window, as well as a special group of dignitaries gathered on the second-floor balcony porch. The parade participants are lined up on Main Street on the west side of the town square. (Courtesy of Pea Ridge National Military Park.)

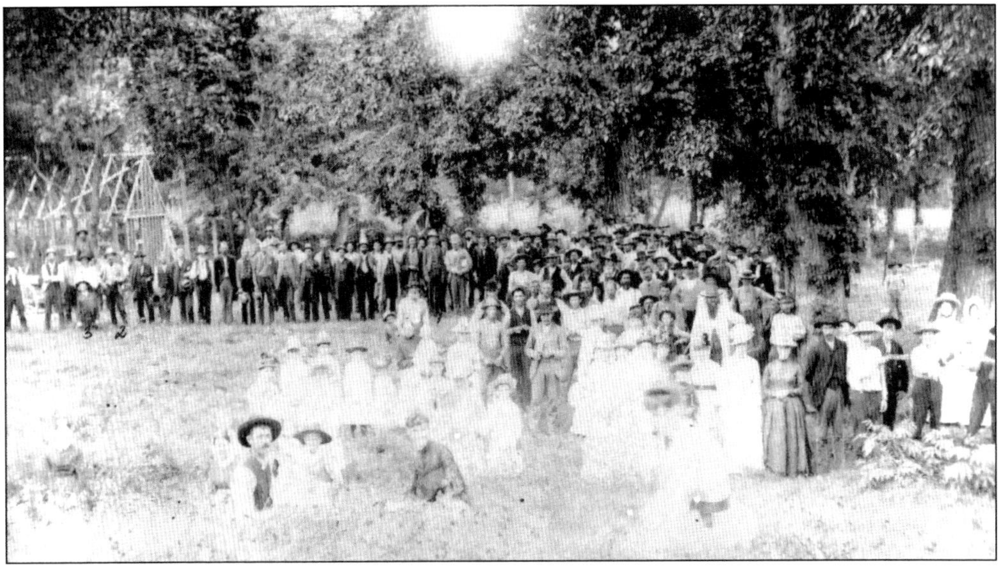

The Old Soldiers Reunion, 1891. This old faded photograph is believed to be the soldiers reunion organized by the Northwest Arkansas Confederate Reunion Association. The program was presented at old Park Springs, and an estimated 2,000 people attended. Past soldiers are lined up in the background, and in the foreground are young ladies dressed in white for a presentation. (Courtesy of Patty Pearce Payne.)

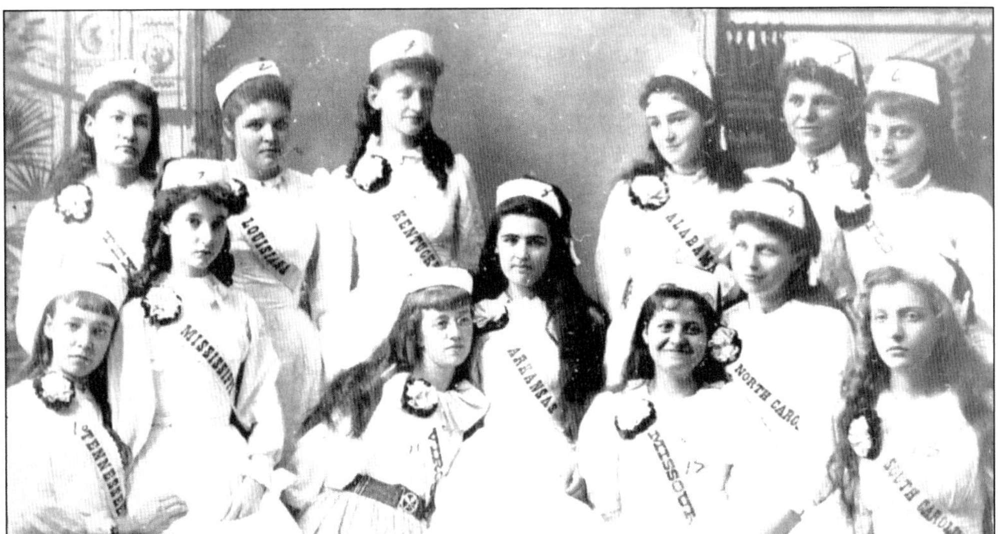

The Historical Drama, 1893. In beauty queen style, each young lady represented one of the 13 Confederate states in a historical drama and also rode on a decorated float in the parade. From left to right are (first row) ? Hines (Tennessee), Katherine Watson (Mississippi), Carrie Henry (Virginia), Jennie Berry (Arkansas), Minnie Robinson (Missouri), Ophelia Bates (North Carolina), and Olive Suggs (South Carolina); (second row) Mabel Clark (Texas), Etta Jackson (Louisiana), Effie Morris (Kentucky), Kitty Smartt (Alabama), Nannie Whayne (Georgia), and Mary Woods (Florida). (Courtesy of Gary Black.)

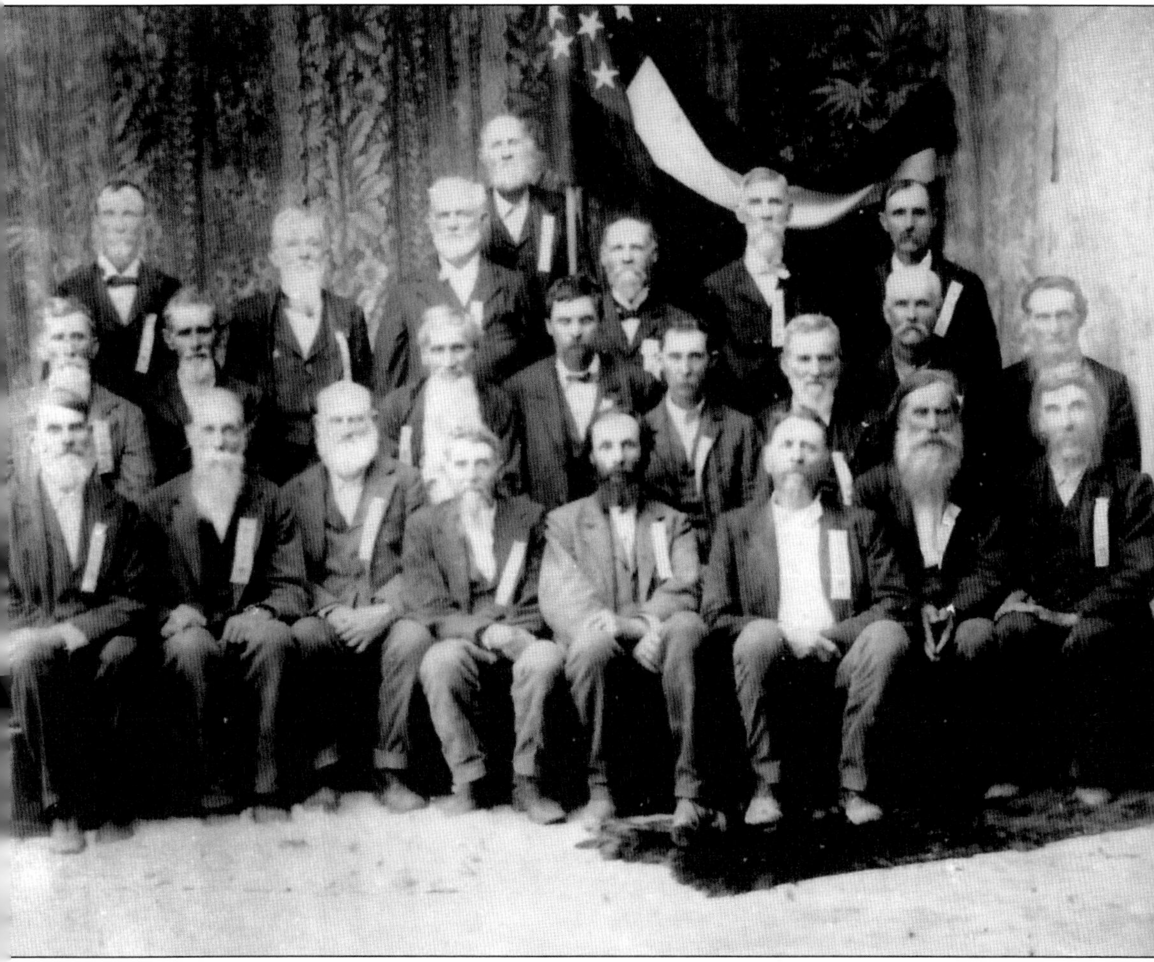

A Reunion Portrait, 1895. The Confederate veterans from Company F, 34th Arkansas Infantry, CSA, gather for a reunion portrait. They were the last surviving members of their regiment at that time. Included are Capt. Joe Dickson, Capt. J. W. McClinton, Capt. C. L. Pickens, John Black, Major Earle, Rev. Peter Carnahan, George Breathwaite, William Cash, Frank Price, Lemuel Cash, Dick Gamble, William Eggleston Gould, John Pace, Joe Ford, William Threet, John Weaver, Bob D. Woods, Dave Young, John Blevins, Wash Gamble, Jesse Blevins, Bill Ricketts, and John Hileman. (Courtesy of Gary Black.)

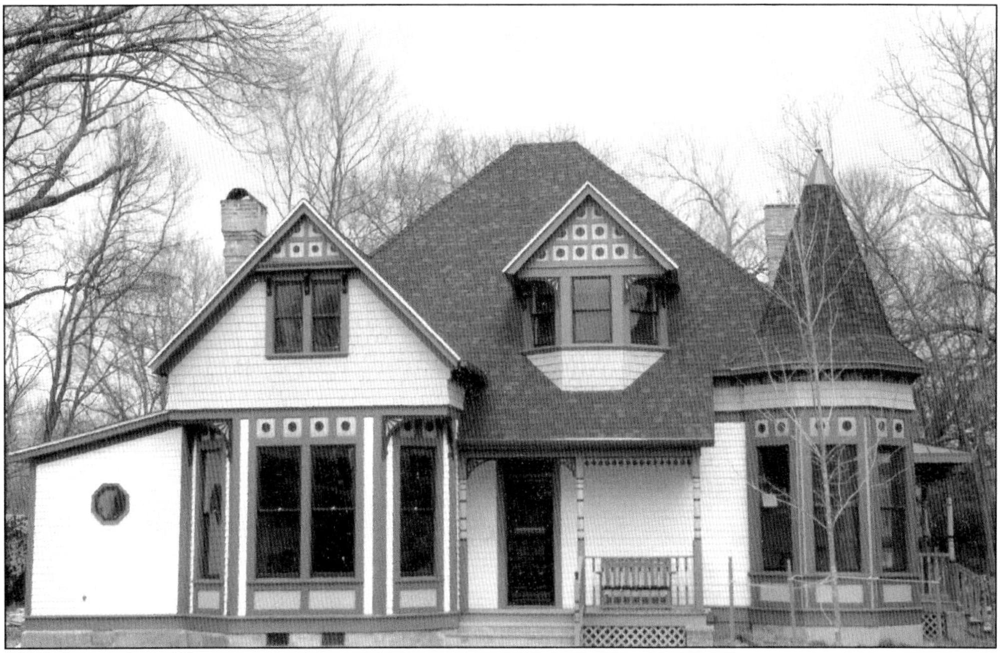

THE LAUGHLIN HOUSE. Ebe Laughlin lived most of her life in this beautiful house located at 102 Northwest Third Street. Music was often heard coming from the Laughlin House, as Ebe practiced several instruments and performed in programs at the opera house and in her church. (Courtesy of the author.)

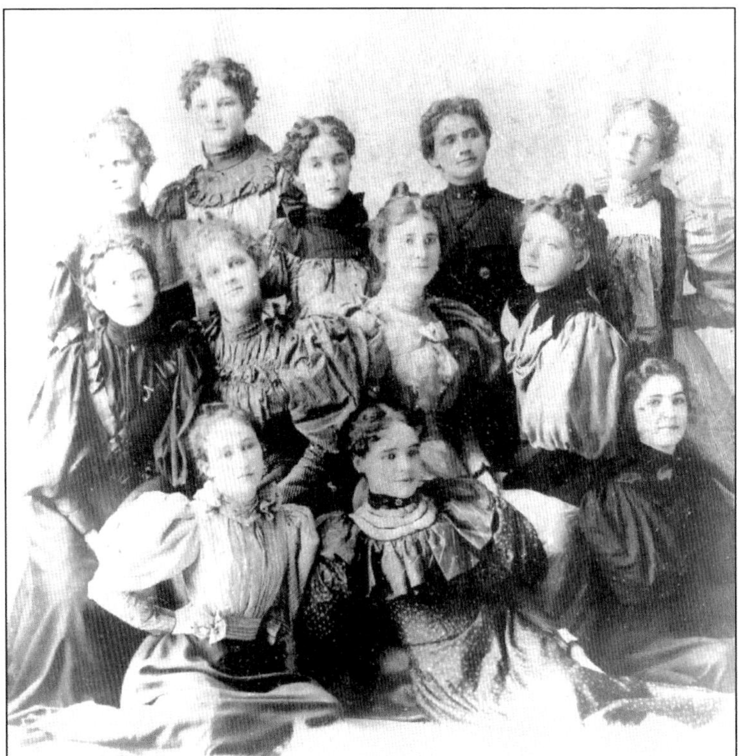

PHOEBE LAUGHLIN AND CLASSMATES. Phoebe Laughlin, at right in front, was known as "Ebe" by her friends. The Laughlin family moved to Bentonville in 1881. Her father, Reuben J. Laughlin, sold clocks, watches, jewelry, and silverware. Beginning at a young age, Ebe was recognized for her musical talent, which she may have inherited from her grandfather, who was a fifer in the Battle of New Orleans. (Courtesy of Gary Black.)

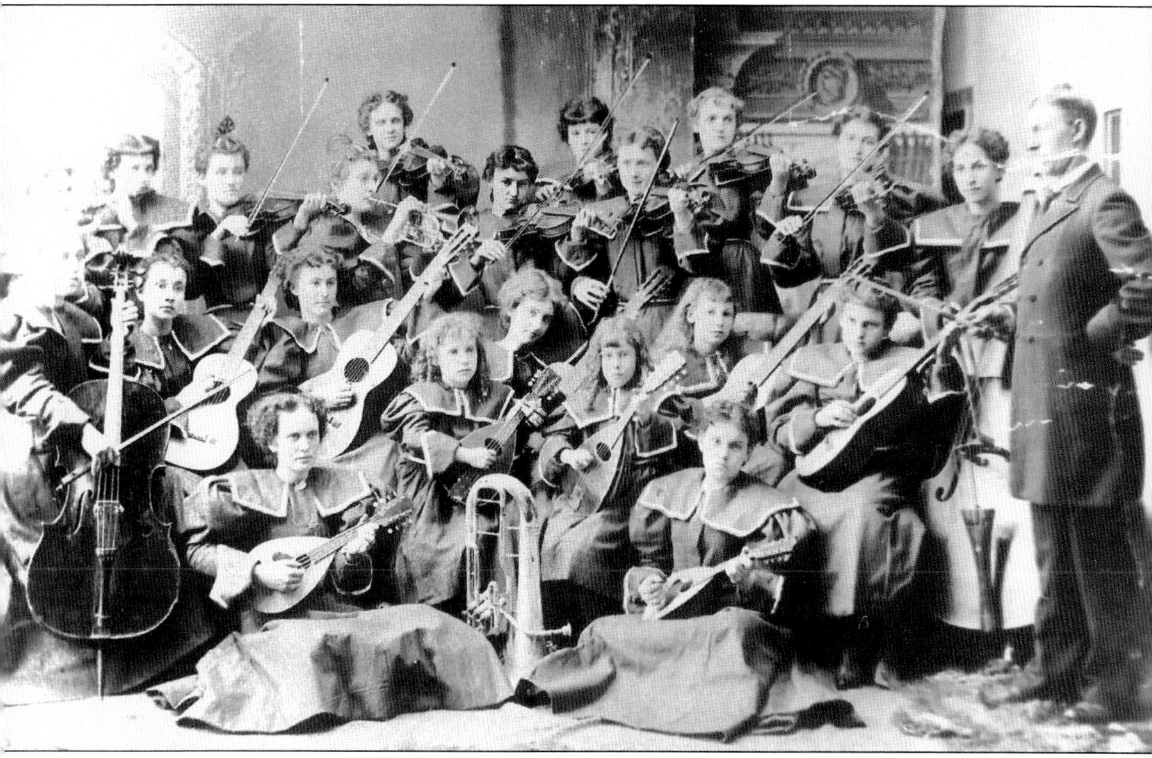

BENTONVILLE LADIES ORCHESTRA. Pictured here is one of Bentonville's musical groups who were likely attending the Bentonville Academy, which offered an array of classes in the arts. Ebe's father was an avid supporter of the school. From left to right are (first row) Betty Blake with mandolin, (later in life, Betty married Will Rogers, famous performer, satirist, and cowboy), Alma Langford, ? Langford (Alma's twin sister), and Ebe Laughlin (who generally played piano but is posed with a mandolin); (second row) cellist Helena Kryer, Lillie Stahl, Mary Hindman, Agnes Rice, Betty Cook, and Josie Shields; (third row) Agnes James, Oma Blake on piccolo, Mrs. Michelltree, Olive Suggs on cornet, Montie Blake, Kitty Smartt, Ada Haney, Mrs. Mobberly, Leah Shibley, and Minnie Clark. Vina Clark stands with a bass violin next to Prof. Victor Kryer. (Courtesy of Rogers Historical Museum.)

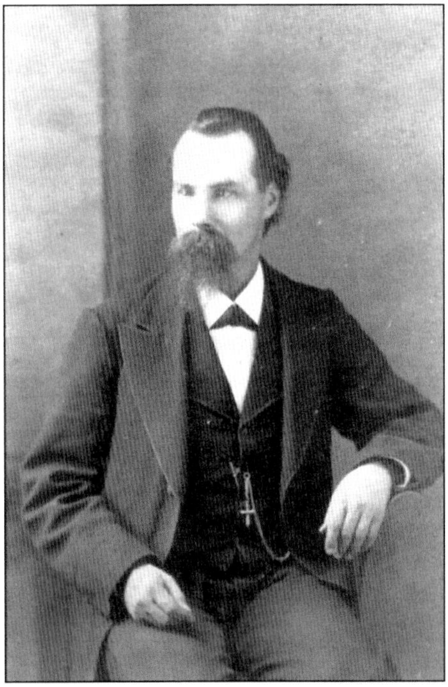

Photographer Raphael Hansard. At left is a self-portrait of professional photographer Raphael W. Hansard, who learned photography from his brother in Fayetteville, Arkansas. Raphael and his brothers were Confederate army veterans who moved to northwest Arkansas from Missouri after the Civil War. Raphael opened his first photography portrait studio on the east side of the town square in the 1870s. (Courtesy of Rogers Historical Museum.)

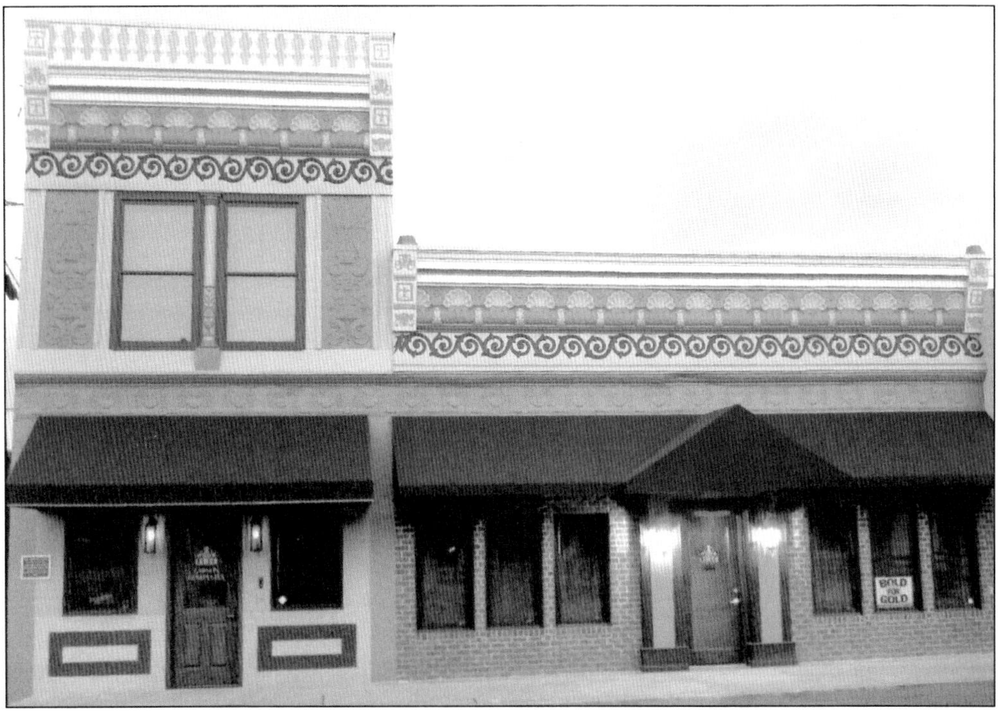

Hansard Photography Studio. The two-story section of this well-preserved commercial building is where Raphael Hansard moved later in his professional photography career. His new studio was complete with slanted glass window for proper northern light exposure in the second-story studio. Today, that building houses Lawco Exploration at 113 South Main Street. (Courtesy of the author.)

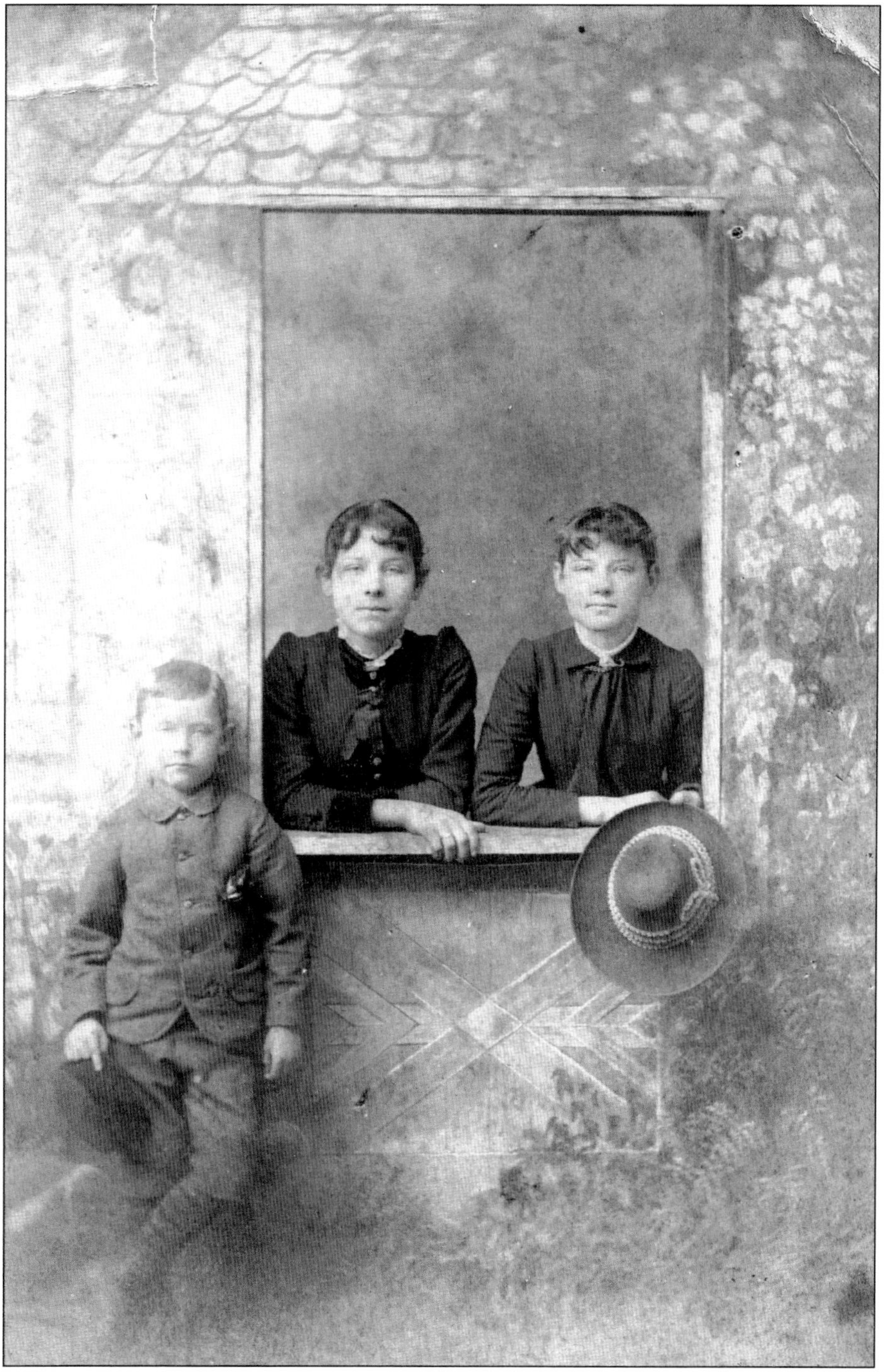

Hansard Photograph. There are many old photographs that have survived with the Hansard Photography Studio logo stamped on the front or back. Unfortunately very few of the subjects are identified, including the young people in this very early creative example of the photographic work of Raphael Hansard in Bentonville. Two girls lean on a hand-painted backdrop, and a little boy poses for the photographer. (Courtesy of Gary Black.)

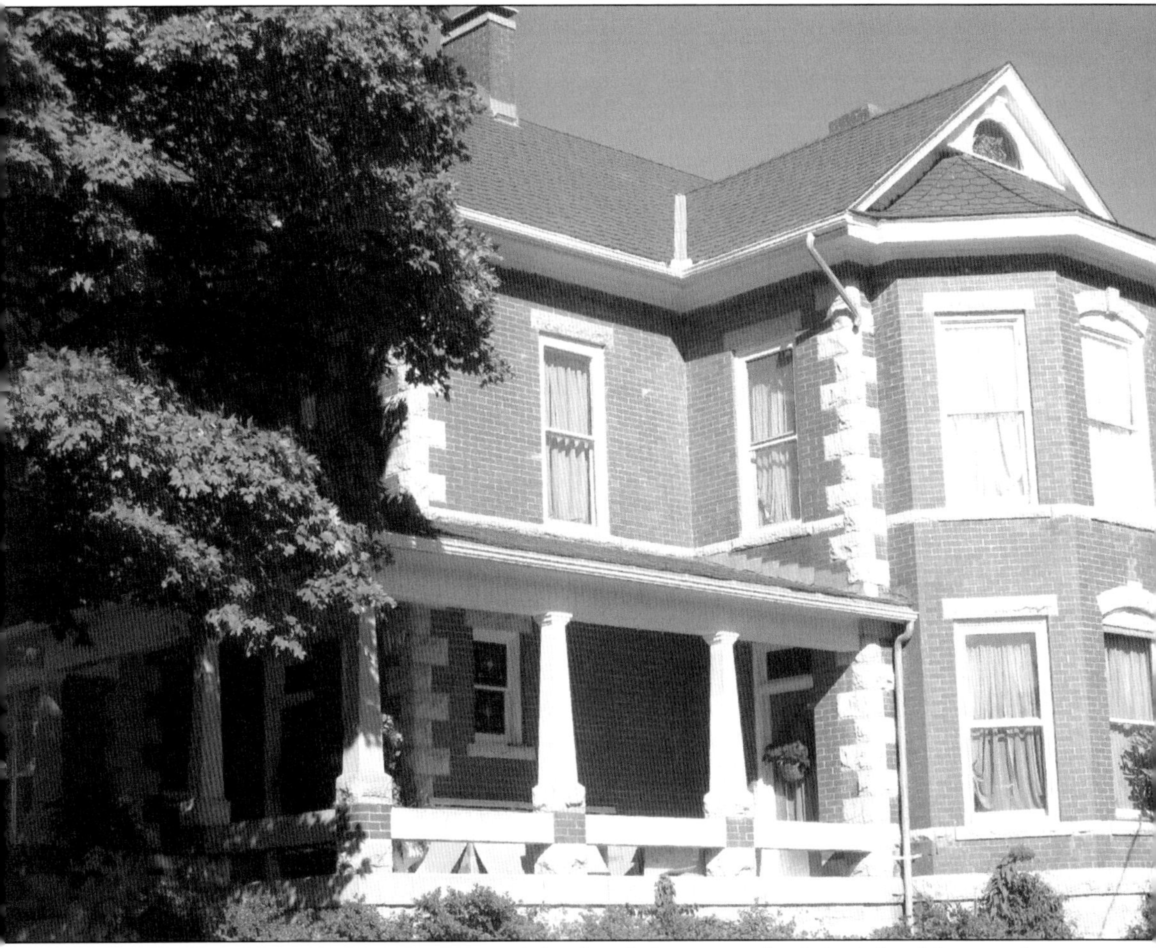

THE MACON-HARRISON HOUSE, 1910. This lovely home was built by John Macon, who was part owner of the Macon-Carson Distillery, located next-door. Later the house was the home of Luther Harrison, who opened the Harrison Variety Store in 1924 on the west side of the square. Harrison sold his merchandise to newcomer Sam Walton in 1950, when Walton decided to move his Ben Franklin store from Newport, Arkansas. (Courtesy of the author.)

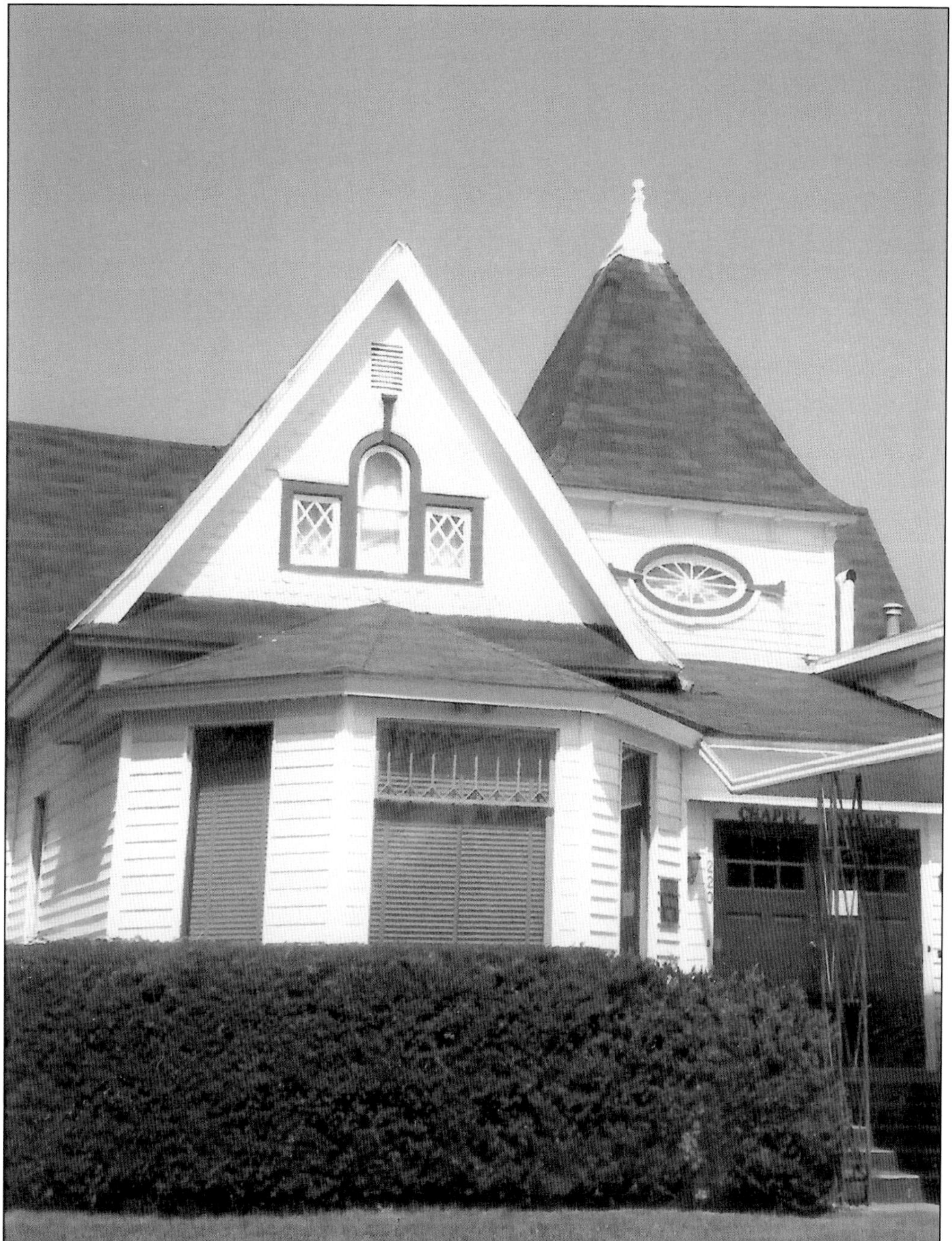

THE PICKENS FAMILY HOME, 1907. The old Pickens family home was built by the grandfather of Dr. James L. Pickens, who was born in this beautiful home that was once located on South Main Street. Dr. James L. Pickens was a well-respected doctor for many years, as was his father. After the Pickens family moved, the building housed the Burns Funeral Home for many years before the structure was torn down. (Courtesy of the author.)

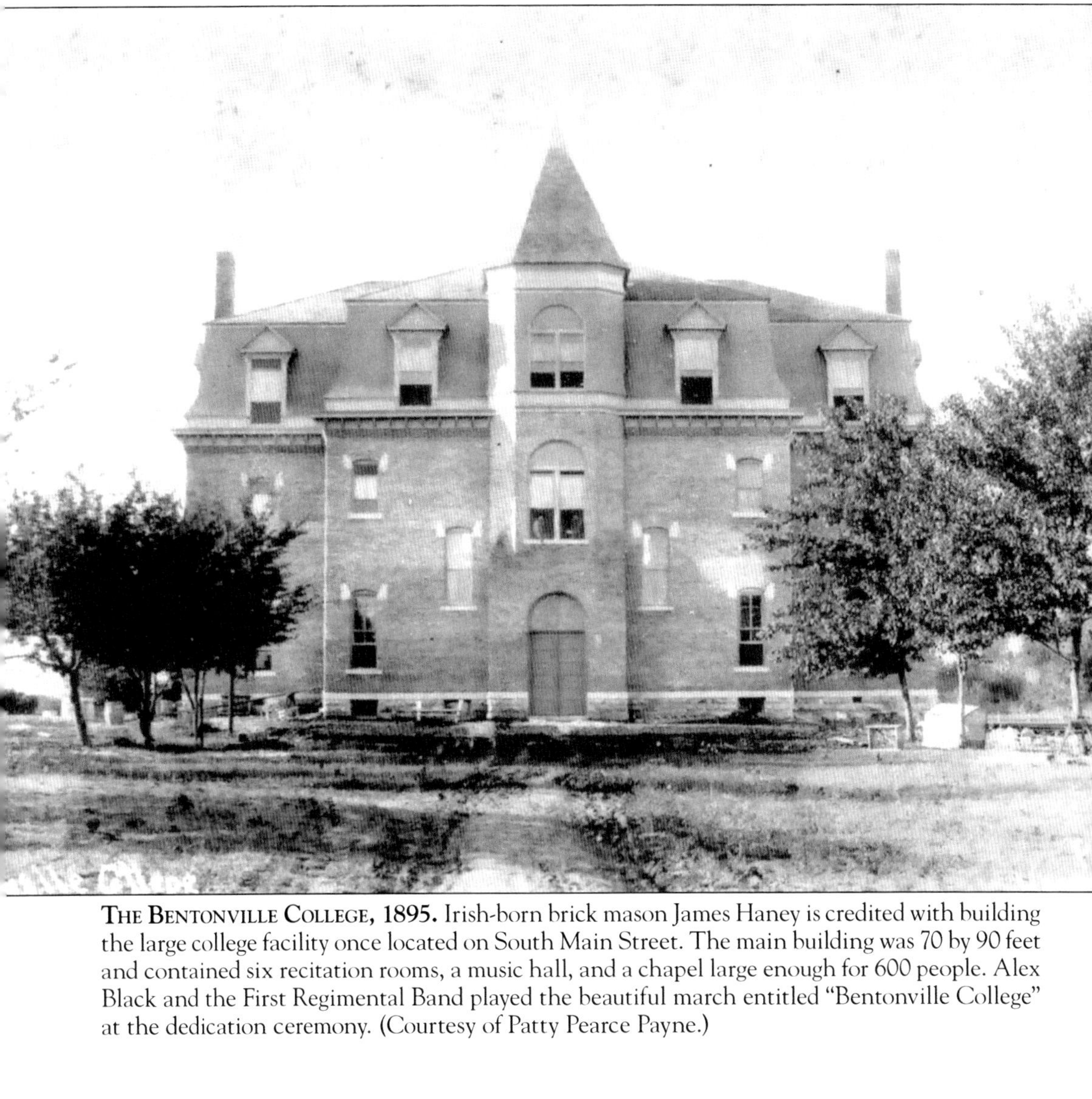

THE BENTONVILLE COLLEGE, 1895. Irish-born brick mason James Haney is credited with building the large college facility once located on South Main Street. The main building was 70 by 90 feet and contained six recitation rooms, a music hall, and a chapel large enough for 600 people. Alex Black and the First Regimental Band played the beautiful march entitled "Bentonville College" at the dedication ceremony. (Courtesy of Patty Pearce Payne.)

Four

The Apple Years 1891–1920

The Macon and Carson Brandy Distillery was located east of the town square and was at one time the largest distillery west of the Mississippi. It was said that if a person knew where the right spigot was located, he could help himself to as much applejack brandy as he wanted for free after dark. Dozens of horse-drawn wagons loaded with apples were brought to the distillery every day. In 1914, the O. L. Gregory Vinegar Company bought the business and started producing apple cider, which was shipped to the Rogers plant. In 1920, the plant was buying 50,000 to 150,000 pounds of apples a day. Today, only the remains of the foundations that held the large vats and barrels can still be seen at the site of this large distillery.

The main railroad line was completed east of Bentonville along a high plateau through the nearby town of Rogers, Arkansas. A railroad spur was built off the main line and served the commercial apple industry and other businesses, such as J. Alvin Dickson's tree nursery and farm. In fact, the spur was named the Dickson Spur. It is still used today and is located along the north side of the J. Alvin Dickson's two-story brick home on Highway 102.

On the square in Bentonville, the merchants were busy expanding their inventories, as their customers had more cash to spend. The Bentonville Academy was in full operation, and students were studying drama, music, and recitation, as all good Victorians were expected to do at the time.

The commercial apple industry years also brought many improvements to the infrastructure of Bentonville. By the 1920s, the highways were being paved, as more people were driving cars instead of horse-drawn buggies.

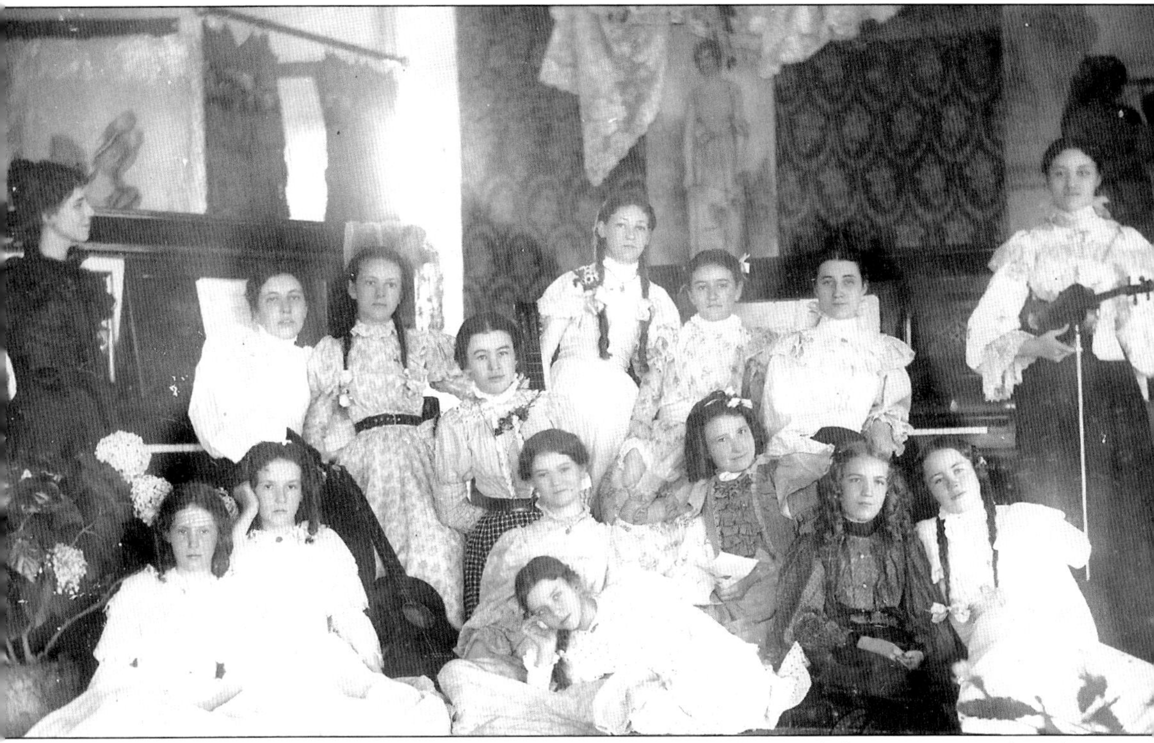

A Music Class, 1895. Seen here is an unidentified group of young ladies in a music class that was probably part of the curriculum at the Bentonville Academy. It was important for young ladies to be well educated in the cultural arts of the day. (Courtesy of the author.)

Bud Dickerson. Bud Dickerson was the father of Arthur "Rabbit" Dickerson. Bud worked for the Bryan family in various business capacities. He also owned a farm north of town near Bella Vista. (Courtesy of Shiloh Museum of Ozark History/ Elizabeth Robertson Collection.)

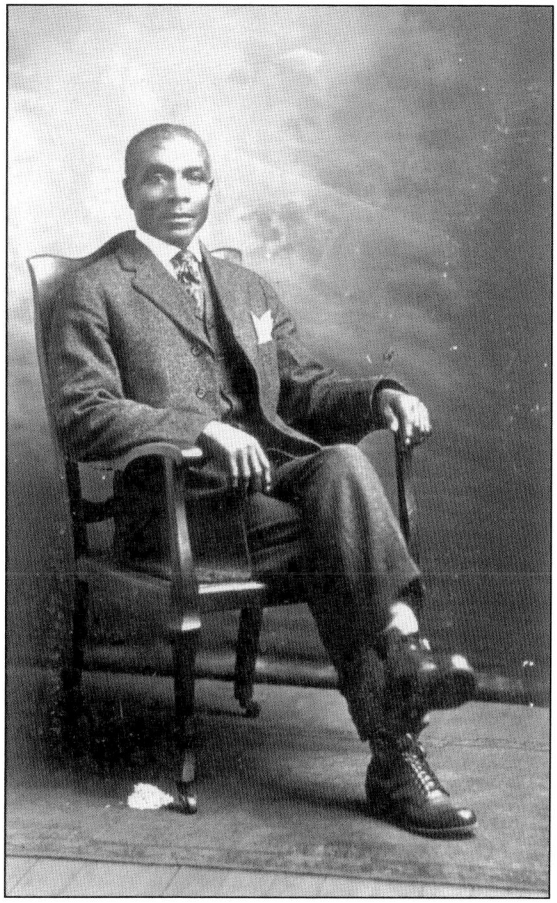

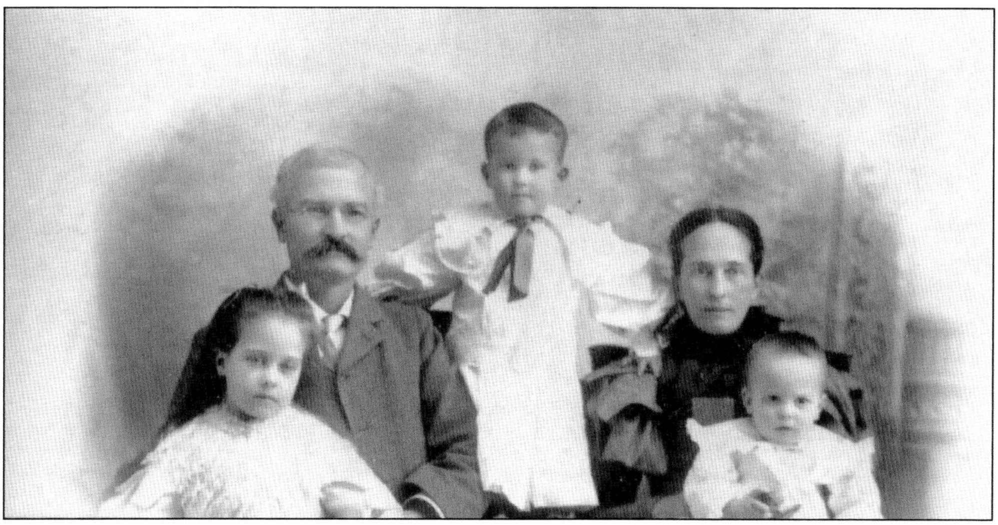

Dr. Charles H. Cargile and Family. Dr. Cargile was known all over America for his development of the Cargile membrane, which significantly improved efforts in surgical procedures for certain operations. He and his beautiful family were citizens of Bentonville for many years. (Courtesy of Rogers Historical Museum.)

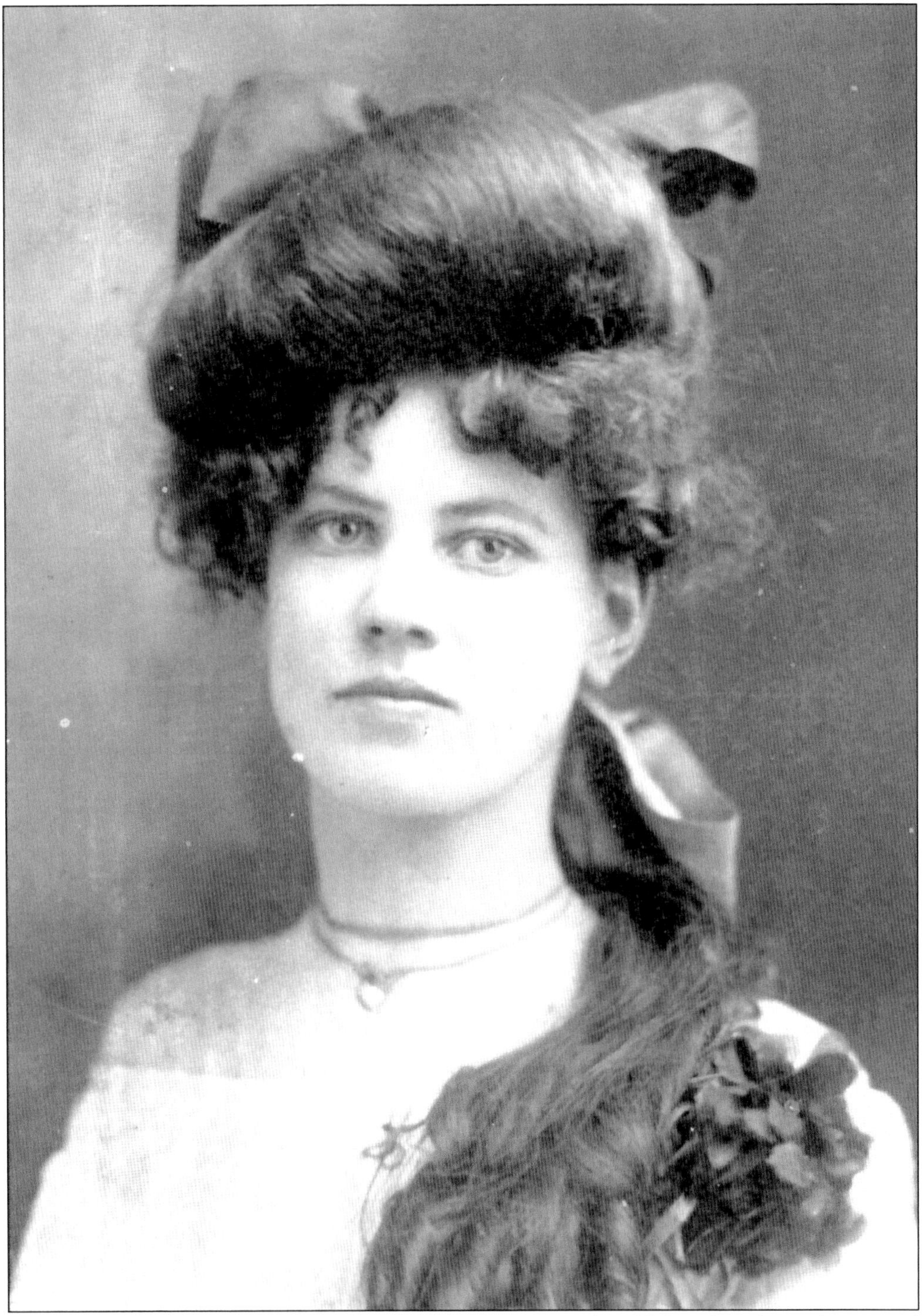

MAUDE BLACK. There may have been a lot of work to do in the old days, but there also seemed to be time to dress up for special occasions. Like today, there were plenty of church, school, and community events that called for the latest styles in fashion. Maude Black models a popular hairdo of her day. (Courtesy of Gary Black.)

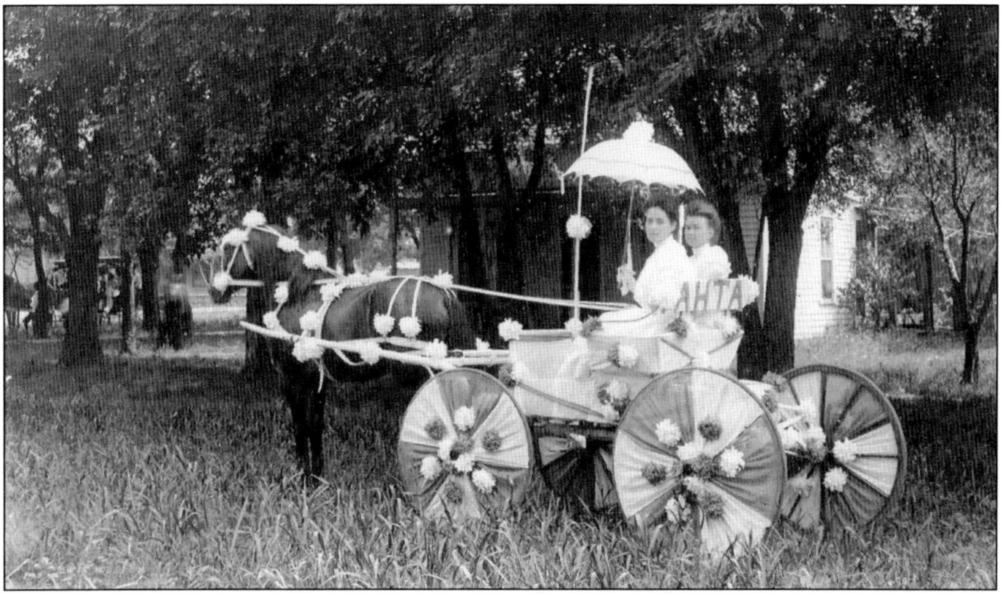

A Well-Decorated Buggy. This well-decorated buggy is ready for a Bentonville parade; however, the organization AHTA could not be identified. The two ladies are beautifully dressed and look to be quite capable to drive the horse-drawn buggy. (Courtesy of Gary Black.)

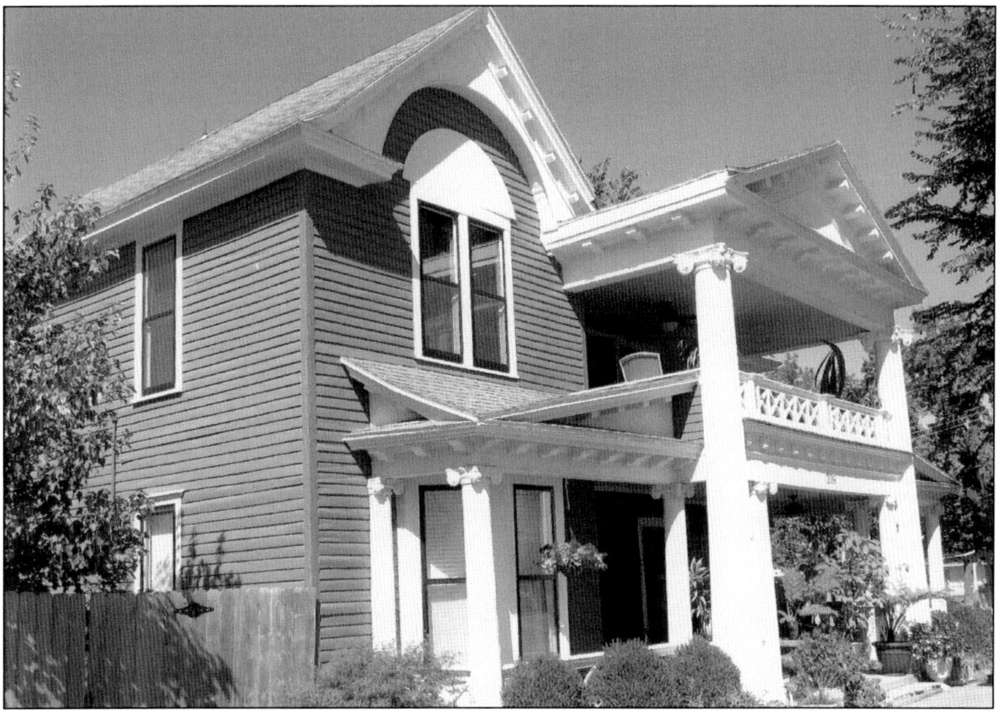

The Bain-Rife House. This house was originally built as a plain white two-story home. It is believed that architect A. O. Clarke designed the neoclassical-style porch addition. The house has been used for many commercial ventures, including offices for the newspaper, a trendy gift shop, an interior designer's office, and a real estate appraiser's office. The house was beautifully renovated by Tom and Donna Rife. (Courtesy of the author.)

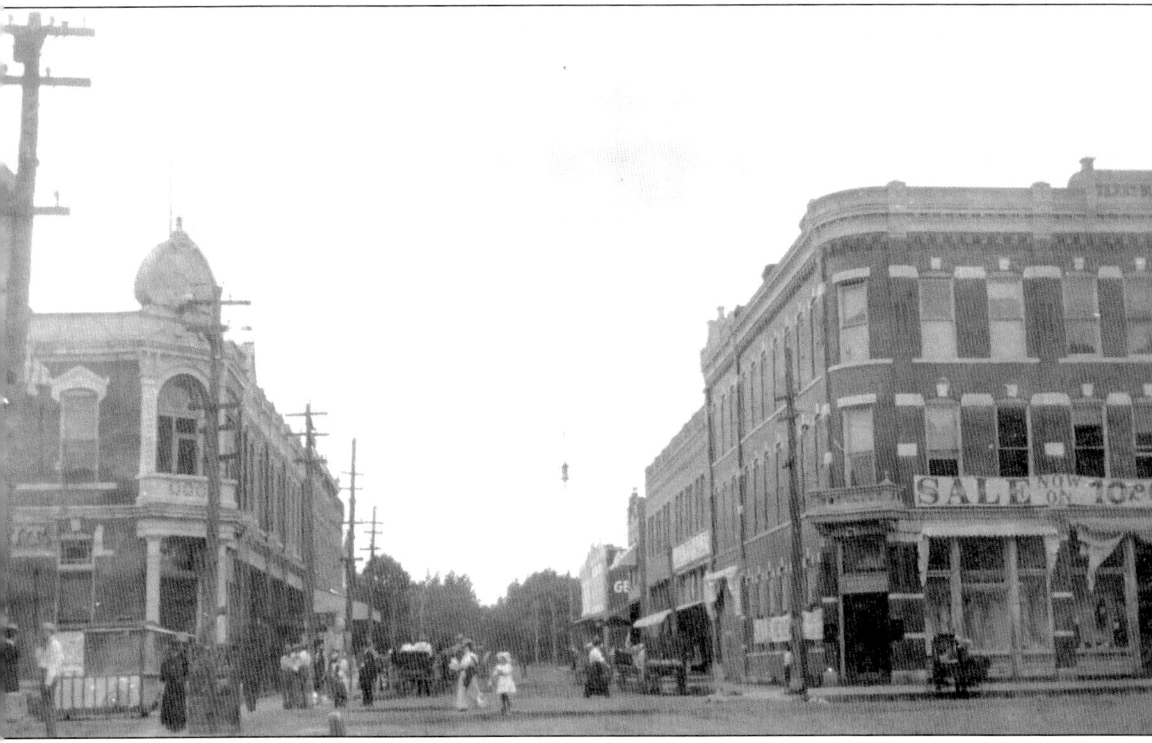

SPRING STREET/CENTRAL AVENUE. Central Avenue was once known as Spring Street, probably because the road led to the spring in a hollow east of the town square. The photographer was facing west when this picture was taken. (Courtesy of Patty Pearce Payne.)

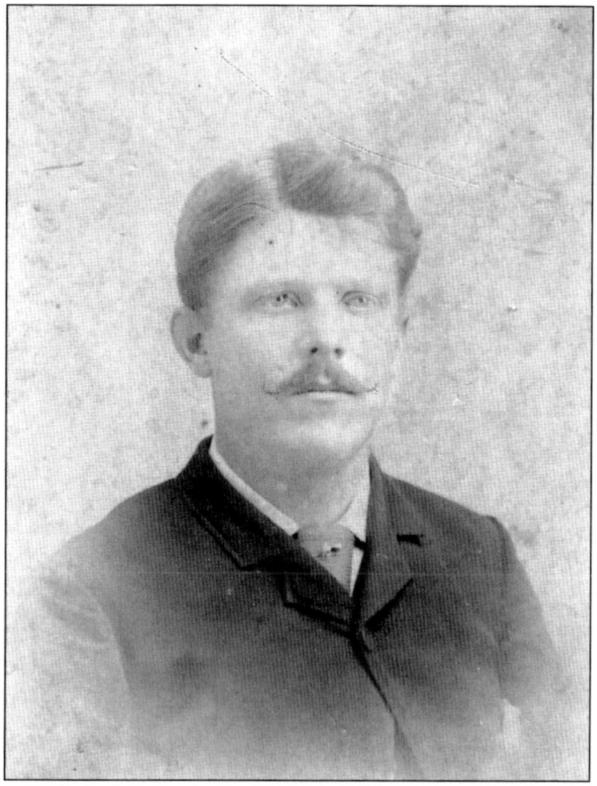

JERRY LEFORS. The People's Bank of Bentonville was robbed in June 1893. Jerry Lefors was one of the men who rode with the posse attempting to apprehend the bank robbers. The posse was not far from the robbers when Jerry's horse was shot out from under him. The same thing happened to another man with the group. Needless to say, the bank robbers were not caught that day. (Courtesy of Gary Black.)

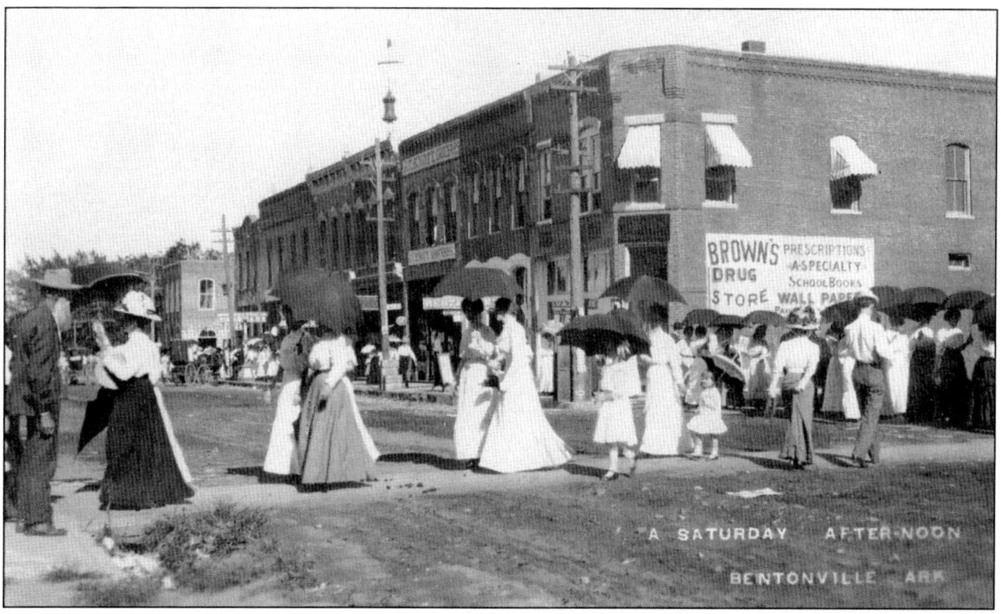

SATURDAY AFTERNOON IN BENTONVILLE, 1900s. Parasols must have been a hot sale item on this particular sunny Saturday on the square. The ladies parade across the street on a walkway designed to help protect long skirts and shoes from unpaved streets in the early 1900s. The first power poles are lined along the streets, and an early traffic light hangs precariously over the intersection of Main Street and Central Avenue. (Courtesy of Patty Pearce Payne.)

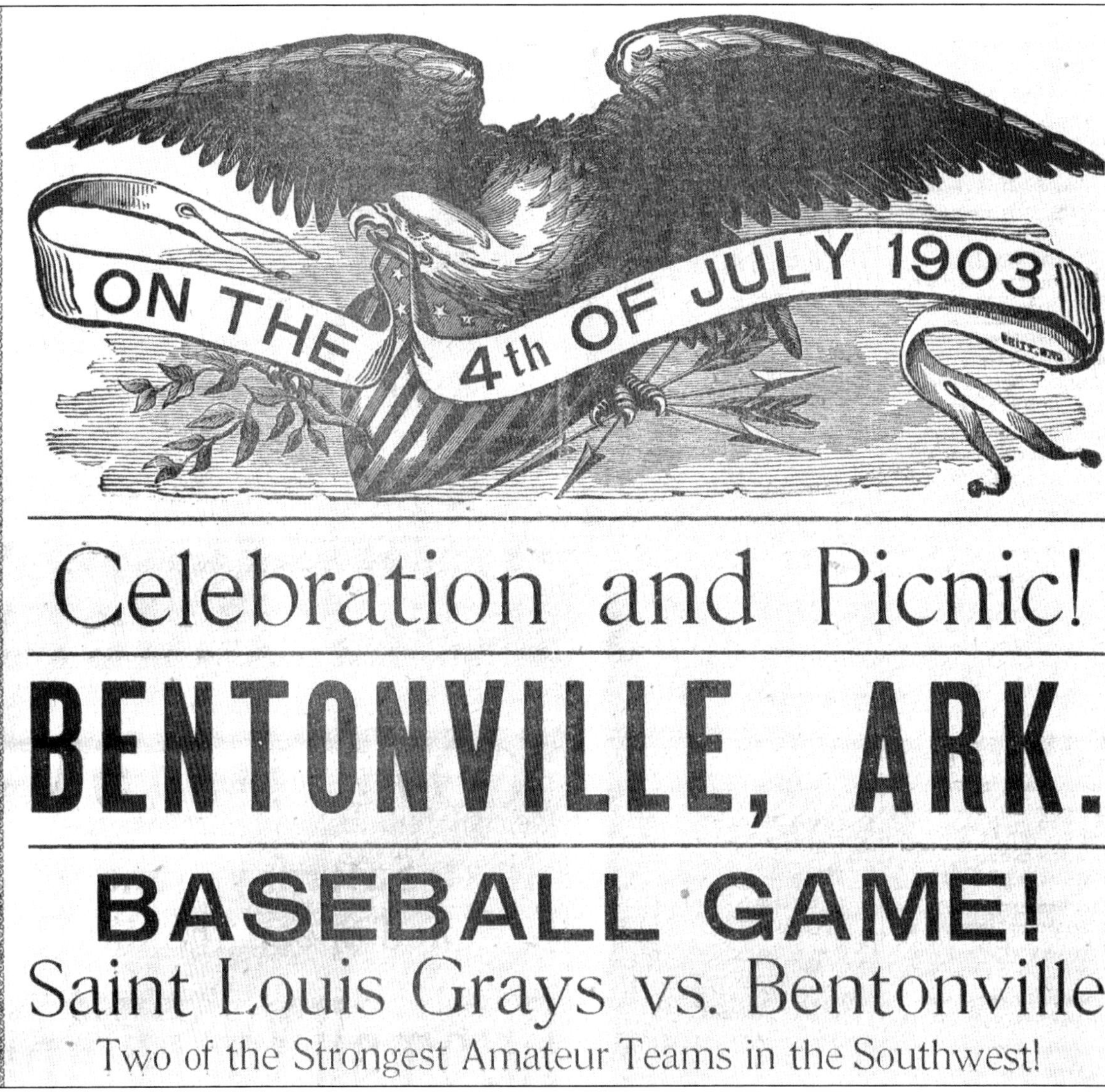

THE FOURTH OF JULY PICNIC, 1903. A Bentonville newspaper advertisement invited the public to picnic and celebrate the Fourth of July with an amateur baseball game. Unfortunately the final score or whether the St. Louis Grays team or the Bentonville baseball team won are unknown today. (Courtesy of the author.)

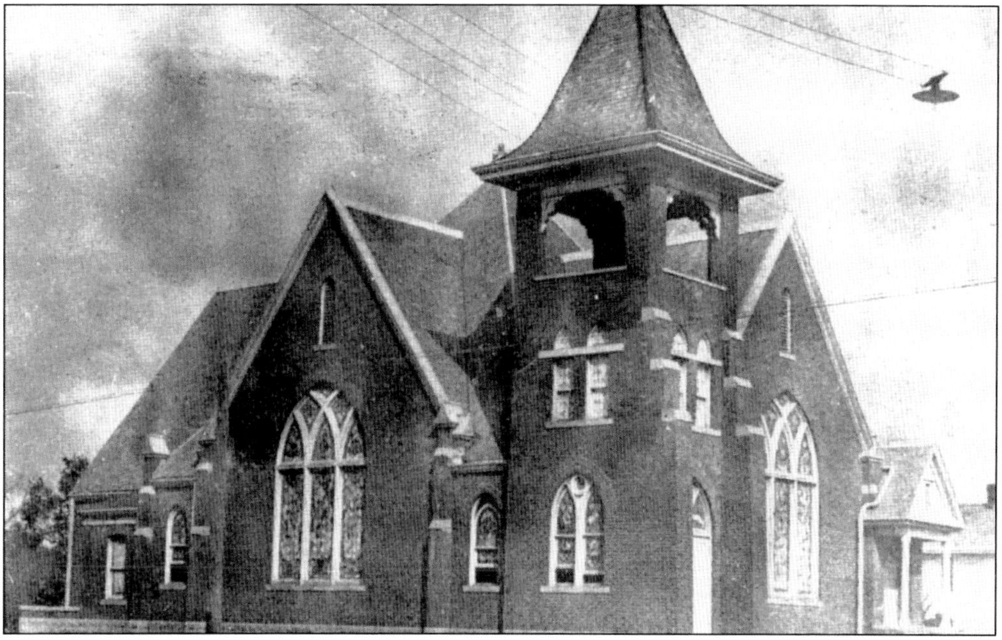

First Christian Church, 1906. The congregation of the First Christian Church held its inaugural service on January 14, 1906. The architect is unknown, but the floor plan was based on the popular design known as the Akron Plan for Sunday School. The Akron Plan called for the Sunday school classrooms to be built with large folding doors that could be opened if extra seating space was needed in the auditorium. Today, this is the oldest standing church building in Bentonville. (Courtesy of the author.)

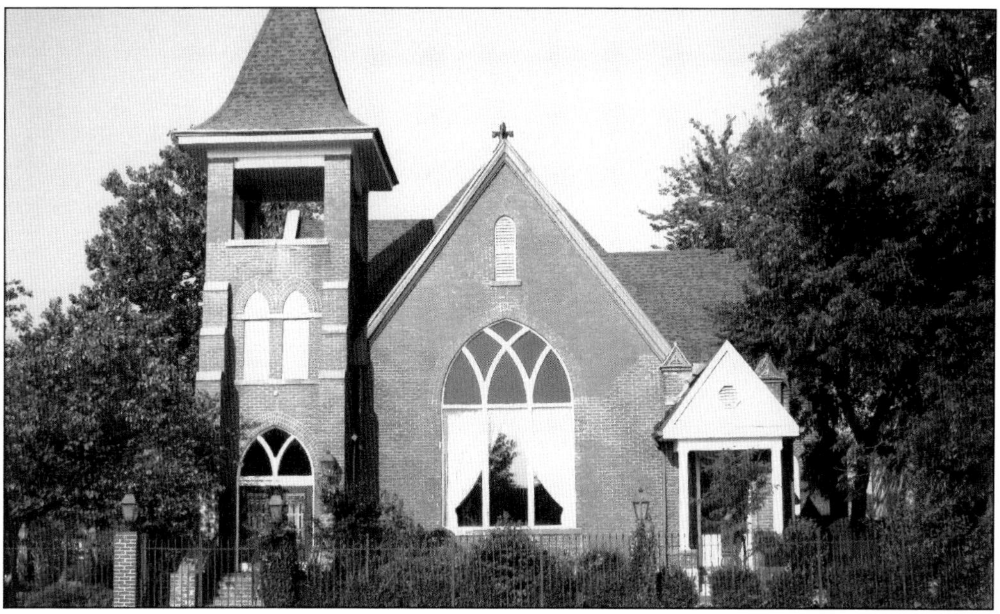

Old Christian Church Building Today. The original stained-glass windows were removed when the congregation sold the historical building in 1979. The old church auditorium was known for having perfect acoustics, which was important in the days before electronic amplifiers. There is a beautiful bell tower, but apparently there has never been a bell. (Courtesy of the author.)

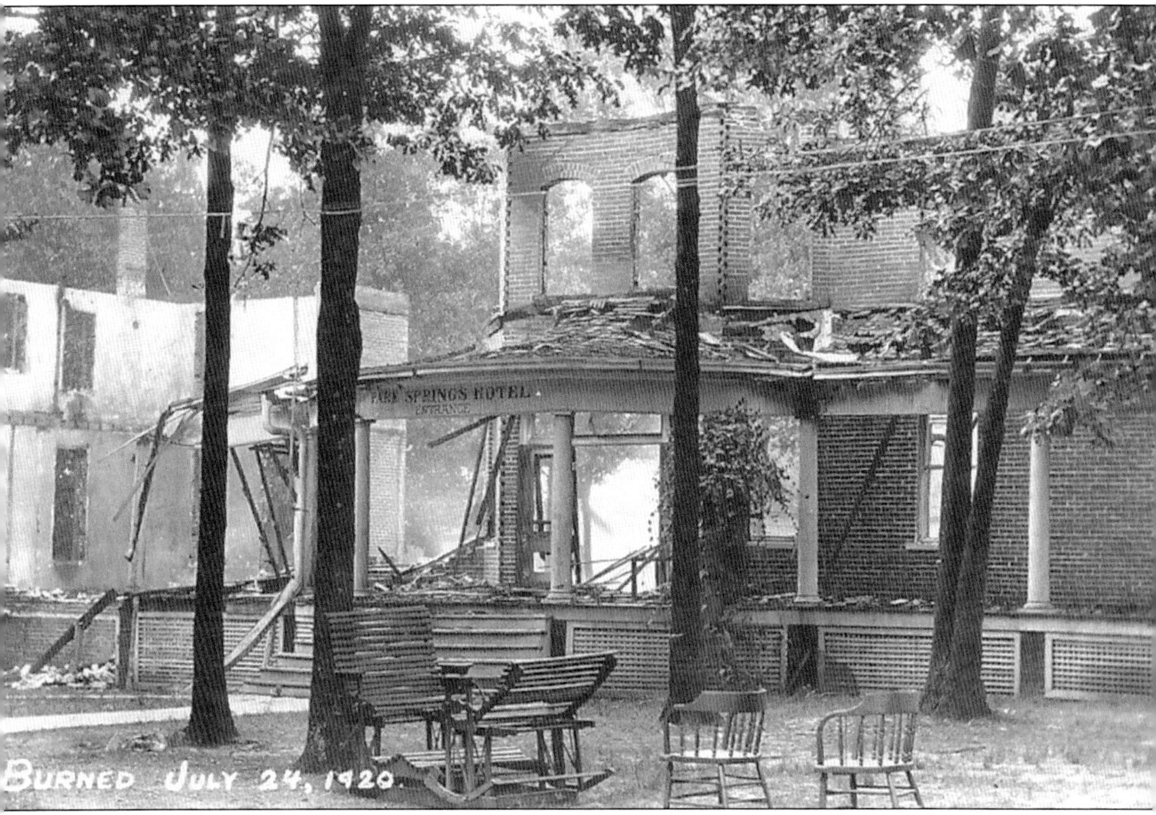

PARK SPRINGS HOTEL FIRE, 1920. The large brick building at Park Springs was first built as a health resort and osteopathic sanitarium by A. T. Still in 1910. There were also six private cottages with two rooms each located on the north side of the 10-acre wooded property. When the sanitarium business closed, the Crowder family purchased the property in the 1920s with plans for an upscale tourist hotel. Unfortunately a fire totally destroyed the hotel building a short time after the Crowder family purchased Park Springs Hotel. (Courtesy of Jack Crowder.)

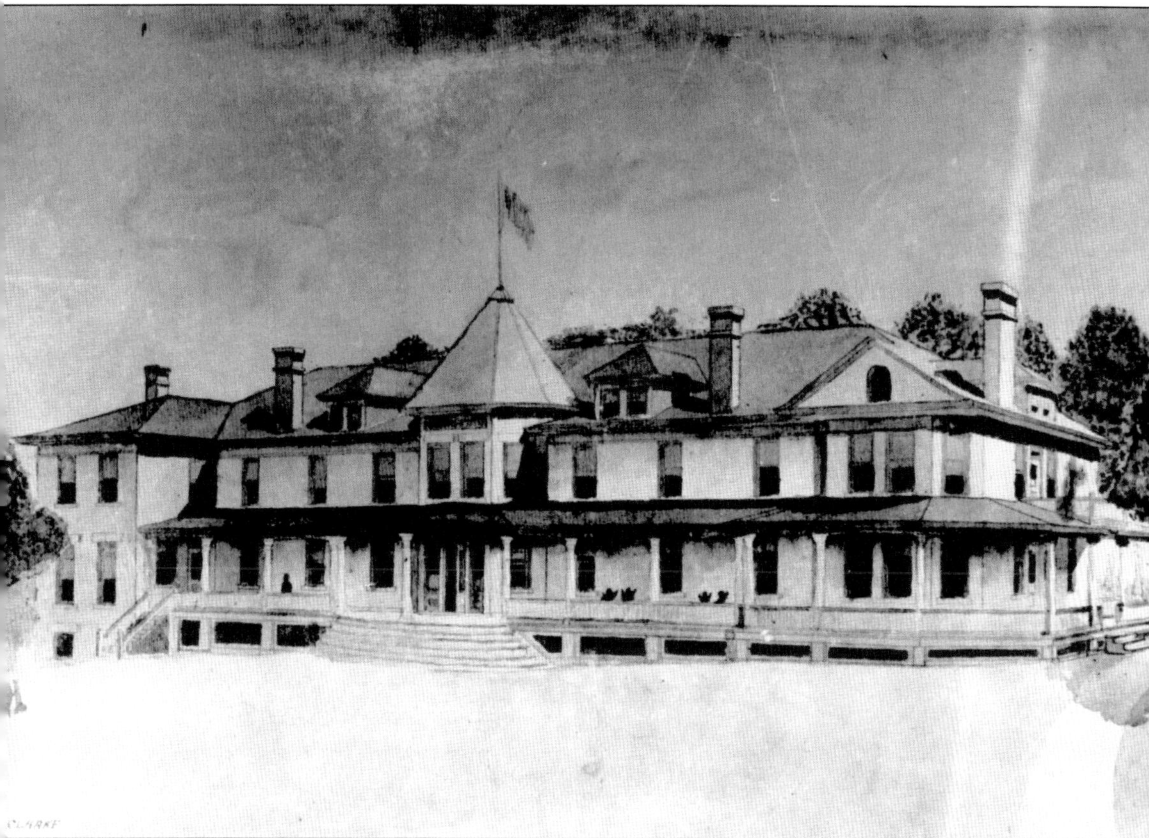

The Park Springs Hotel. It is not known if the above drawing by Architect A. O. Clarke was prepared for the original hotel built by A. T. Still or if it was for the Crowder family and the rebuilding of the hotel after the fire in 1920. The Crowder family later sold the property, and the building was used as a nursing home for several years before it was torn down. (Courtesy of Shiloh Museum of Ozark History/Tom Duggan Collection, S-2008-5-1.)

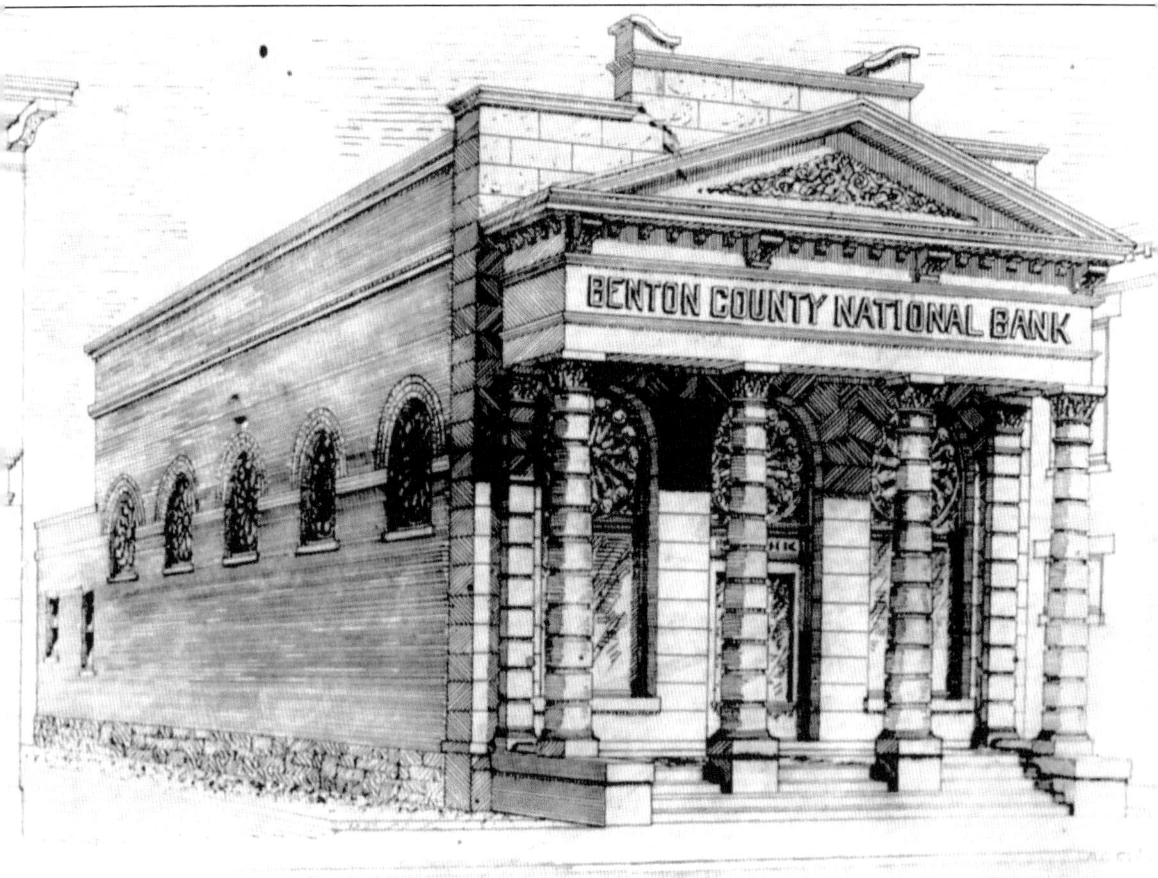

THE PLAN FOR THE BENTON COUNTY BANK, 1908. Architect A. O. Clarke's idea for the design for the Benton County Bank building at 115 West Central Avenue was considerably more detailed than the toned down version accepted as the final plan. Upon completion, the building was considered the most beautiful in Benton County, and it is still admired as an exquisite historical architectural landmark. (Courtesy of Patty Pearce Payne.)

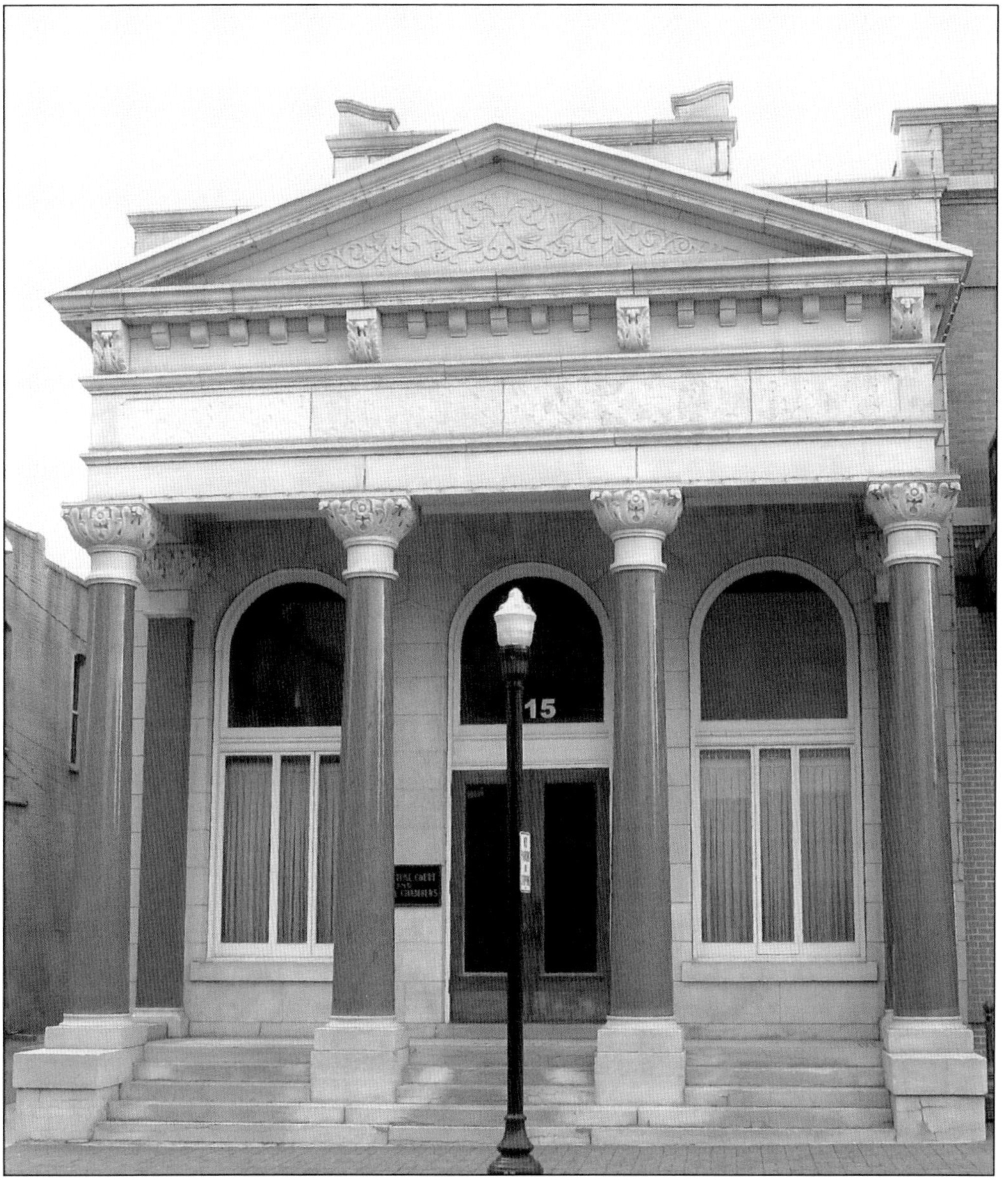

The Benton County Bank Building Today. There is an interesting difference between architect A. O. Clarke's plan and the end result of the bank building, which still stands at 115 West Central Avenue. The gleaming red granite columns are believed to have been from Carthage, Missouri. The building once housed offices for the City of Bentonville and the library. Later the building was used for the municipal court and city council chambers. There are many elegant interior features, including a skylight and an intricate sunburst tile floor. (Courtesy of the author.)

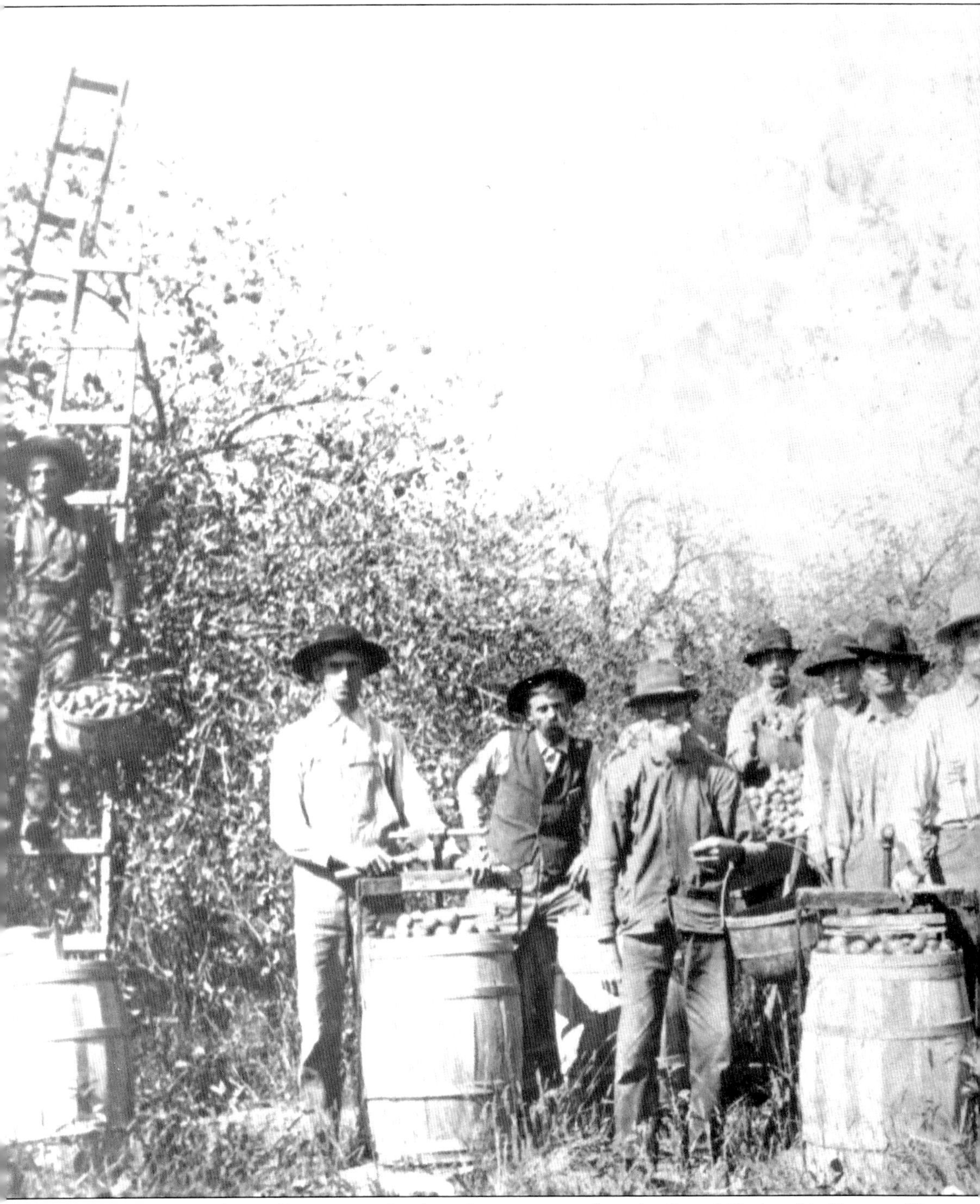

Bentonville Apple Orchards. Apple pickers are at work at the Sneed Orchard in Bentonville with apple barrels, apple-picking ladders, and a culling table. At one point in time, northwest Arkansas was the apple-producing capital of the world, but changes in the weather, disease, and

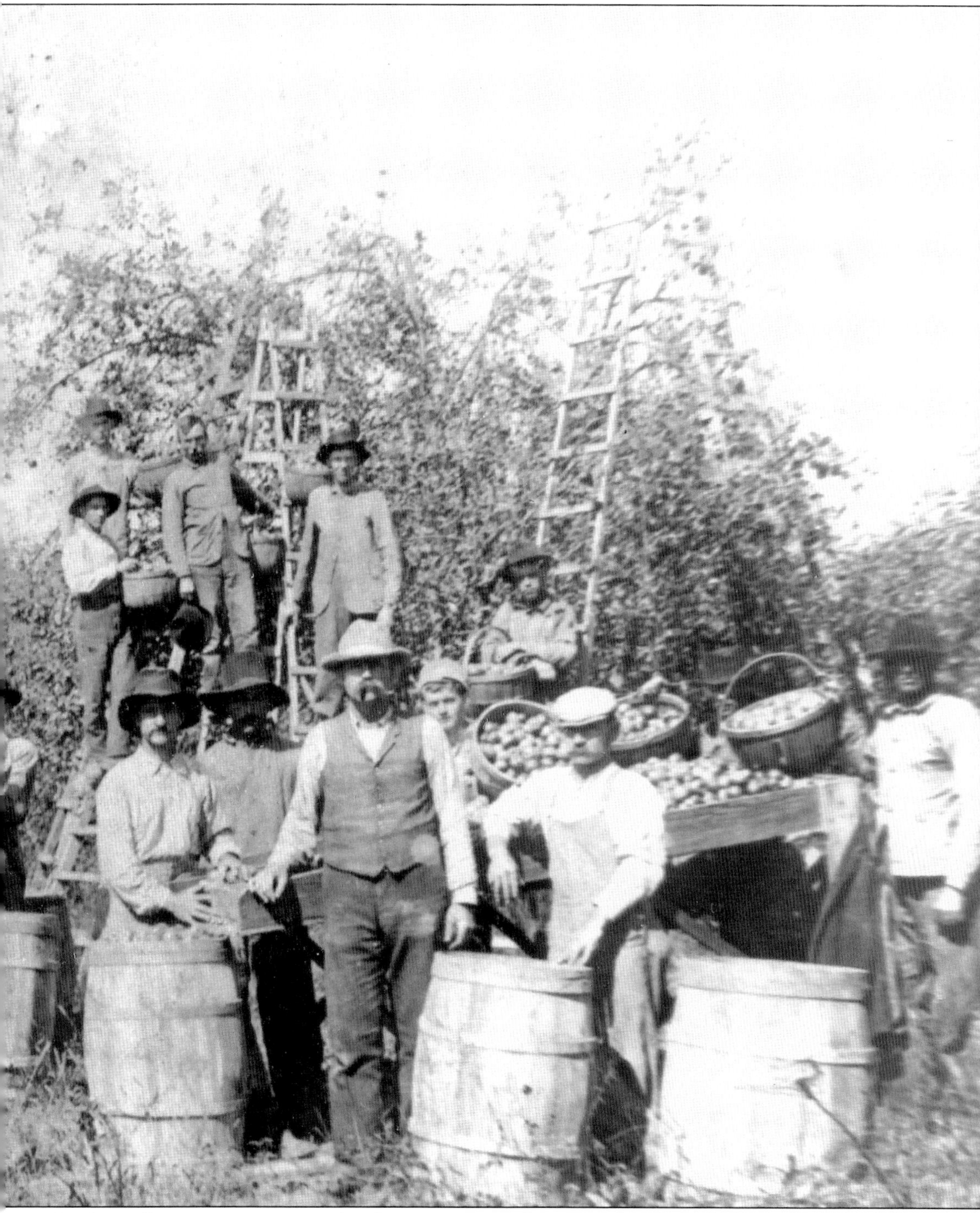

the Great Depression put an end to large commercial apple orchards in the area. (Courtesy of Rogers Historical Museum.)

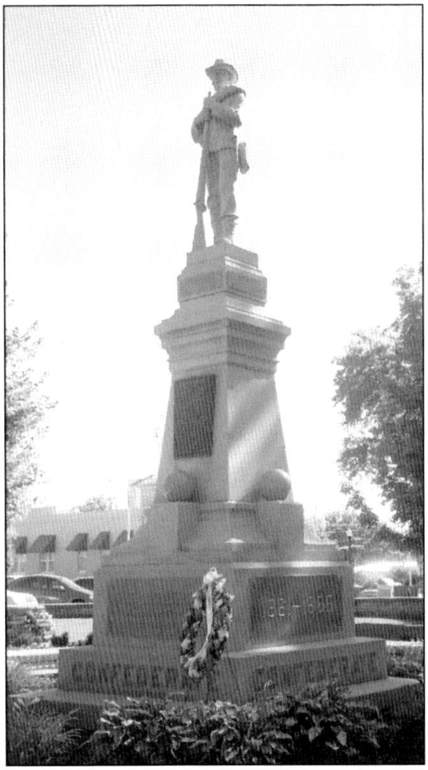

THE CONFEDERATE STATUE, 1908. The United Daughters of the Confederacy, with the help of Bentonville's citizens, erected the statue that is located in the town square. The statue is often mistakenly identified as a depiction of Sen. James H. Berry, but the statue is a generic soldier at parade rest gazing westward. The outdoor commemorative sculpture marks one of the most important chapters in Bentonville and American history. The granite statue was made in Barre, Vermont. The statue is included on the National Register of Historic Places. (Courtesy of the author.)

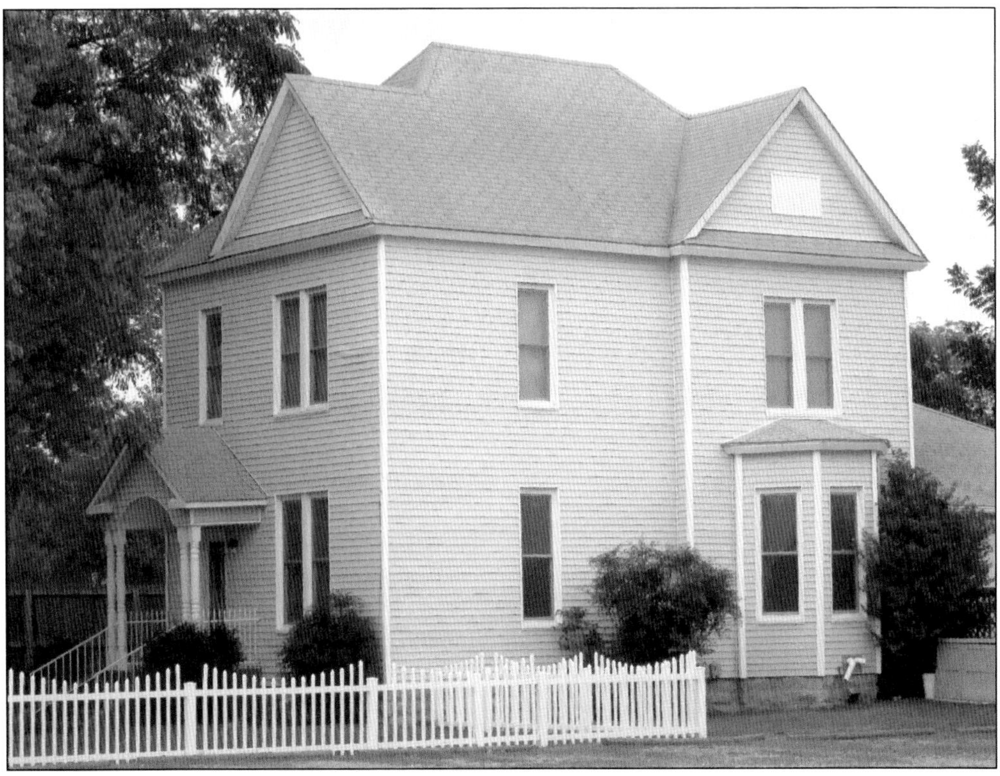

THE BATES HOUSE. This is the house of Andrew Jackson Bates, who moved to Bentonville after the Civil War. He was in the grocery business, as well as other profitable projects. He helped organize one of the first banks in the county and later, with George P. Jackson and D. W. Peel, established the First National Bank in Bentonville. In 1942, the Bates Memorial Hospital was built with money donated by Andrew Jackson Bates and his wife, Ellen T. Bates. By 1964, Bates Memorial Hospital moved to a larger facility, and the original site is now the Bentonville Manor, a residential home for the elderly. (Courtesy of the author.)

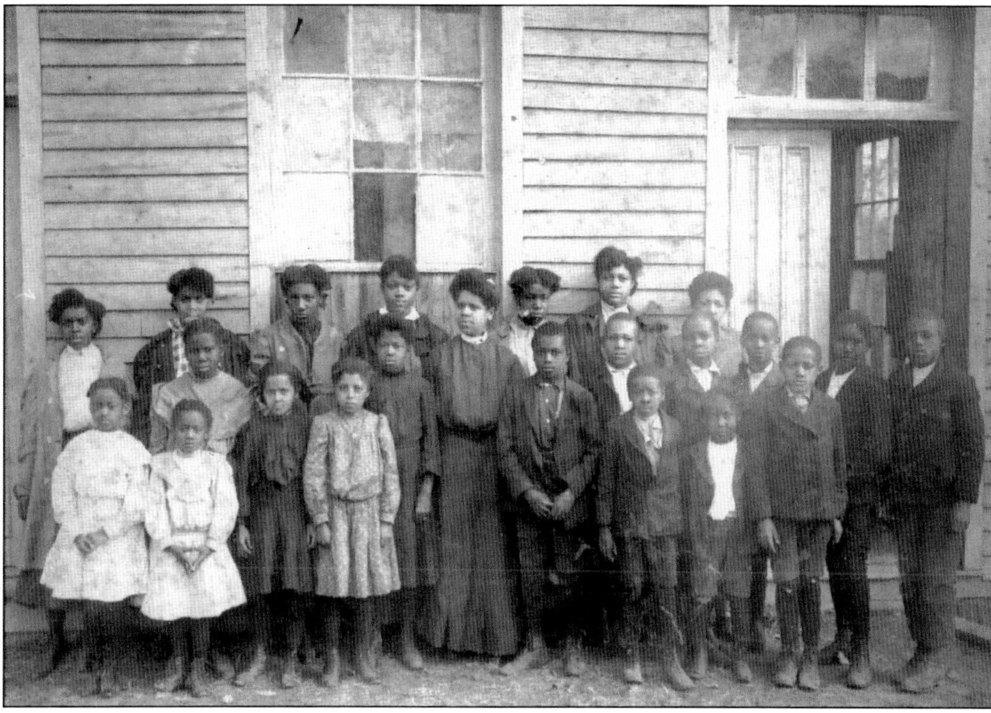

Bentonville African American School, 1909. The African American community operated a school for several years in the north part of town. Pictured from left to right are (first row) Arnette Finney, Florence Gilbert, Mattie Evans, Anna Mae Perry, teacher Florence Quinn, James Finney, Arthur "Rabbit" Dickerson, ? Van Winkle, and Hobart Claypool; (second row) Lula Van Winkle, Ella Pope, Yates Claypool, Marion Finney, John Barker, Harry Van Winkle, and Mack Claypool; (third row) Viola Parks, Edna Gilbert, Eula Claypool, Mamie Finney, Rena Claypool, Thad Whayne, and unidentified. (Courtesy of Shiloh Museum of Ozark History.)

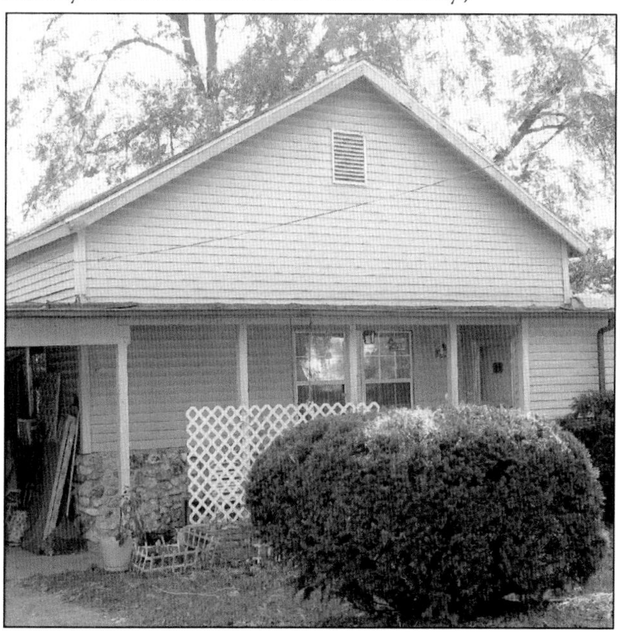

St. Paul's Methodist Church Building. Rev. J. P. Parker was credited with being the lead carpenter in building the church. The building has been renovated over the years but still stands. It is one of the last surviving structures in a neighborhood once nicknamed by the African American community as "the clique." The church building is now a private residence. (Courtesy of the author.)

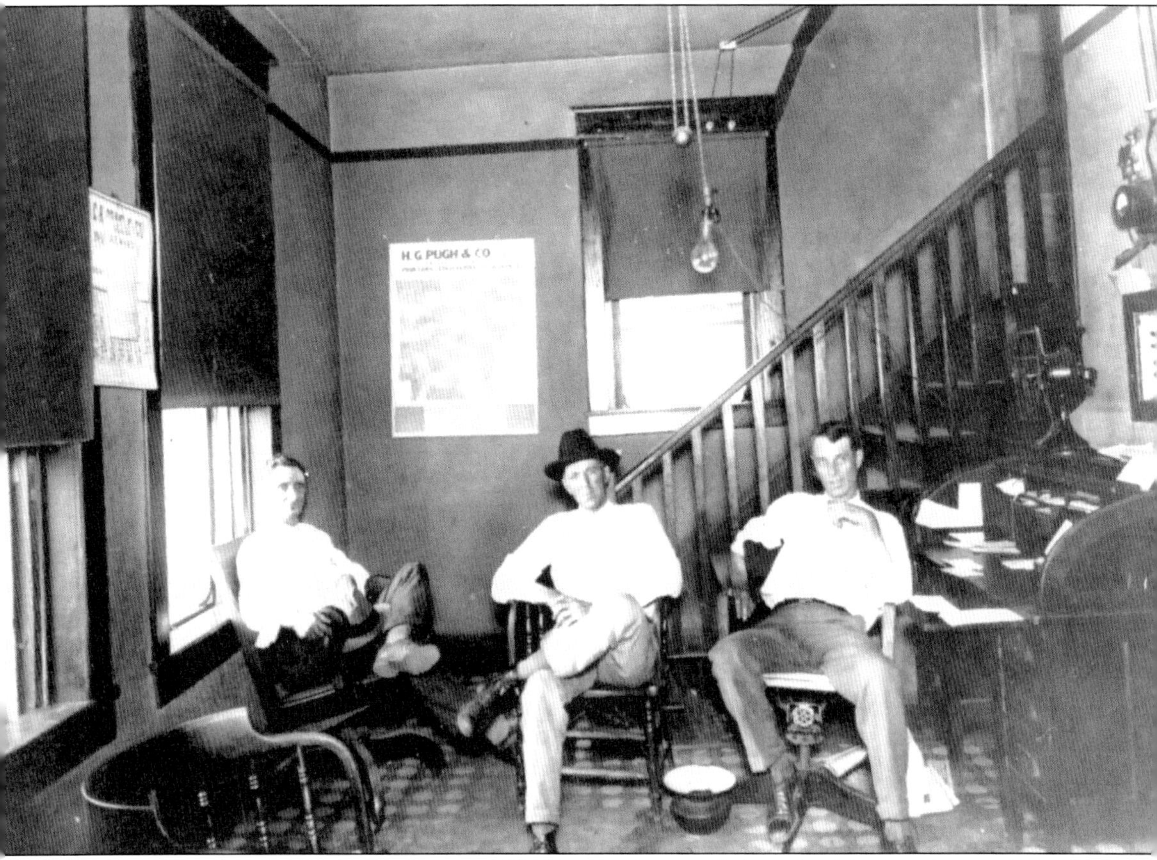

THE OLD BENTON COUNTY JAIL, 1911. The Benton County Jail was built by Lon Pace in 1911 and is located at 212 North Main Street. Architect A. O. Clarke designed the neoclassical structure, which is listed on the National Register of Historic Places. In the old days, the sheriff and his family lived in part of the building. (Courtesy of the author.)

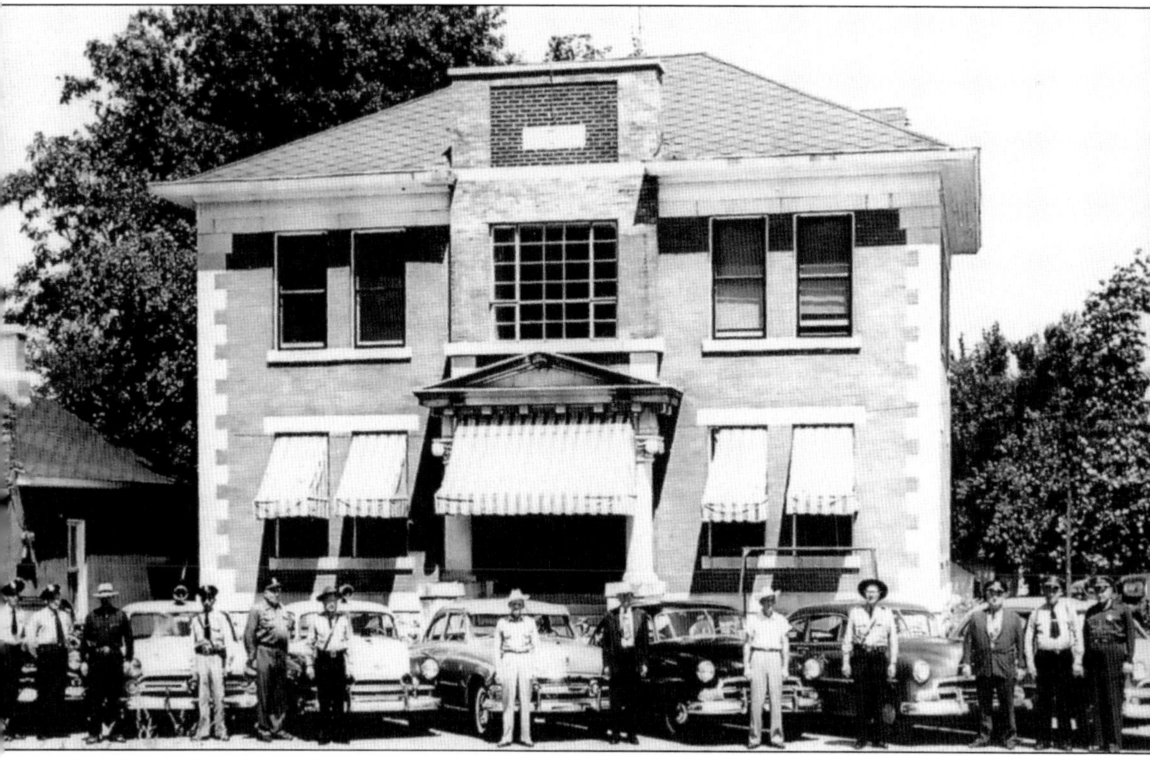

Benton County Sheriff's Office. The sheriff and his deputies worked out of this office, located in the front of the old Benton County Jail building. There were few electronic gadgets available to help law enforcement fight crime in those days. The building still stands and is listed on the National Register of Historic Places. (Courtesy of Gary Black.)

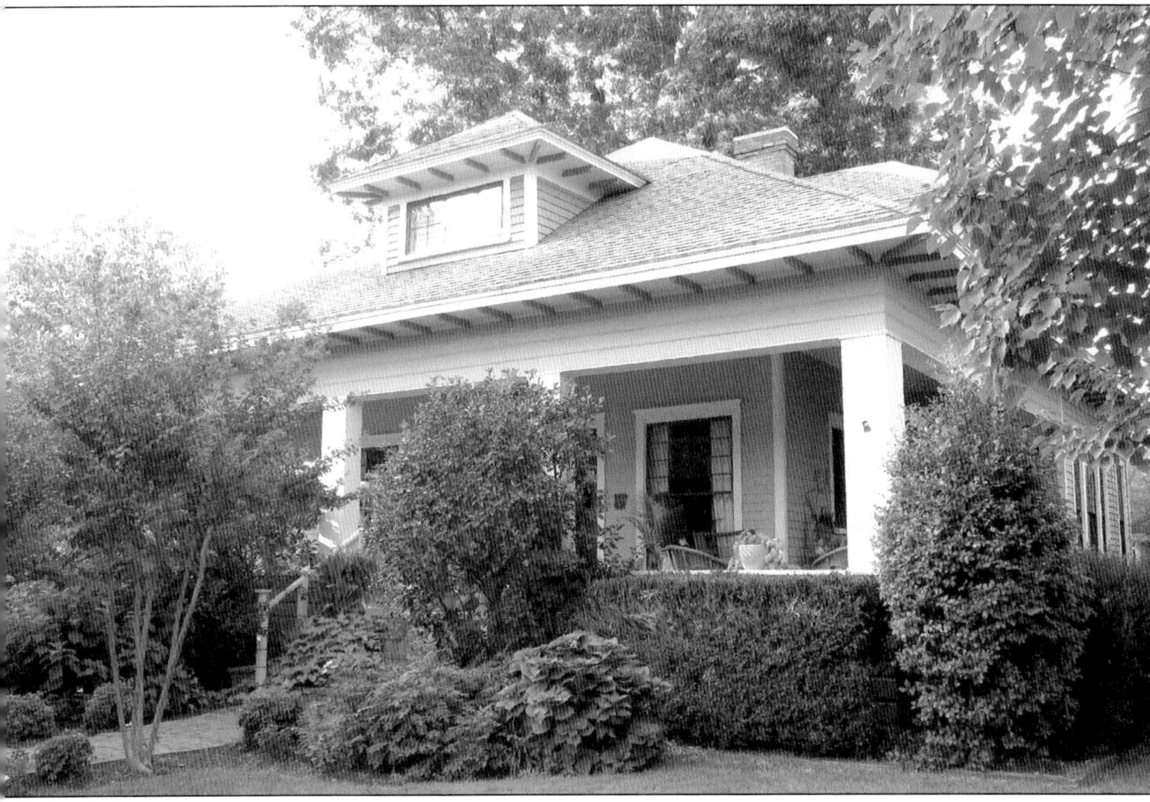

The Peel-Morris House. This house was built around 1913 and is believed to be the first true California Bungalow Craftsman–style home in Bentonville. This is one of five historical houses in Bentonville credited to the Peel family. This sturdy, meticulously preserved home has been listed on the National Register of Historic Places since 1992. (Courtesy of the author.)

Five

A Time of Economic Challenges 1921–1950

There were problems developing in the apple orchards and other signs of worry in the national news as well. Throughout northwest Arkansas, there were more and more reports of a apple tree disease known as blight, which affects the leaves and blossoms. The heavy spring rain made it even easier for the blight to spread, and before long, it became a crisis.

Before the apple blight problem could be solved, the Great Depression hit the whole country, spreading fear and worry, but the full impact was not felt in Bentonville until December 1930, when both Bentonville banks closed their doors. In 1931, Jackson Dry Goods, the largest dry goods store in Arkansas, closed.

The bright economic sun rose again over the Bentonville town square on the morning of February 28, 1931, when a new bank opened on the southwest corner of the square with a capital of $30,000 provided by a group of Fort Smith, Arkansas, businessmen. The new bank was named the Bank of Bentonville, and no one could have imagined at the time what a long and influential life this institution would have.

According to a newspaper account, students at the Bentonville school saw television for the first time on February 28, 1939, during a Parent Teacher Association–sponsored exhibit of a transmitting screen on one side of a stage and a receiving screen on the other. Of course, it would be a few more years before anyone in Bentonville had their own television at home.

Like everywhere else in America, life drastically changed when automobiles arrived in Bentonville. Anna Patton is remembered as the first lady to buy her own personal automobile, which was a 1940s green Packard. Patton was the first female to hold political office in Benton County when she was elected county clerk.

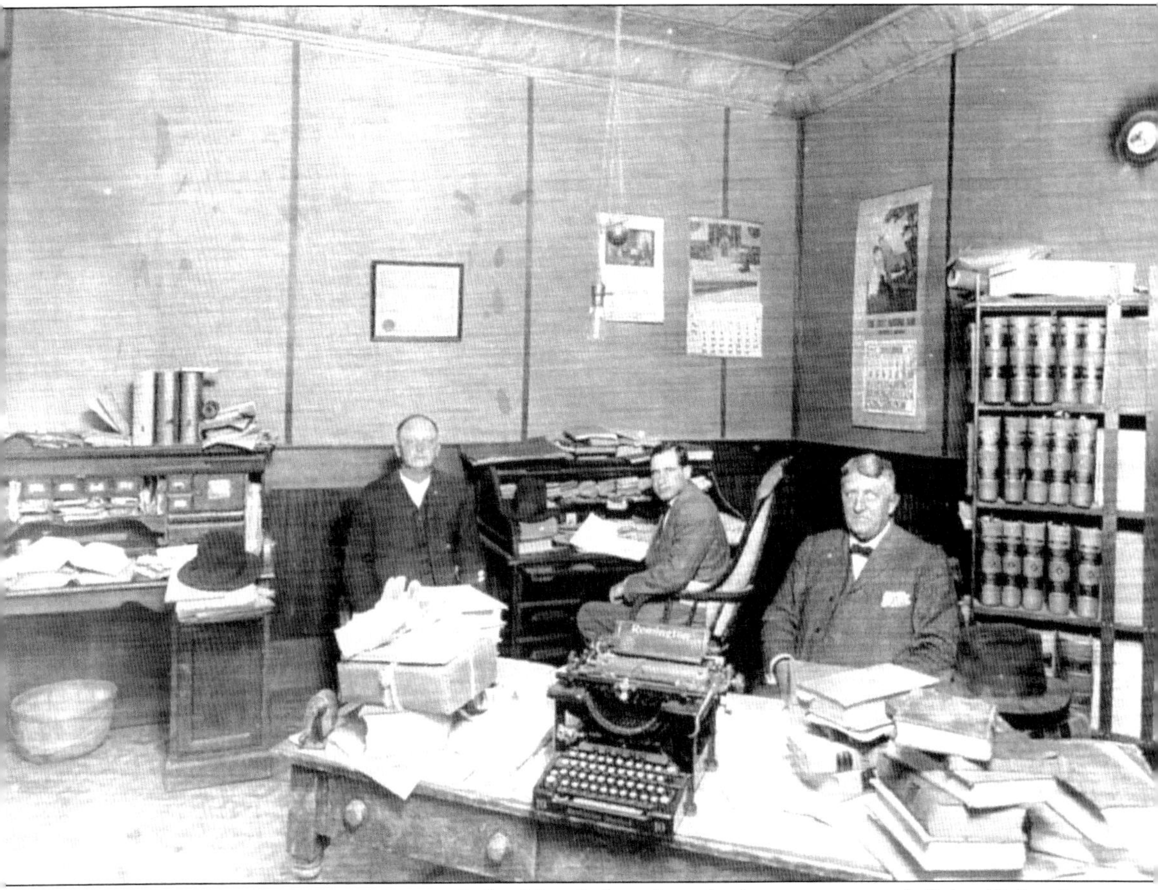

JUDGE WILLIAM DUDLEY MAUCK. Judge Mauck first shared a law practice with Felix G. Lindsey before opening his own law office. His wife, Emma, liked to paint china dishes and was considered to be a fine landscape designer as well. Judge Mauck was well respected and a mentor to many young Bentonville lawyers, such as Eugene Coffelt. (Courtesy of Gloria Coffelt Moore.)

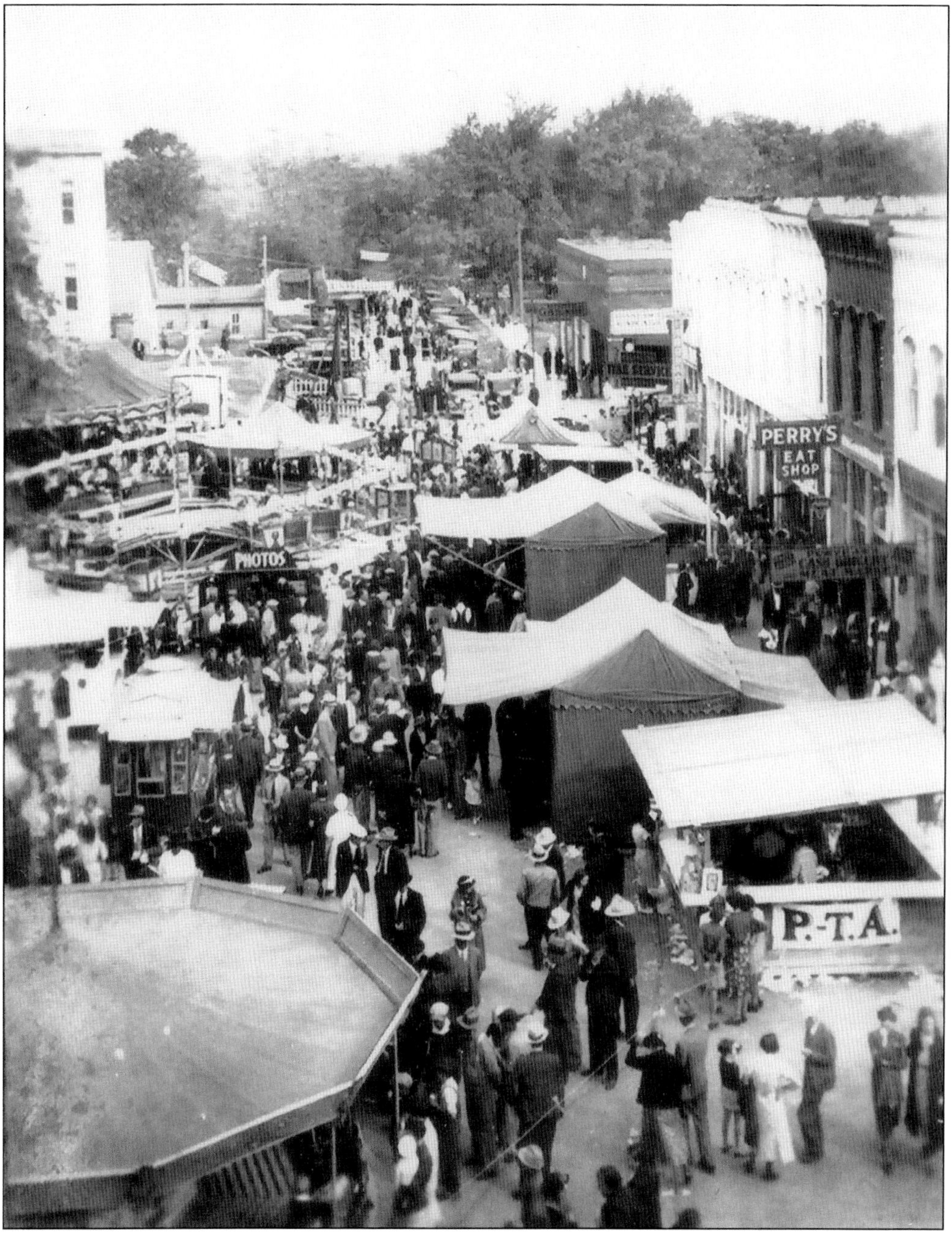

The Fair at the Square. Over the years, the town square has been the center for many community activities, including fairs and carnivals. At this particular event, the crowd enjoyed several carnival rides, including the merry-go-round, and could have their pictures taken in an automatic photograph booth. The Parent Teacher Association booth in the right foreground was probably a fund-raising project. (Courtesy of Mary Marquess.)

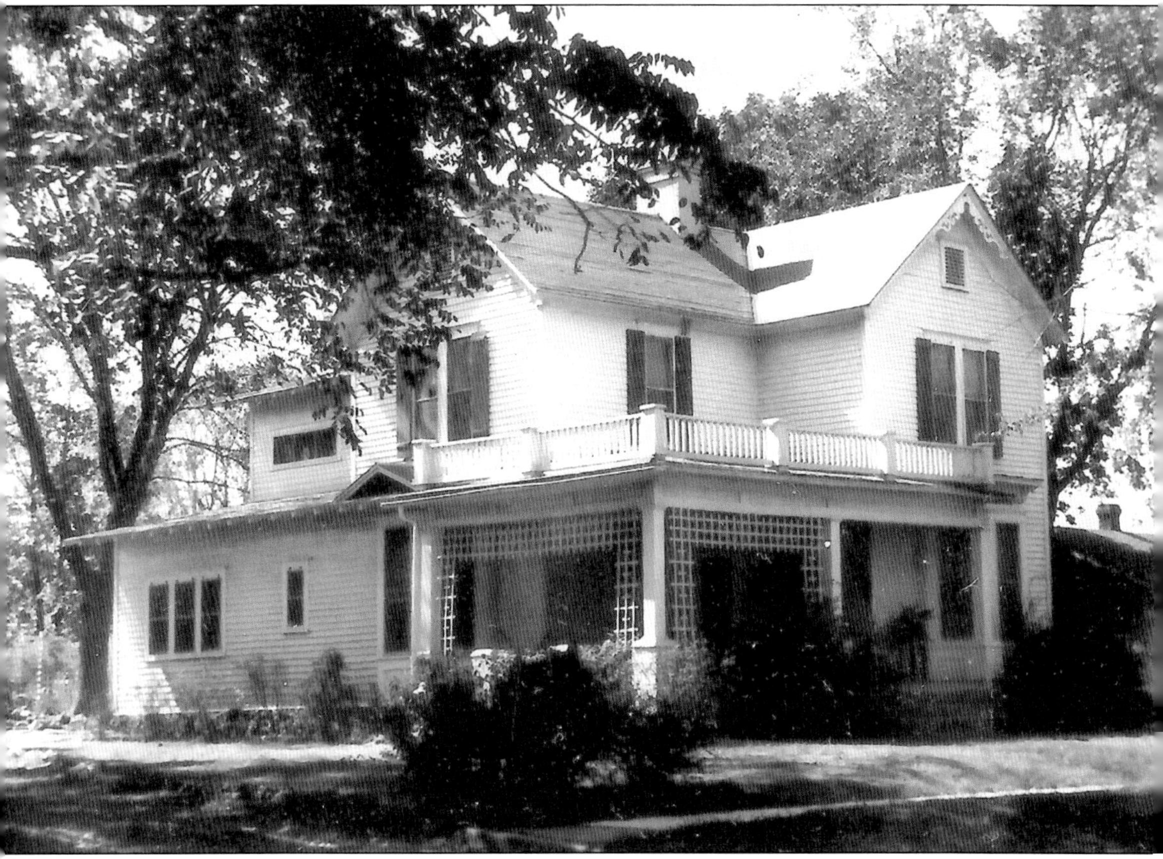

THE MCPHETRIDGE FAMILY HOME. The McPhetridge family moved to this home when their daughter Louise was 14 years old. Louise dreamed of learning to fly airplanes while living in this large and spacious house. The original fireplace is adorned with beautiful quartz crystal mined from Crystal Cave in the Bella Vista area. The staircase may have been renovated later, as it is said to have been salvaged from the old Benton County Courthouse when it was torn down. (Courtesy of Rogers Historical Museum.)

LOUISE MCPHETRIDGE THADEN. Teenager Louise and her friend Ruth Barker bought a ticket for a flight over Bentonville in a barnstormer-style plane. From that day on, Louise not only learned to fly but won more aviation competition events than the legendary Amelia Earhart during her career. Louise and Amelia worked together to promote aviation opportunities for women and organized the 99 Club especially for lady pilots. Amelia Earhart once visited Bentonville but stayed at the Lane Hotel in Rogers because it was, at the time, the nicest facility in the area. The Bentonville airport is named in honor of Louise McPhetridge Thaden. (Courtesy of the Thaden family.)

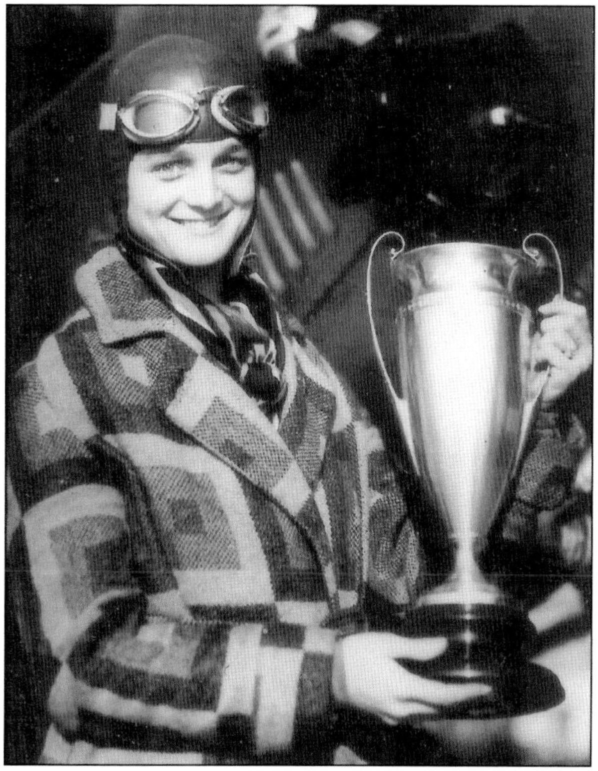

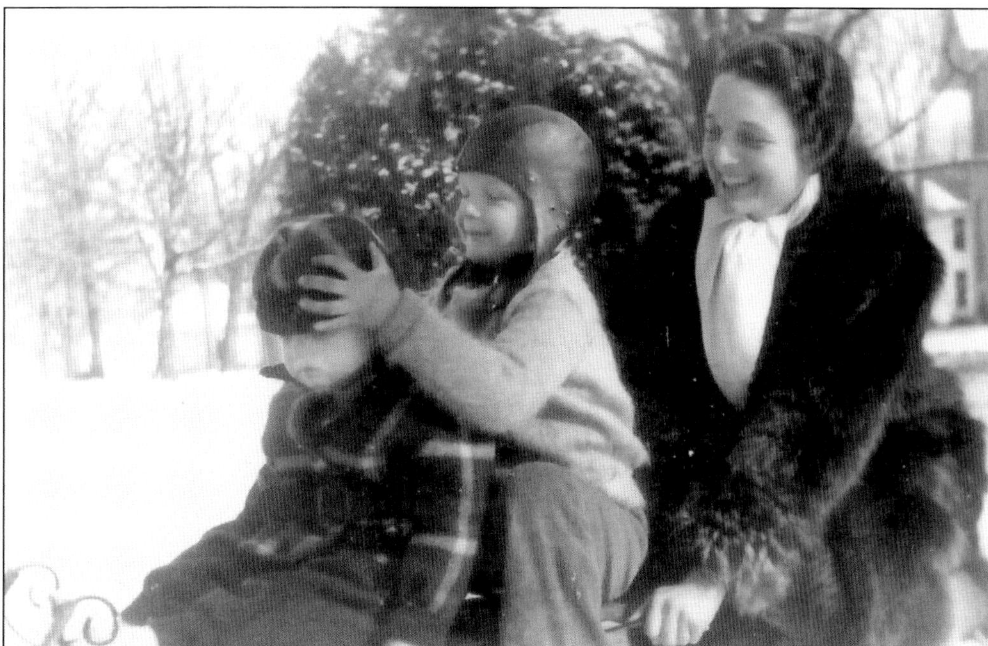

LOUISE AND CHILDREN IN BENTONVILLE. Louise Thaden's daughter Pat has her cap adjusted by her older brother Bill as they prepare to sled in the snow. This photograph was taken in front of Louise's childhood home on West Central Avenue. (Courtesy of the Thaden family.)

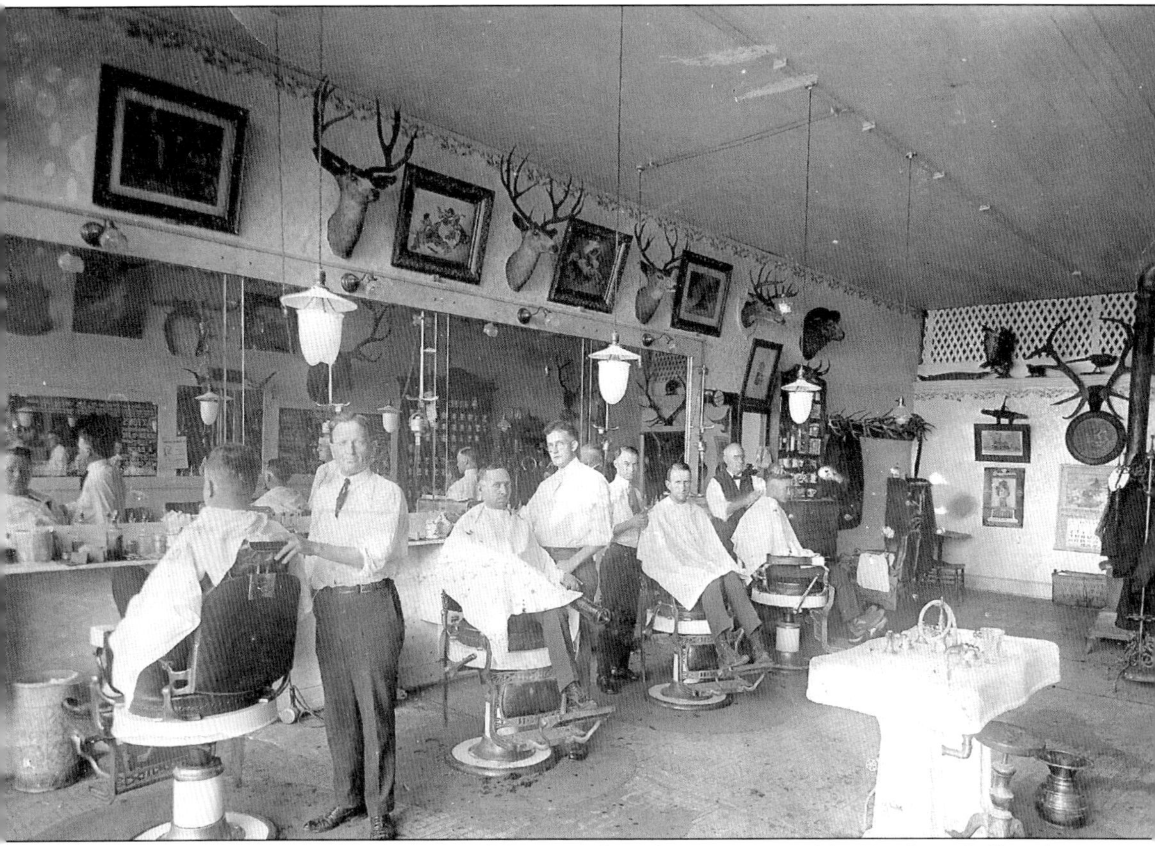

The Elkhorn Barber Shop. The Elkhorn Barber Shop was owned by Kit Campbell and was located on the south side of the square. This picture was taken on April 15, 1920, and the barbers are identified, from front to back, as Amos Cavness, Erby Rogers, Jimmy Harris (the author's father), and Kit Campbell, owner of the Elkhorn Barber Shop at the time. Unfortunately the customers could not be identified. (Courtesy of the author.)

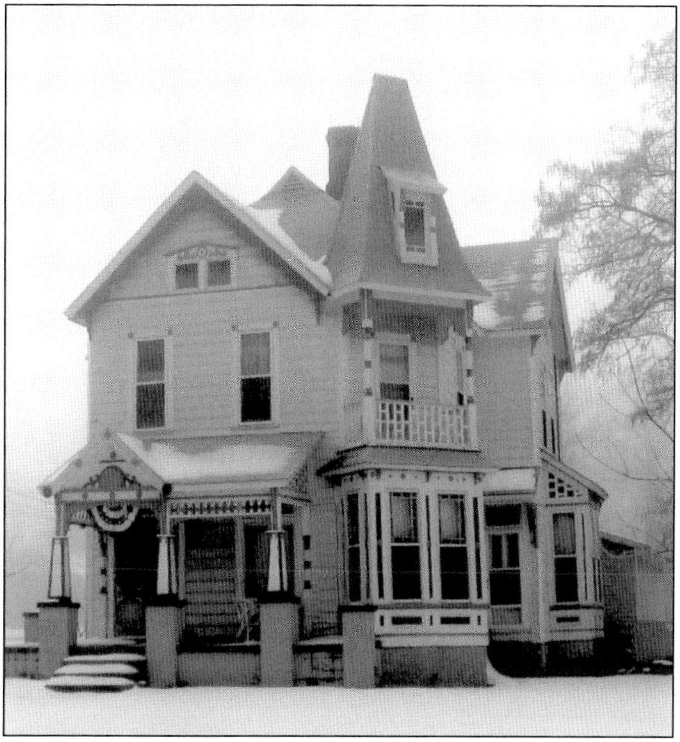

The Kit Campbell House. Kit Campbell was a barber for many years in Bentonville. He first operated a barbershop in the back of the People's Bank, which was owned by Jack Bates. Bates returned from Colorado hunting trips with elk and deer, and the mounted specimens ended up on the wall of the barbershop. When Congressman Sam Peel and Sen. James H. Berry brought their own shaving mugs for sanitary reasons, everyone else had to have his own mug, and so began the mug and hunting trophy collection that became the signature of the Elkhorn Barber Shop. (Courtesy of the author.)

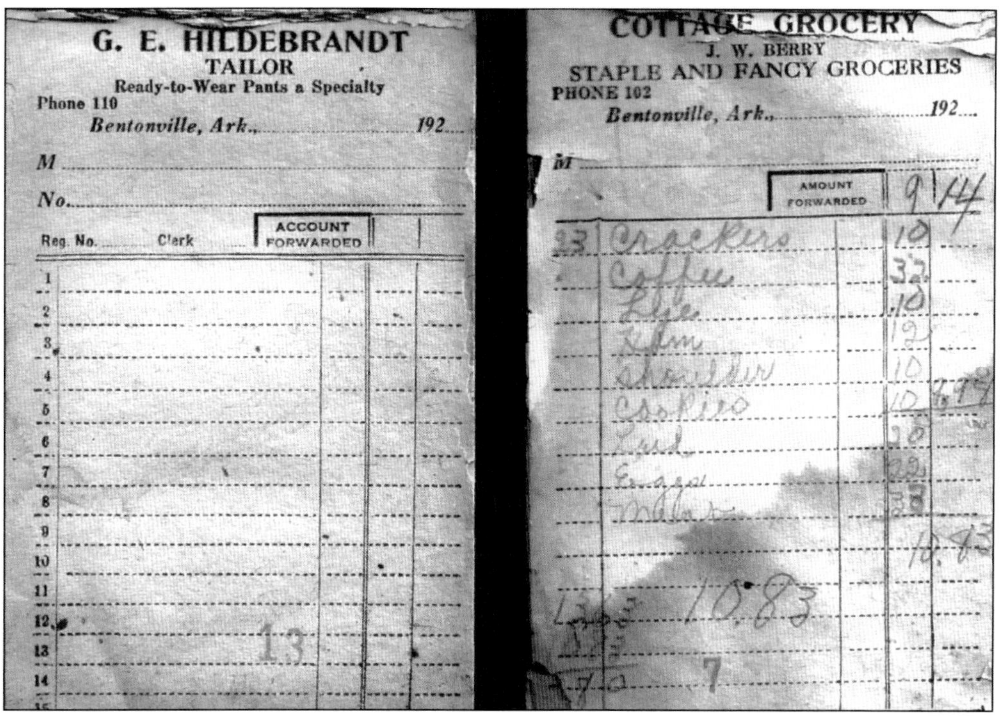

G. E. HILDEBRANDT
TAILOR
Ready-to-Wear Pants a Specialty
Phone 110
Bentonville, Ark. .... 192...
M ....
No. ....
Reg. No. ...... Clerk | ACCOUNT FORWARDED

COTTAGE GROCERY
J. W. BERRY
STAPLE AND FANCY GROCERIES
PHONE 102
Bentonville, Ark. .... 192...
M ....
AMOUNT FORWARDED

Old Bentonville Store Receipt Books, 1920. G. E. Hilderbrand specialized in tailored-to-fit pants, while J. W. Berry sold staple and fancy groceries. It is not certain where Hilderbrand's shop was located, but the grocery was on the square. (Courtesy of the author.)

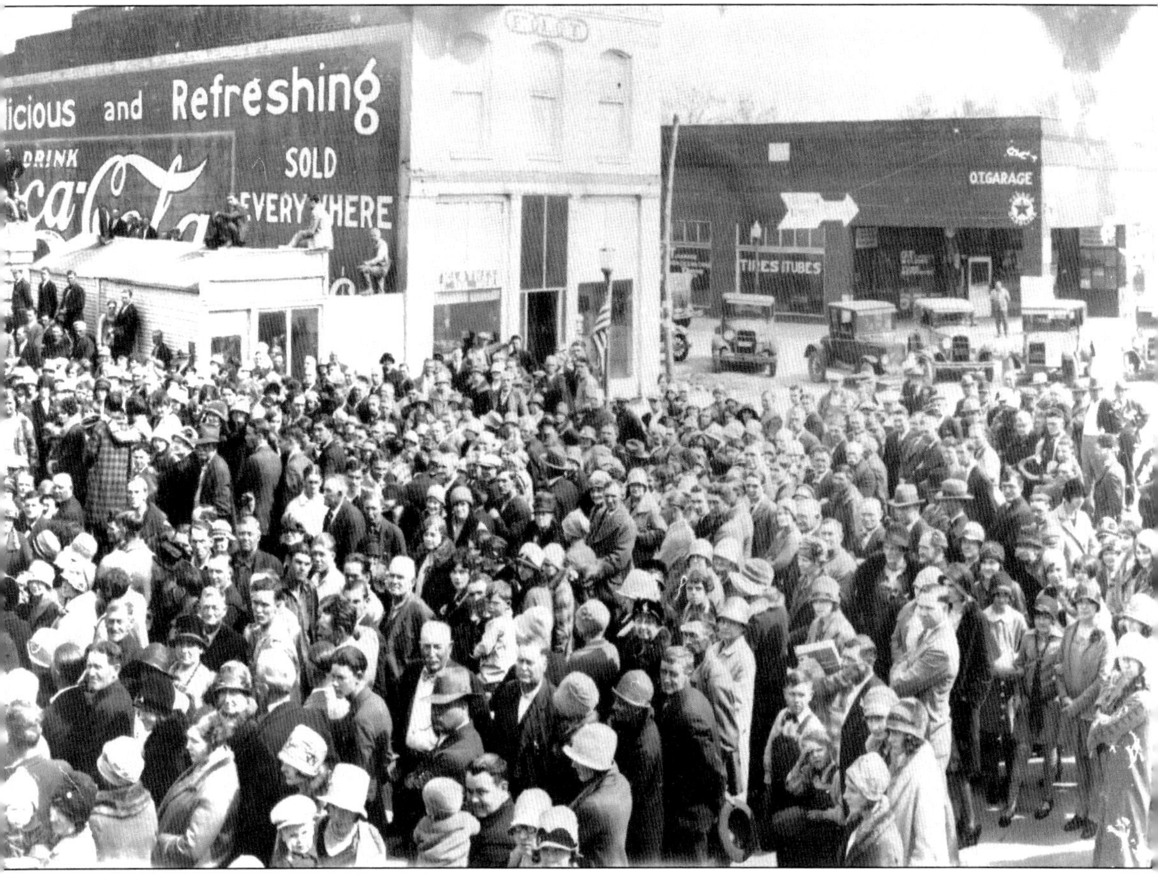

THE COURTHOUSE CORNERSTONE, 1927. The laying of the cornerstone for the Benton County Courthouse, located on the east side of the town square, signifies the beginning of construction. This image shows several post–Civil War buildings that were later torn down to make room for the new building. On the side of one building is an early Coca-Cola sign. (Courtesy of Rogers Historical Museum.)

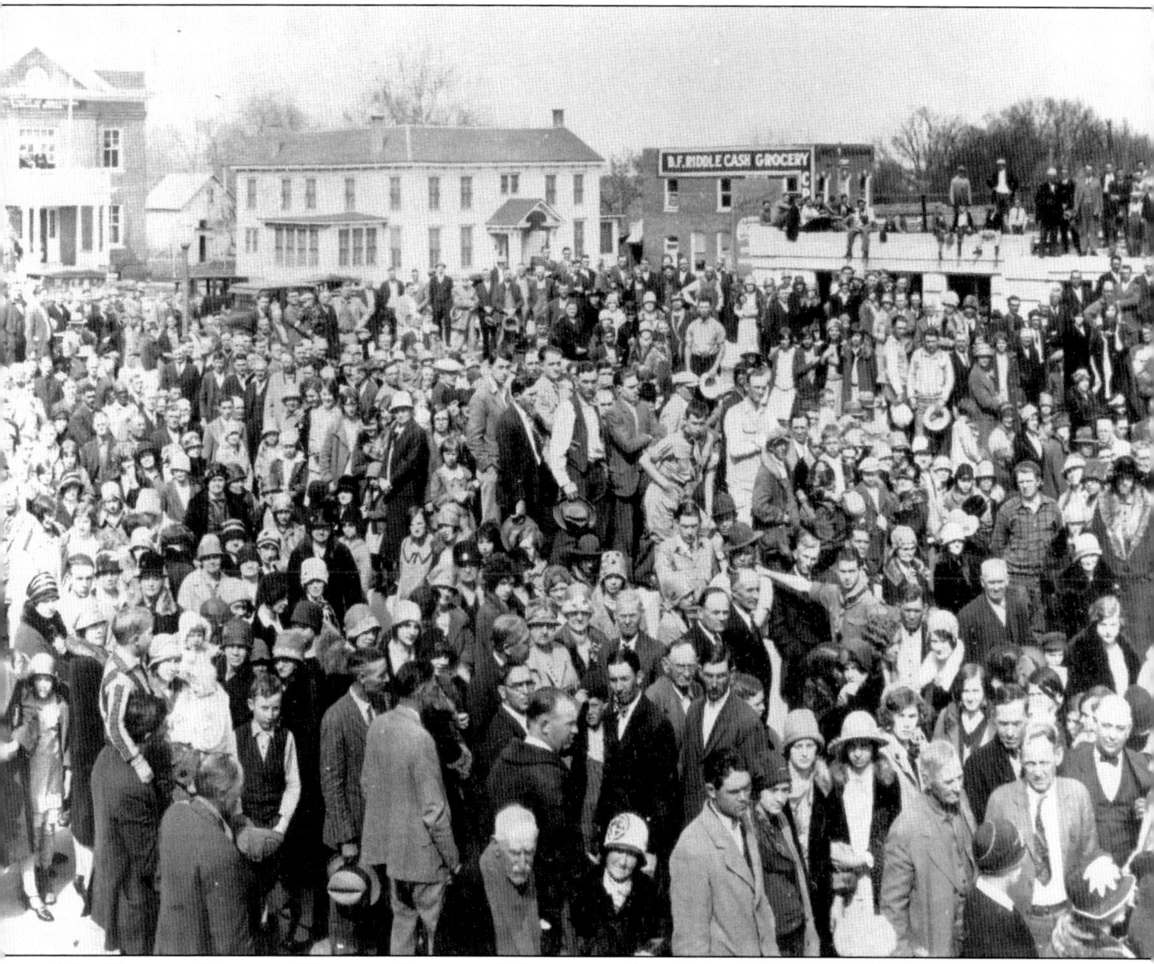

The Benton County Weather Bureau. A large crowd gathers on the square for the ceremonial laying of the cornerstone of the Benton County Courthouse. The Benton County Weather Bureau is shown at left in the background, and to the right is a large boardinghouse that once stood on South East Second Street. Few small towns had their own weather bureau, but it was necessary to help protect hundreds of acres of fruit orchards at that time. (Courtesy of Rogers Historical Museum.)

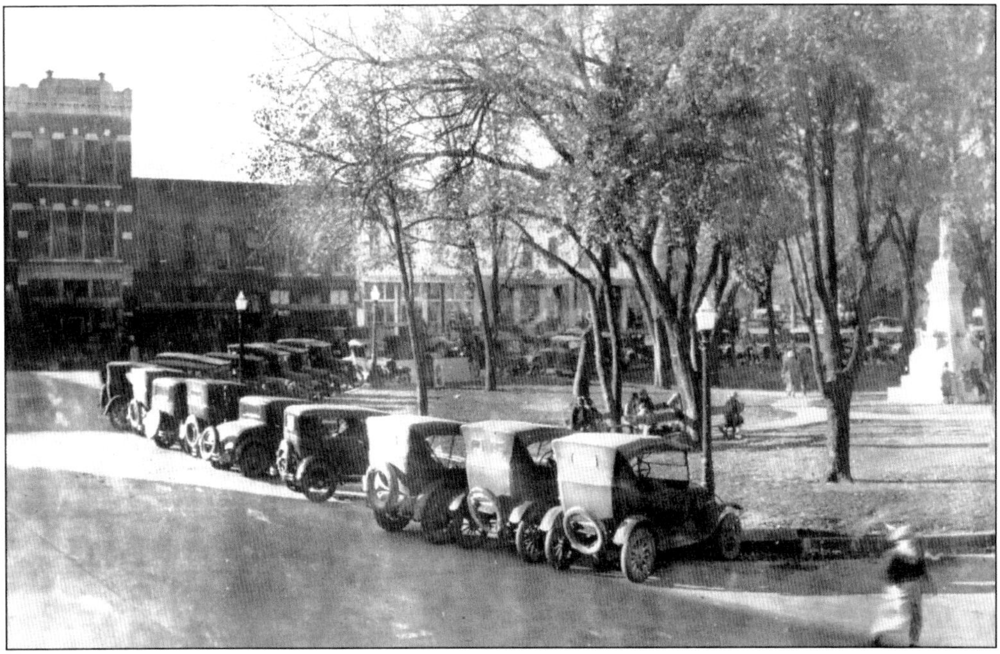

AROUND THE SQUARE, 1928. This is a view of the town square with lovely old streetlamps and an array of automobiles. This photograph shows several people enjoying the park while the dedication ceremony is conducted for the newly constructed Benton County Courthouse. (Courtesy of the author.)

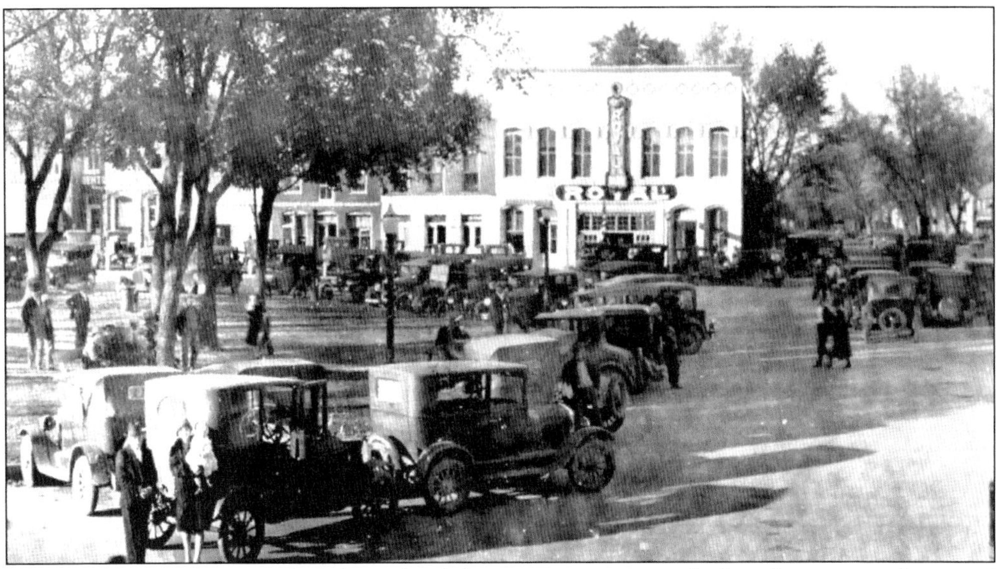

THE ROYAL THEATRE. On the other side of the square, cars are parked in the street as the crowd gathers for the dedication ceremony of the new courthouse in 1928. In the background is the Royal Theatre, which was the latest business to operate in the old opera house building. Traveling vaudeville musicians and entertainers performed and Chautauqua educational programs were presented at the opera house. Later the Park Theatre was located in the building for several years before it was torn down and the Bank of Bentonville was built on that corner. (Courtesy of the author.)

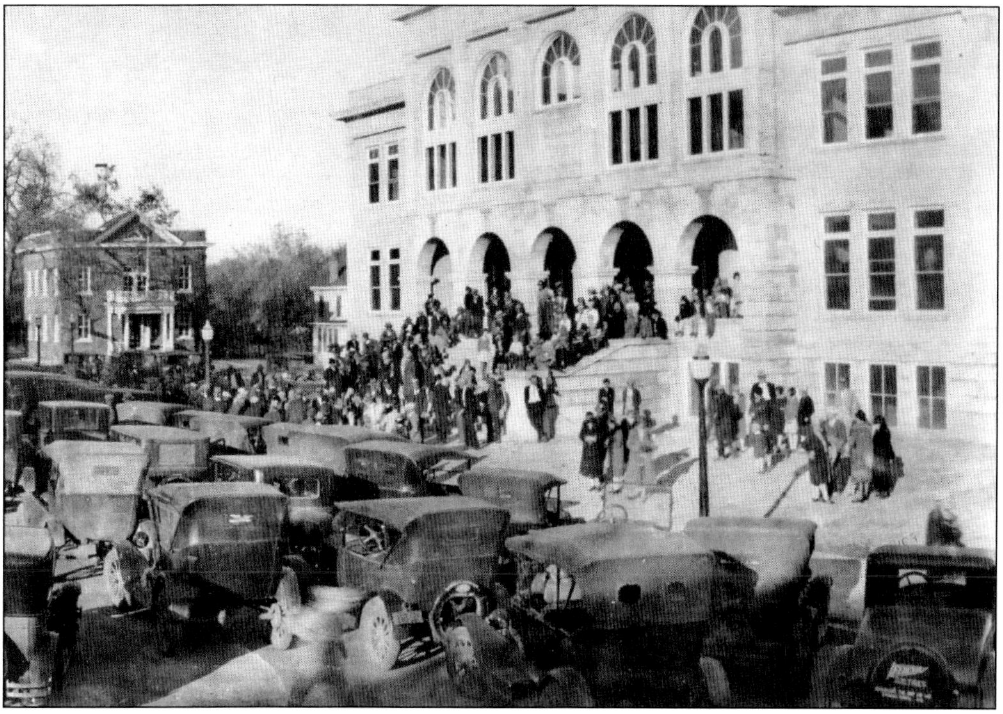

BENTON COUNTY COURTHOUSE, 1928. This is the dedication of the new courthouse in 1928 on the town square. The architect was A. O. Clarke, who had been brought to northwest Arkansas by Coin Harvey, famed developer of a summer resort named Monte Ne. The building cost $200,000, and lighting and fixtures cost another $10,000. It took 12 train carloads of cut stone, 30 cars of bricks, 40 cars of crushed stone, 4 cars of reinforcing steel, 12 cars of cement, and 16 cars of sand to construct the 36-room building. (Courtesy of the author.)

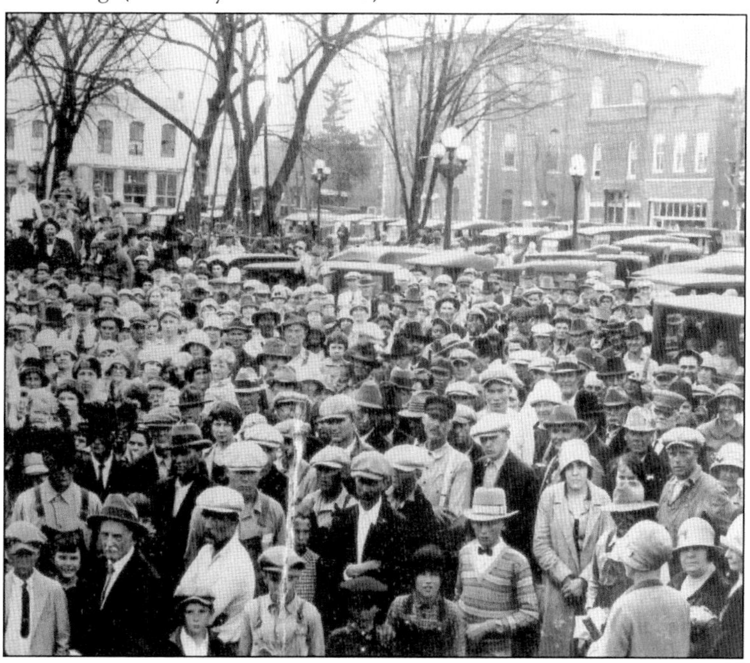

TRADES DAY CROWD ON SQUARE. In the old days, most people did their shopping in town on Saturday, which might include a chance to win a prize from the Trades Day drawing held on the square. In the background, the 1874 Benton County Courthouse is clearly visible in what is one of the last pictures of the large brick structure before it was torn down. (Courtesy of the author.)

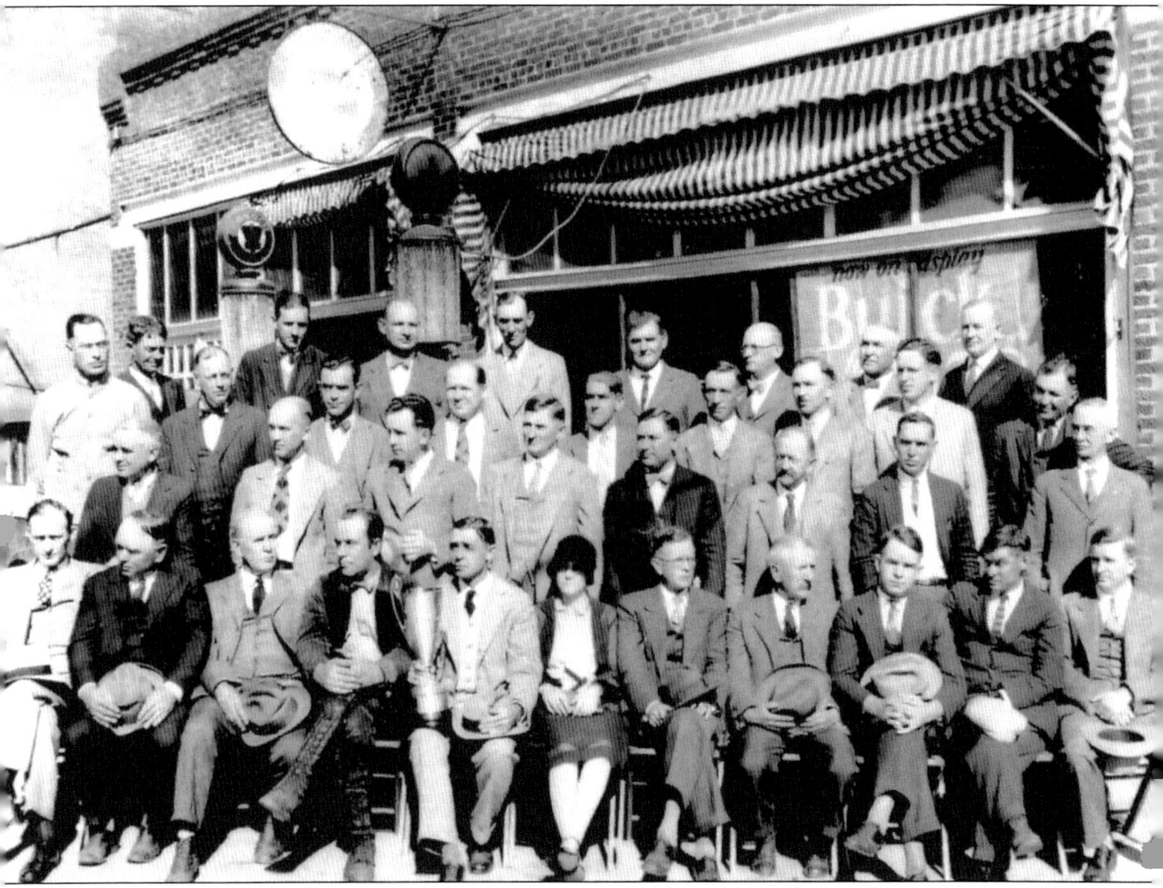

CHAMBER OF COMMERCE GROUP. Although it is not known exactly when this photograph was taken, members of the Bentonville Chamber of Commerce are posing outside the Bentonville Buick dealership and celebrating some type of award. Bess Pace was once president of the Chamber of Commerce and is the only person who can be identified in the group. (Courtesy of Patty Pearce Payne.)

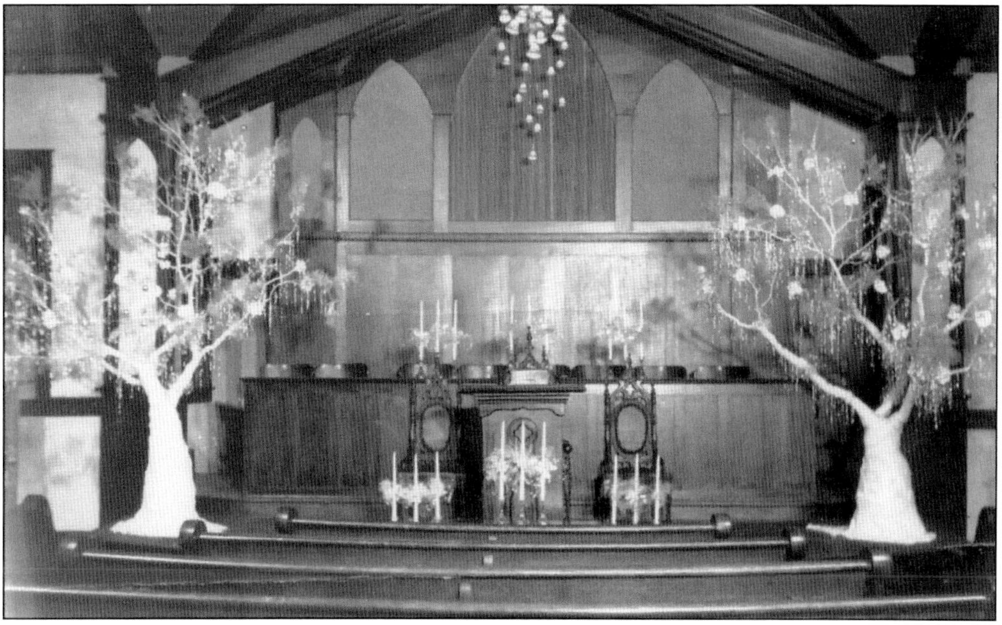

Presbyterian Church Christmas, 1936. This photograph provides a look at the sanctuary of the old Presbyterian church during Christmastime. The trees are creatively wrapped in white and feature snowflake ornaments. The beautiful velvet vesper chairs and preacher's pulpit have been lovingly cared for and today are in the new church on J Street. (Courtesy of the First Presbyterian Church.)

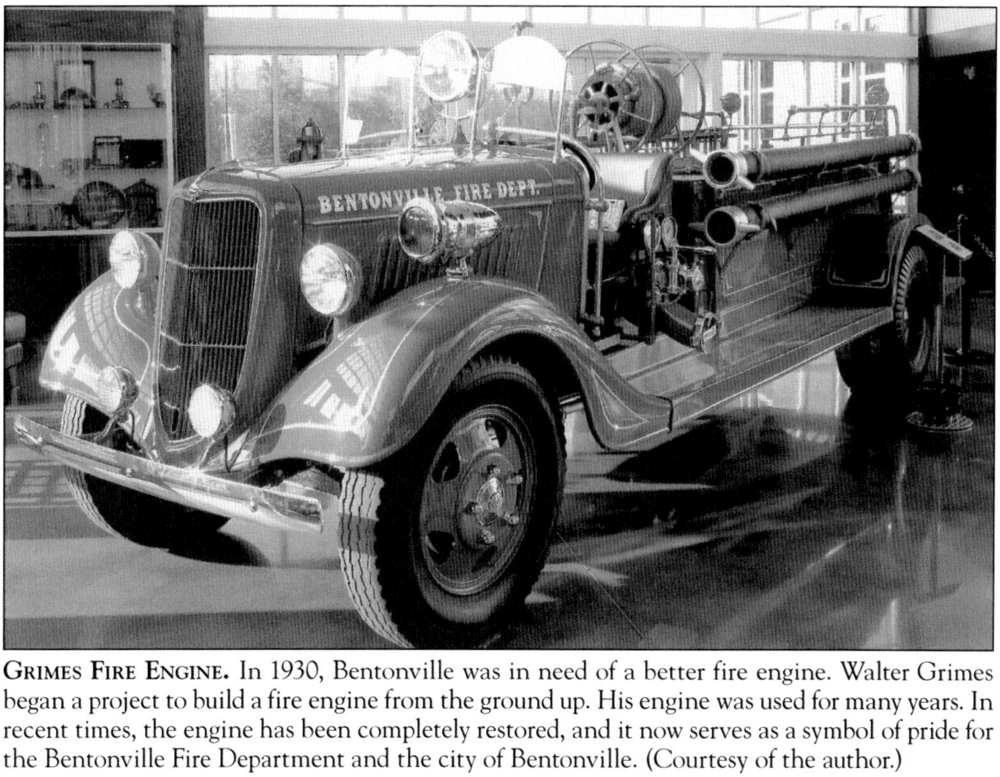

Grimes Fire Engine. In 1930, Bentonville was in need of a better fire engine. Walter Grimes began a project to build a fire engine from the ground up. His engine was used for many years. In recent times, the engine has been completely restored, and it now serves as a symbol of pride for the Bentonville Fire Department and the city of Bentonville. (Courtesy of the author.)

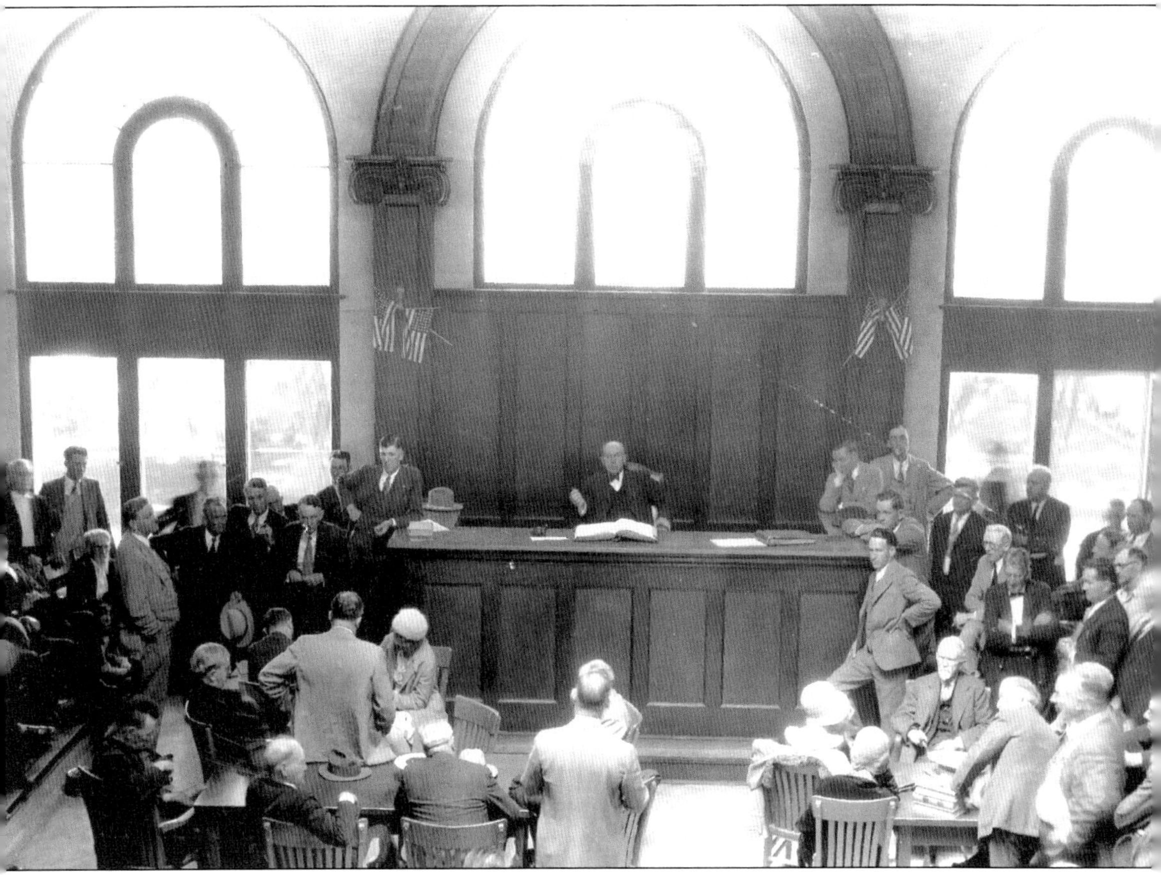

Murder Trial. This is a rare photograph of a murder trial in progress in the Benton County Courthouse in April 1930. Retired dentist Dr. A. J. Bass of Columbia, Missouri, pled guilty to the murder of William R. Pearman, who was found dead near Gravette, Arkansas, with three bullets in his head. Dr. Bass received a life sentence. Sheriff Edgar Fields is standing left of the judge's bench while Judge Earl Blansett presides over the trial. Defense attorney John R. Duty and Boyle Clark are seated in the foreground to the left. Prosecuting attorney John S. Combs and his assistants are to the right. (Courtesy of Shiloh Museum of Ozark History/Washington County Historical Society Collection P-26-72.)

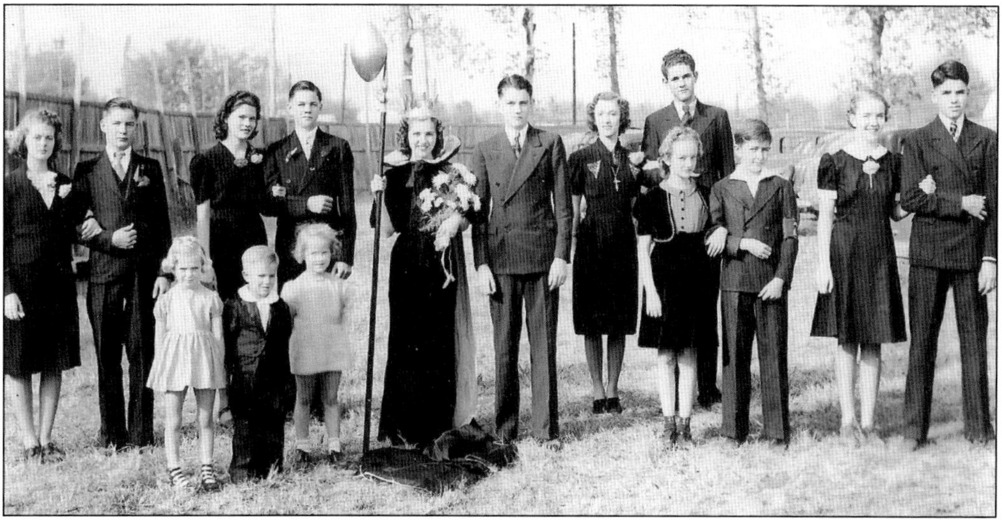

HOMECOMING QUEEN, 1938. This is the Bentonville High School homecoming queen of 1938 and her court. From left to right are Jane Fisher, Bill Bryan, Loraine Butts, unidentified, Alberta Allred (homecoming queen), Alfred Smartt, Waniese Radler, Bill Austin, Dorothy Peel, David Peel, and an unidentified couple. The children in front are unidentified. (Courtesy of Mary Marquess.)

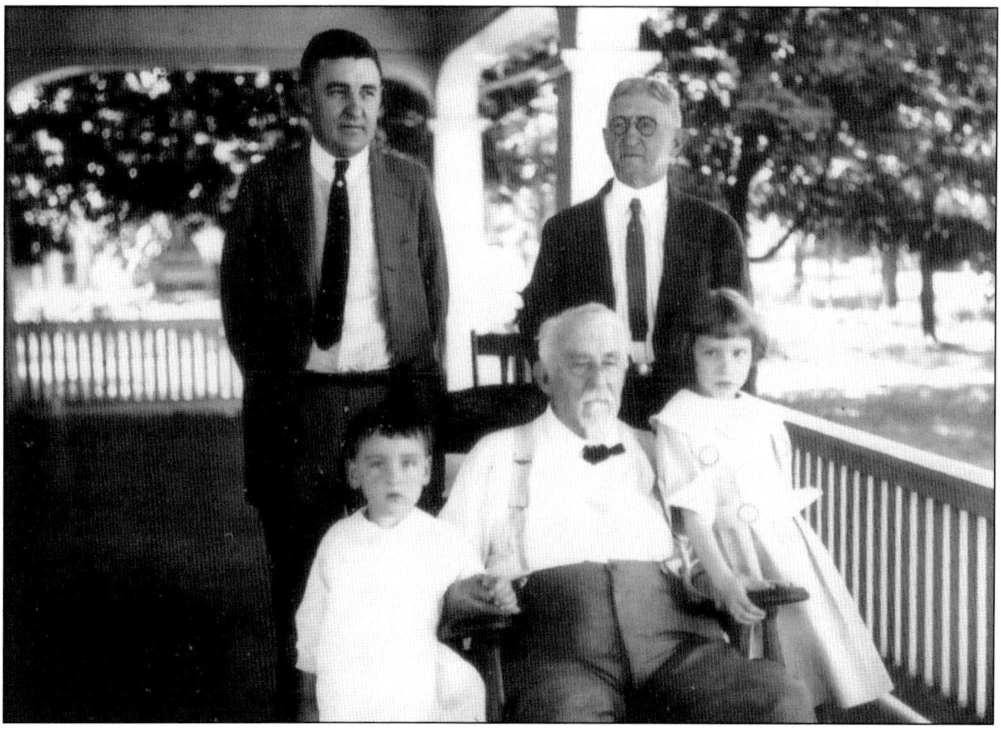

THE PEEL FAMILY ON THE PORCH. Col. Sam Peel (sitting) poses on the porch with his grandson Jeff Rice Jr. on the left, his granddaughter Mary Elizabeth Peel on the right, and his sons Rex W. Peel (left) and David Walker Peel standing behind him. This house was owned by Sam's daughter and was where he resided when he died. In the 1980s, the house was moved from its original location, which was directly across from the First United Methodist Church. (Courtesy of Mary Marquess.)

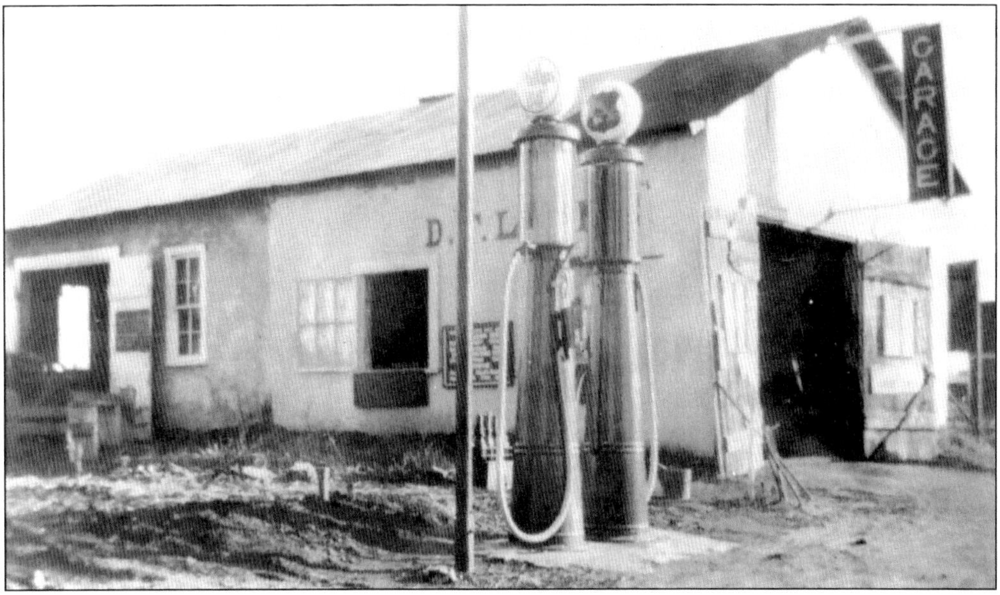

The Laine Garage. The Laine Garage was located just off of East Central Avenue in 1931. It was owned and operated by D. T. Laine and was a Phillips 66 filling station and one of the first auto repair garages in Bentonville. The windows for the garage were salvaged from the old Benton County Courthouse. (Courtesy of Daryl Stroud.)

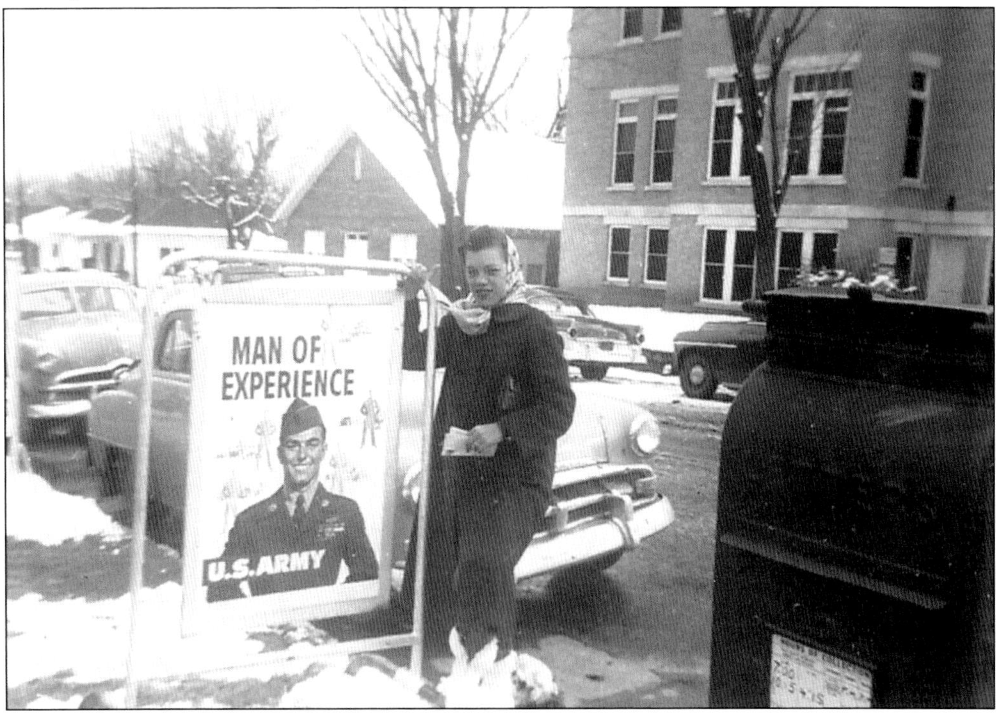

Man of Experience. In the 1940s, it was difficult to find a young man of experience in Bentonville because most of them were away at war. Teenager Tomilee Lindner poses by the sign in front of the post office building where the recruiting office was located. (Courtesy of Tomilee Lindner Lundy.)

World War II Soldiers. John Black and his brother Hugh "Tater" Black answered the call to join the armed services during World War II. After the war, John Black served as Bentonville chief of police and then joined the Arkansas State Police. Hugh also had a career in local law enforcement before moving to Fort Smith and serving as a federal marshal. (Courtesy of Rogers Historical Museum.)

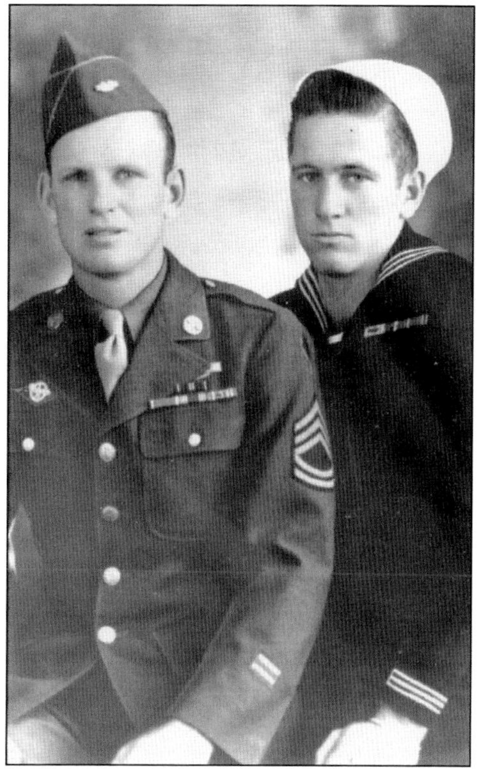

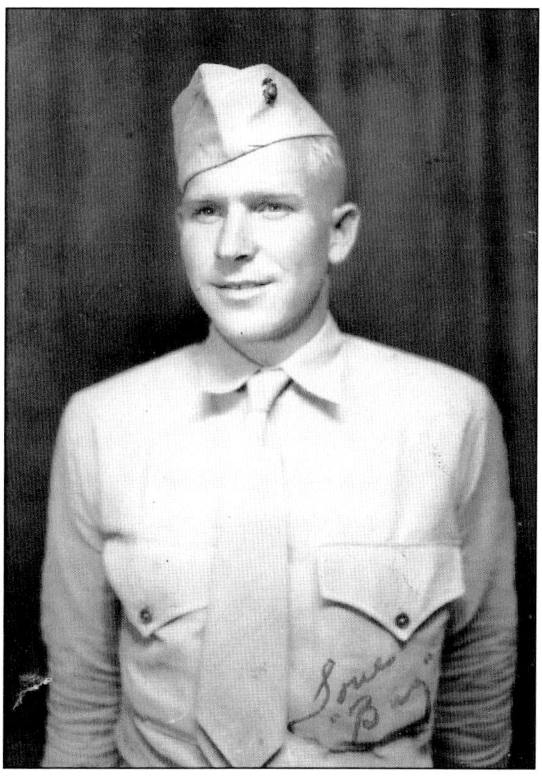

Truman Boling, World War II Soldier. Truman Boling was one of three Boling boys who served in World War II. He was with an engineering unit that built bridges for heavy tank traffic. While Boling was away, he spent all his free time drawing up plans for a house he hoped to build for his young bride when he returned to Bentonville. When he returned home, he did build the house of his dreams. (Courtesy of Lorene Boling.)

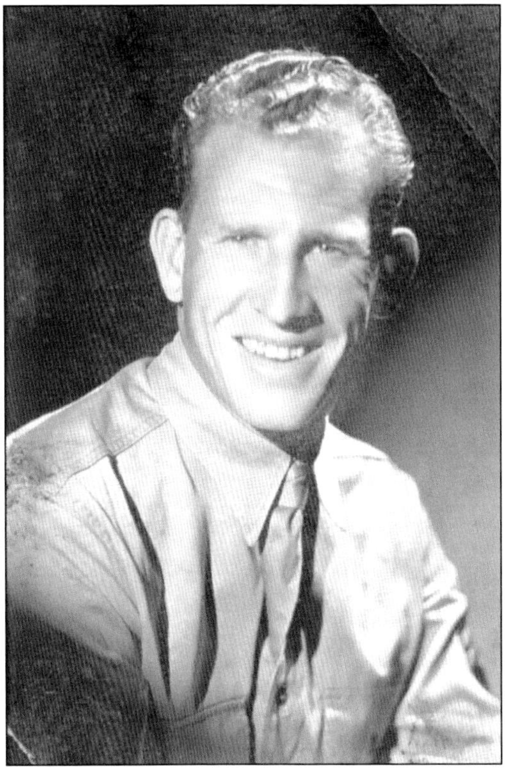

Cleo Boling, World War II Soldier. S.Sgt. Cleo Boling was the oldest of the three Boling boys. He graduated from Bentonville High School in 1933 and was drafted into the army. He served two years overseas during the war, and after returning home from the war, Cleo worked for the Bentonville post office. (Courtesy of David Boling.)

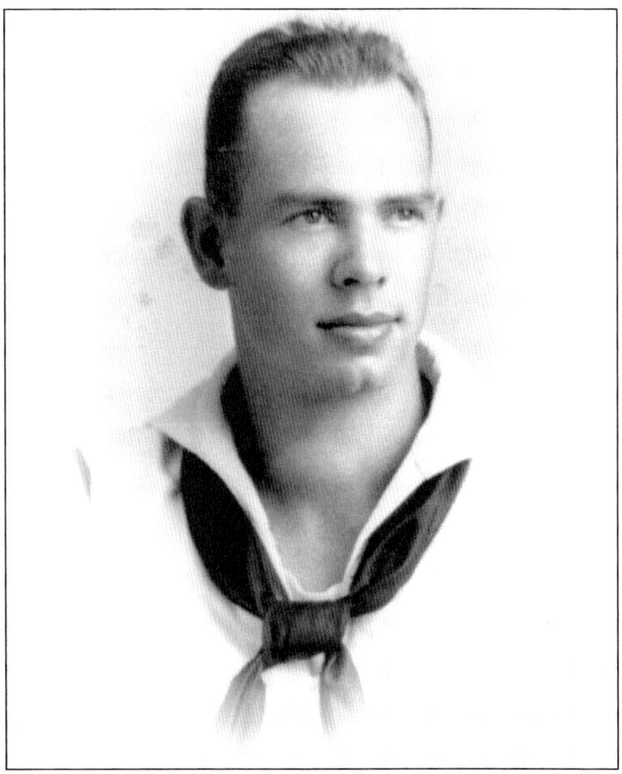

Max Boling, World War II Soldier. Max graduated from Bentonville High School in 1935 and was drafted the same year. Max was not as lucky as his two brothers. Max was an air radio mechanic, second class, for the U.S. Navy. In 1945, he was trapped in the gondola of a blimp when the fuel tanks exploded about 200 feet off the ground as they were heading for the mooring in Santa Ana, California. (Courtesy of Lorene Boling.)

Gold Star Boys. Bentonville mourned the loss of its young men killed in World War II. They were honored as Gold Star Boys, and their pictures were in the 1946 *Bentonville High School Annual*. This group included (from left to right, top to bottom) Dwight Gamble, Max Boling, Vearl Griffin, Clyde Carter, Gordon Sumner, Lewis Hughs, Howard Wolgamot, Raymond Clark, A. J. Yates, Hal Neal Wood, and Frank Morris. (Courtesy of the author.)

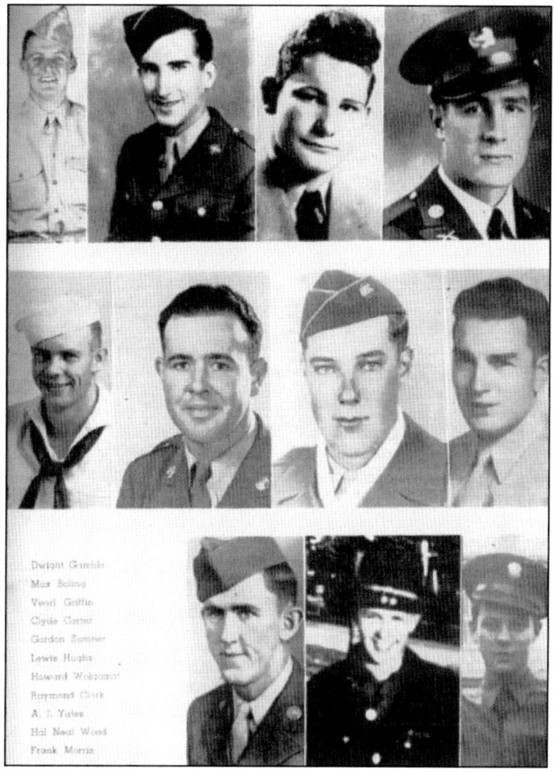

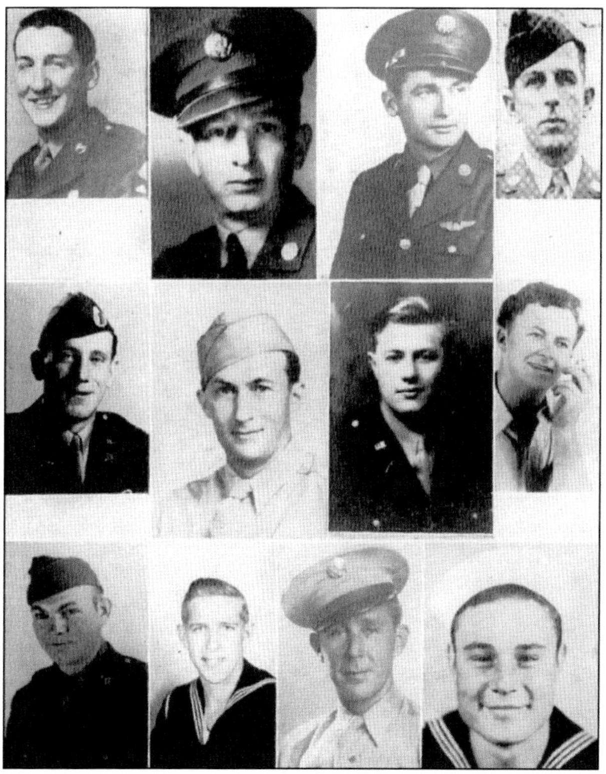

More Gold Star Boys. There was a second page in the 1946 annual with pictures of more soldiers who did not come home from the war. They were (from left to right, top to bottom) Charles David Rice, Eugene Knott, Harvey Back, Walton Shores, Jack Lincoln, Rolland Pipinger, James Hugh Carithers, Dickie Knott, Cevil Conner, Johnny Holmes, Tommy Lincoln, and Milton Ralland. (Courtesy of the author.)

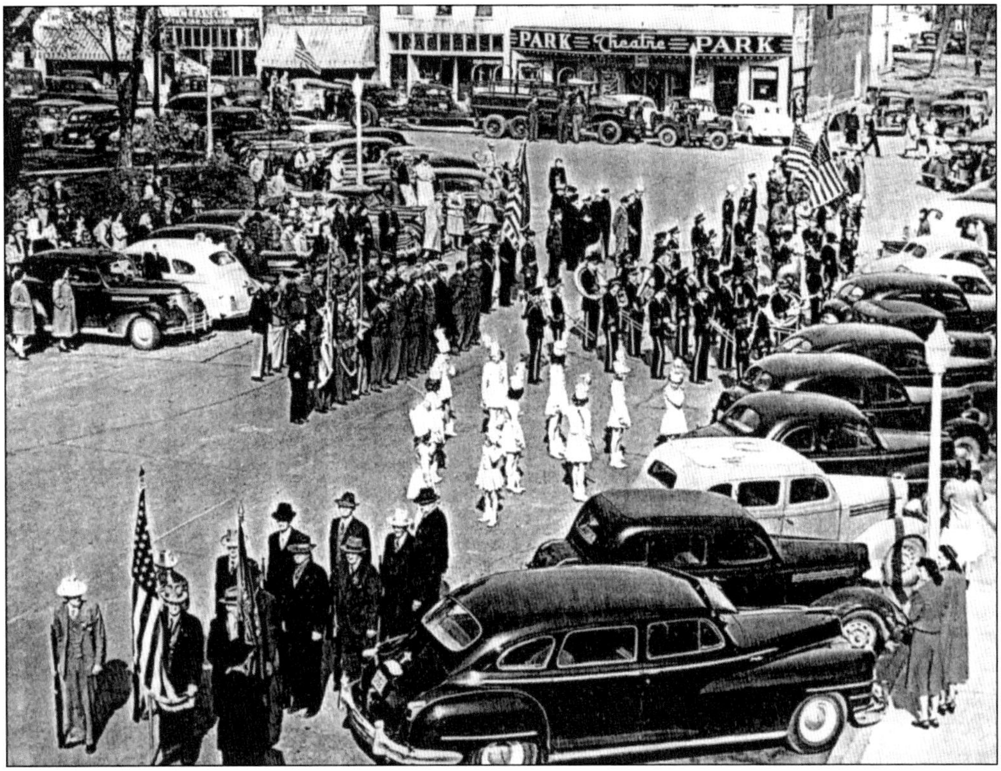

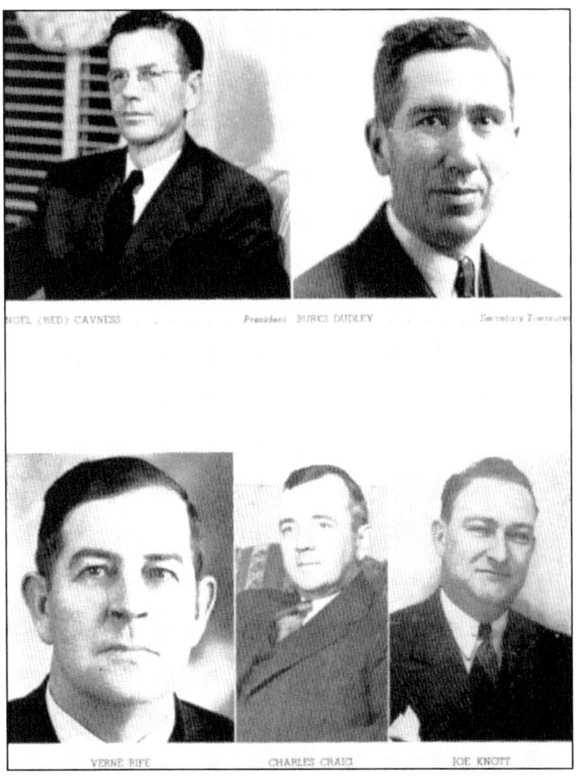

Thanks to the Veterans. A veteran appreciation parade and ceremony took place on the town square in 1947, with music provided by the Bentonville High School marching band. In the background there are several military vehicles parked in front of the Park Theatre, which was in the old opera house building. (Courtesy of Lorene Boling.)

Bentonville School Board, 1946. Noel "Red" Caveness (top left) was mayor for several years. Board president Burks Dudley (top right) owned the Cash Store, which sold fabrics by the yard. From left to right, below, Verne Rife, Charlie Craig, and Joe Knott were well-respected businessmen and longtime leaders in the community. (Courtesy of the author.)

The Chicken Hatchery Business. After the apple industry began to fade, many people took advantage of opportunities in the poultry business. Syble Harris, the author's mother, is shown in a chicken hatchery promotional photograph with her niece, Audrey McCord, and a box of baby chicks. The hatchery was located on Main Street in the 1940s. (Courtesy of the author.)

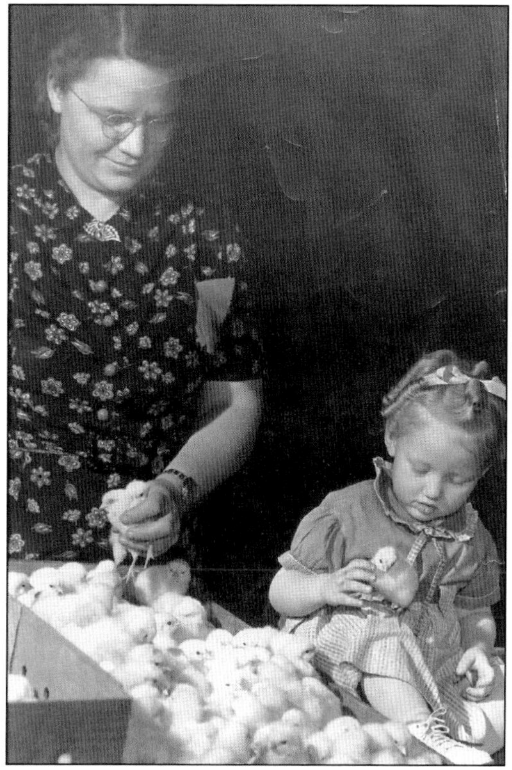

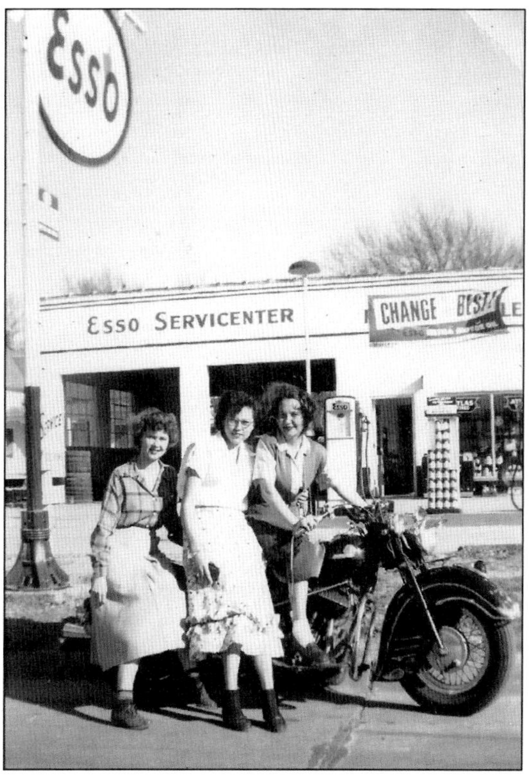

Bentonville Teens. In front of the Esso Station are, from left to right, Rosmond Morris, Jo Ella Carter, and Shirley Gaut posing on a motorcycle. These teenage girls were having fun in the autumn of 1949 in downtown Bentonville. Today, there is a drive-through bank instead of a gas station at this location. (Courtesy of Ray Jefferson.)

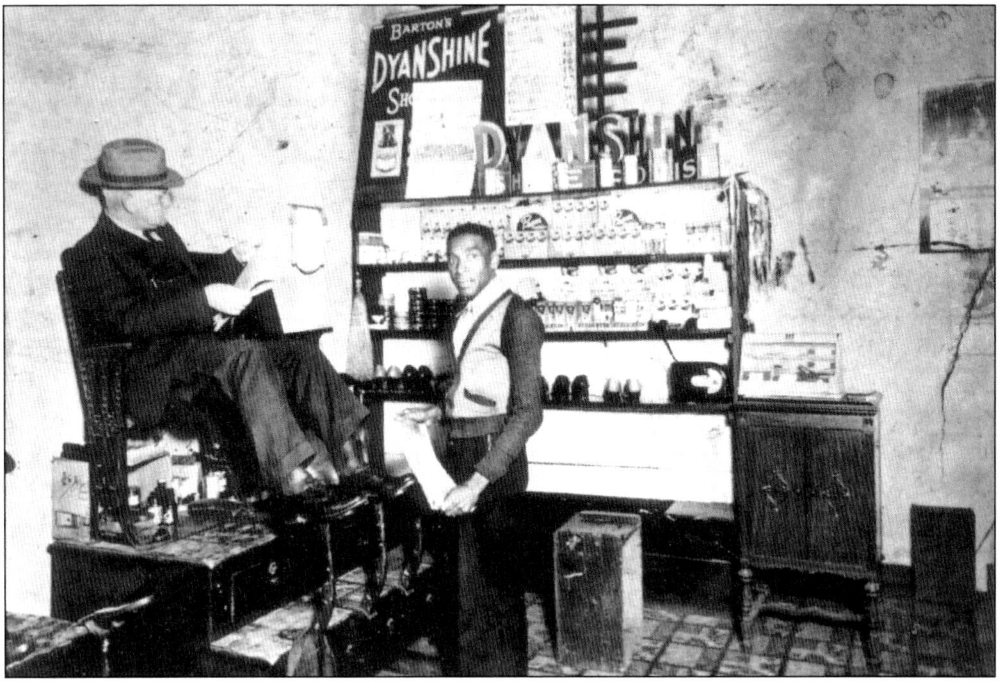

ARTHUR DICKERSON. Arthur "Rabbit" Dickerson owned and operated Rabbit's Shine Parlor in Bentonville for many years. Arthur said he was nicknamed "Rabbit" when he was a child. At one time, Arthur had owned and operated a business longer than anyone else in downtown. He was recognized for his excellent business practices by the Bentonville Chamber of Commerce and was the first recipient of the Arthur "Rabbit" Dickerson Man of the Year Award. (Courtesy of Shiloh Museum of Ozark History S-94-141-22.)

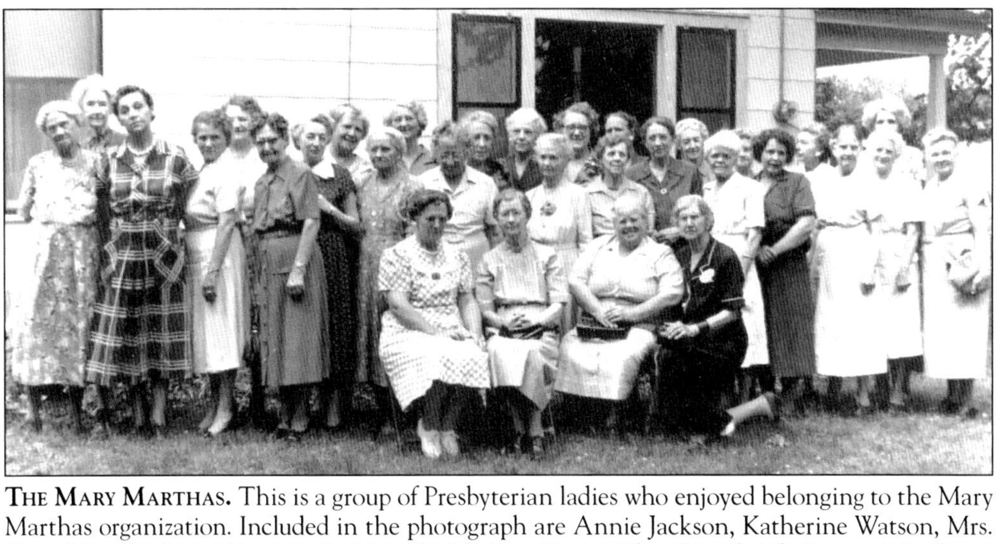

THE MARY MARTHAS. This is a group of Presbyterian ladies who enjoyed belonging to the Mary Marthas organization. Included in the photograph are Annie Jackson, Katherine Watson, Mrs. Gary, Mrs. Cowley and her cousin, Mrs. Shickle, Leta Bryan, Clara Diezel, Ada Fenton, Mrs. Ryan, Mrs. Griffith, Mrs. Rife, Mrs. Beck, Mrs. Rueling, Anna Patton, Mrs. Lincoln, Leota Rankin, Gertrude Schmidt, Nell Patton, Mrs. Stewart, Minnie Strock, Kitty Burks, Mrs. Dudley, Mrs. Deloach, Mrs. Adamson, Gay Coutchie, Mrs. Rosborough, Mrs. Miller, Mrs. Ruth, Anna Mary Jabusch, and Mrs. Phinney. (Courtesy of the First Presbyterian Church.)

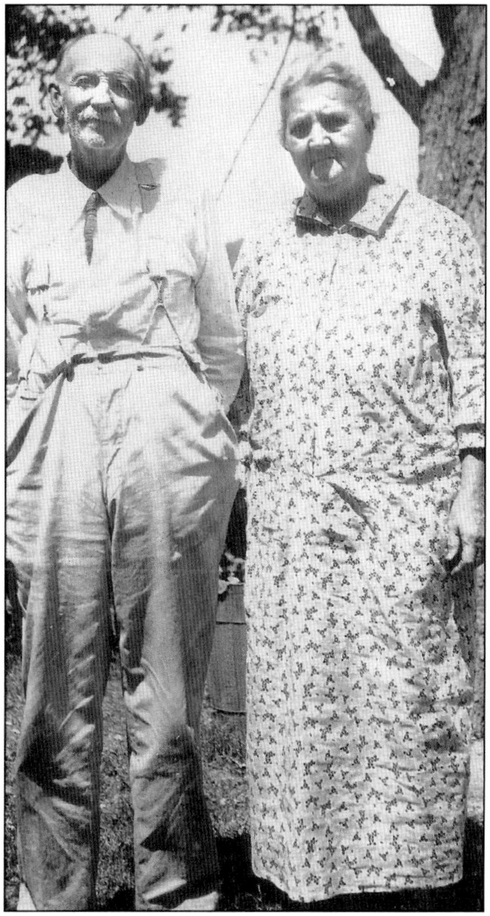

One Generation to Another. Charles and Mary Boling were Bentonville citizens during a much different time. They are examples of how one generation can pass along a strong set of values to their children, as well as the skills needed to help build a town like Bentonville. Through the years, their son, grandson, and great-grandson have built some of the most beautiful and well-crafted homes in Bentonville. (Courtesy of Lorene Boling.)

The Gordon Knott House. When this house was built in 1956 and 1957 by R. D. Boling and his son Truman Boling, it was considered the latest in modern design. The house is located at 403 West Central Avenue and was built for Gordon Knott. Ralph and Peggy Wallis lived in the house for a number of years. Peggy used her teddy bear collection year-round to decorate the large front windows for each holiday. Many neighborhood children and adults enjoyed the teddy bear tea parties and charming window scenes Peggy created. (Courtesy of the author.)

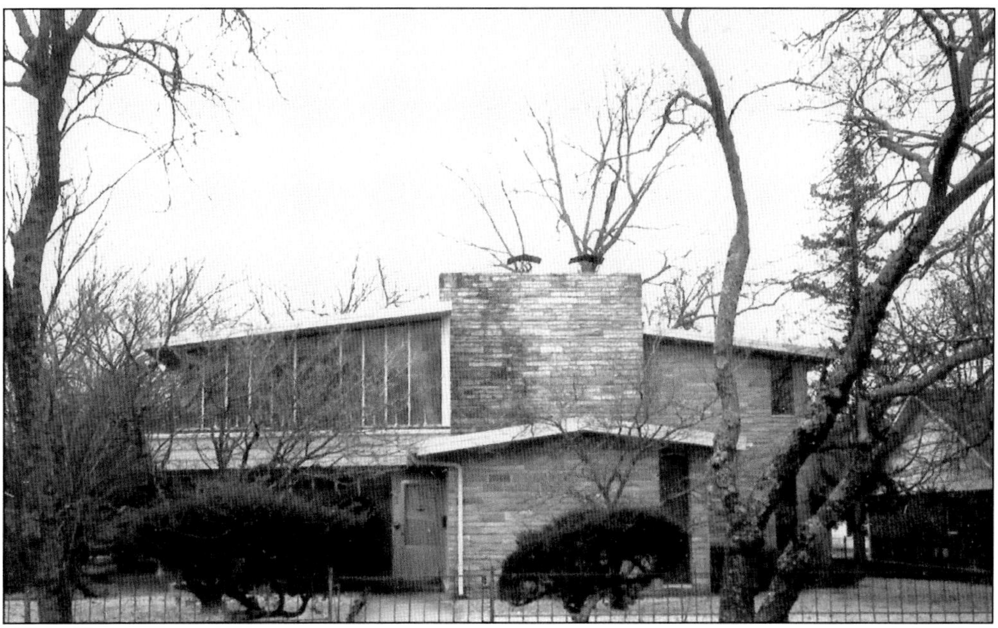

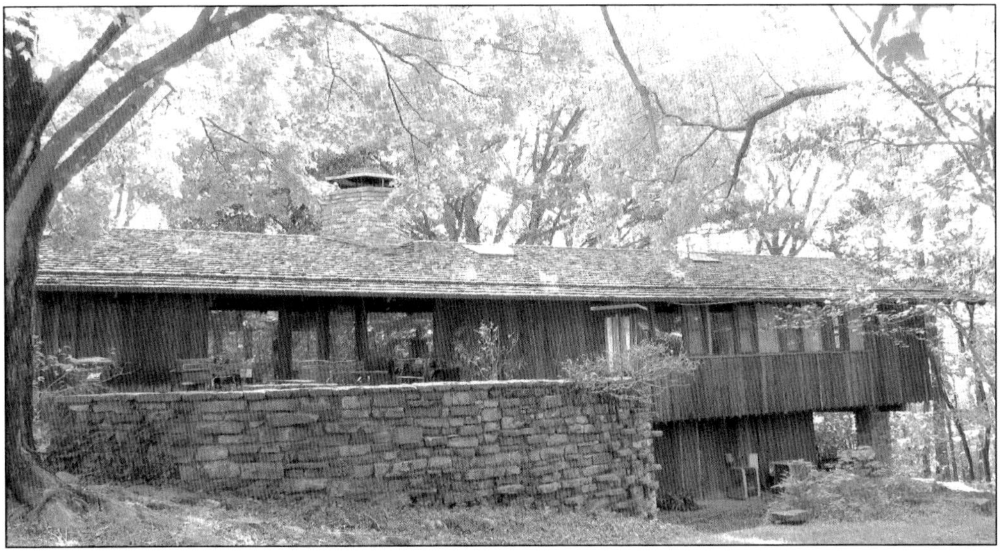

TRUMAN BOLING, MASTER BUILDER. One of Arkansas's most famous architects, E. Fay Jones, was so pleased with Truman Boling's work on the Applegate House that they teamed up to build several Bentonville landmarks, including the Enfield House, pictured here. Jones designed and Boling built the first Sam Walton home, located on the Town Branch Creek. Truman's son Mike continued the Boling tradition of fine craftsmanship when he built a magnificent hilltop home in north Bentonville for Larry Dimmit. (Courtesy of the author.)

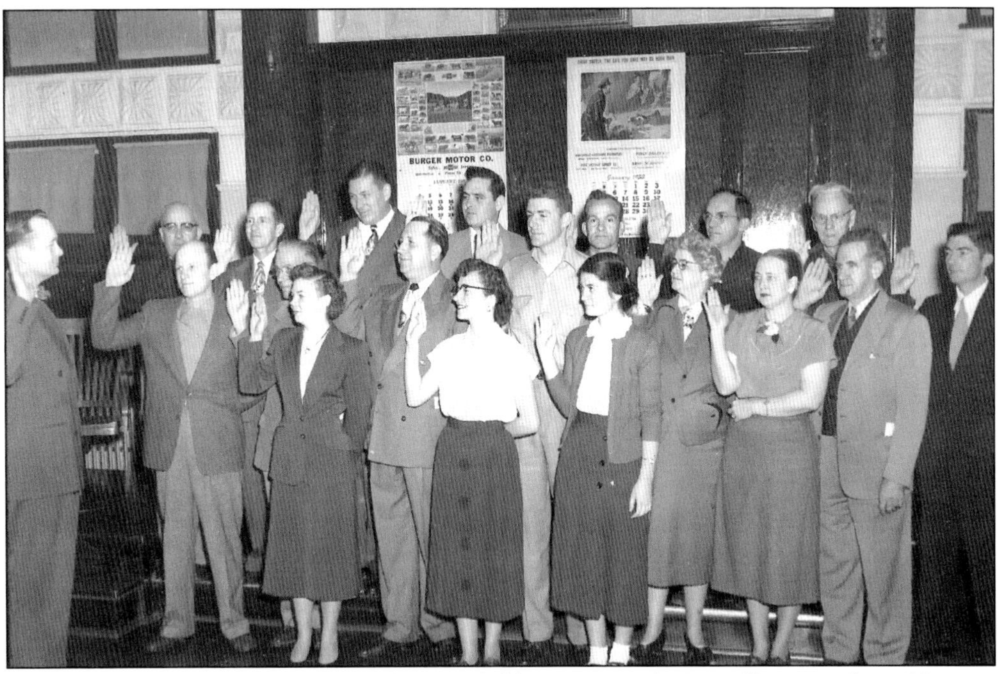

JUDGE WILLIAM H. ENFIELD. Judge William Enfield swears in 1952 City of Bentonville and Benton County officers and deputies. From left to right are (first row) three unidentified ladies; (second row) John Black, unidentified, Craig Holt, unidentified, Josephine Heyland, unidentified, Mayor Alvin Seamster, and unidentified; (third row) two unidentified men, Buddy Burns, Charles Gocio, Ray Jefferson, unidentified, and John Cox. (Courtesy of Gary Black.)

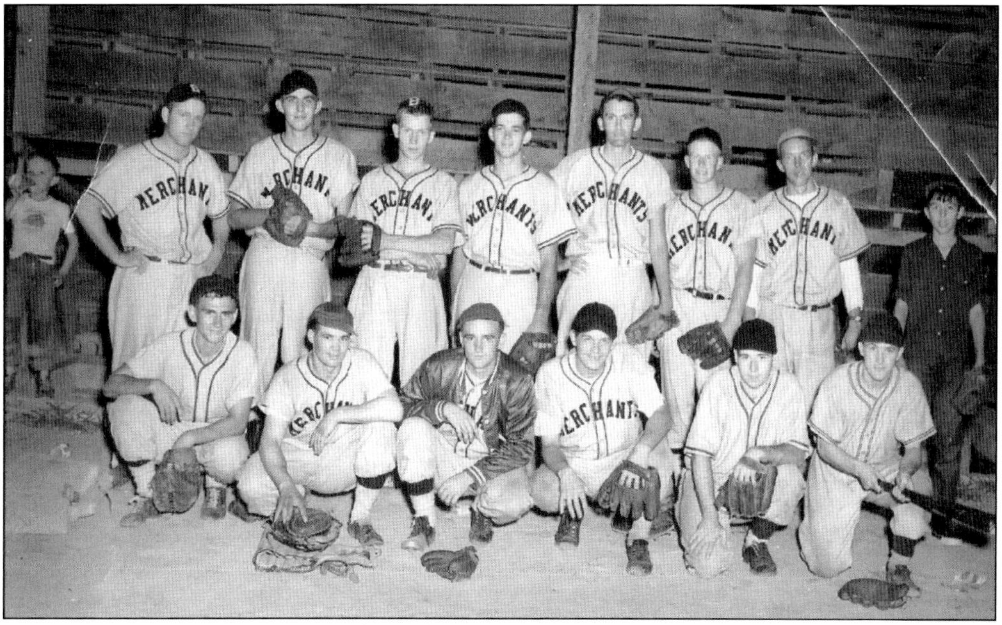

The Bentonville Merchants. This is the Bentonville Merchants baseball team in 1955. From left to right are (first row) Johnny Horton, Charles Kirby, Oliver Bates, Joe Cavness, unidentified, and Bill Gailey; (second row) Mike Mason (little boy), coach Hugh "Tater" Black, C. L. Jones, Truman Boling, unidentified, Bob Norman, Dean Boyles, Edward "Duck" Moore, and Gene Walker (batboy). (Courtesy of Lorene Boling.)

Downtown Fire, 1961. On March 21, 1961, a large fire completely destroyed two establishments and greatly damaged several other businesses on Northwest Second Street and West Central Avenue in downtown. The fire alarm went off at 10:15 a.m., and flames were 200 feet in the air at times. The newspaper reported it as the worst fire in town since 1921, when another building burned at the exact same location. The checkerboard sign to the right was about all that remained of Banks Grocery and Feed Store. (Courtesy of the author.)

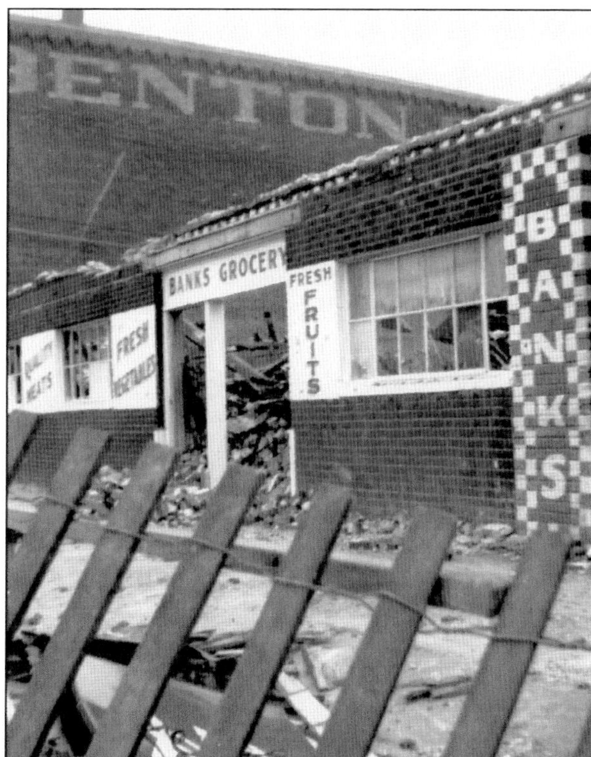

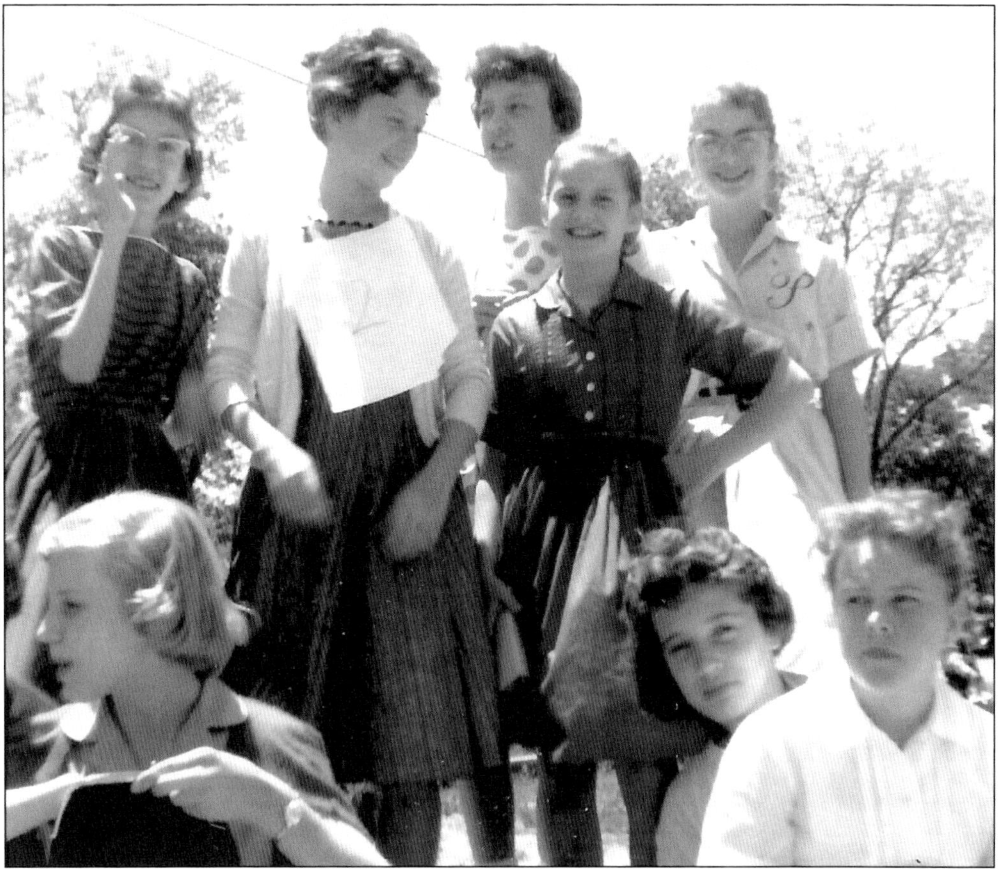

FUN AT BENTONVILLE SCHOOL. In the 1960s, students often gathered after lunch on the front lawn of the Bentonville High School. This group has remained friends and celebrated its 45th class reunion in 2010. From left to right are (first row) Carolyn Boling, Jo Lynn Fisher, and Barbara Harris; (second row) Sarah Harrison, Jerri Sparks, Sharon Adamson, Sharon Fields, and Ann Powell. (Courtesy of the author.)

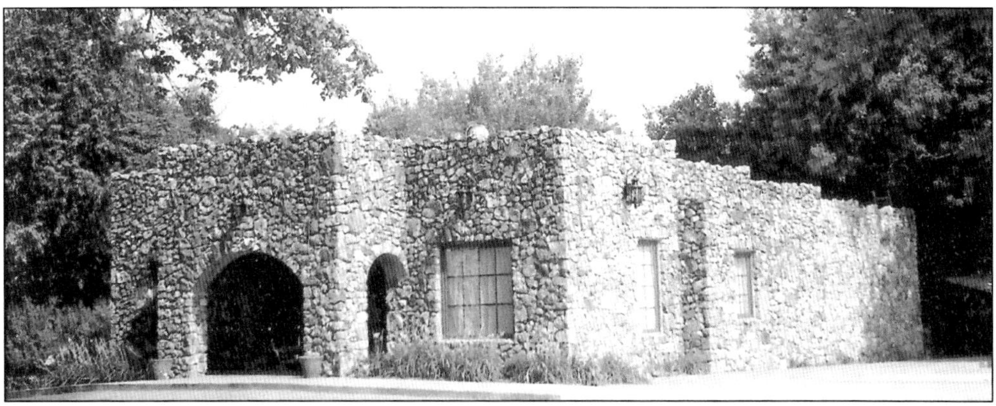

WILLARD BRAITHWAITE HOUSE. There are several homes in Bentonville built by Willard Braithwaite, but the most unusual one is sometimes referred to as the "Bethlehem House." This beautiful structure was built of fieldstone. The structure survived a fire and has been successfully renovated into a day spa. (Courtesy of the author.)

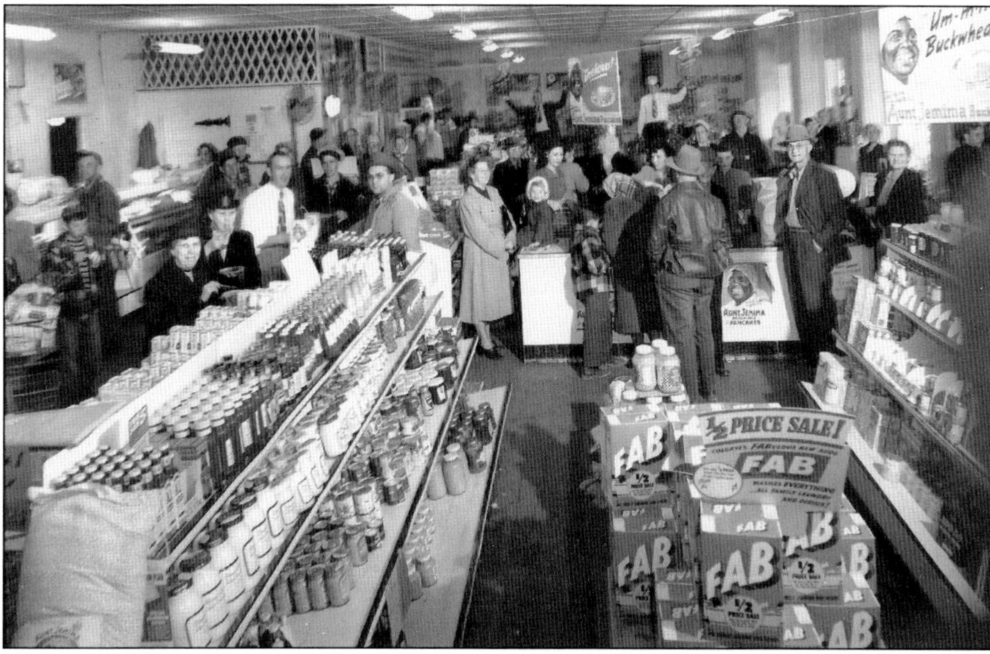

GRAND OPENING OF THE COFFELT'S MARKET. The building was built and the grocery business started by Henry Coffelt, but his children and other relatives helped operate the store through the years. This picture was taken at the grand opening in the early 1950s. Russell Fields was the butcher at that time, and Mildred Potts was the cashier. (Courtesy of Cathy Coffelt Palmer.)

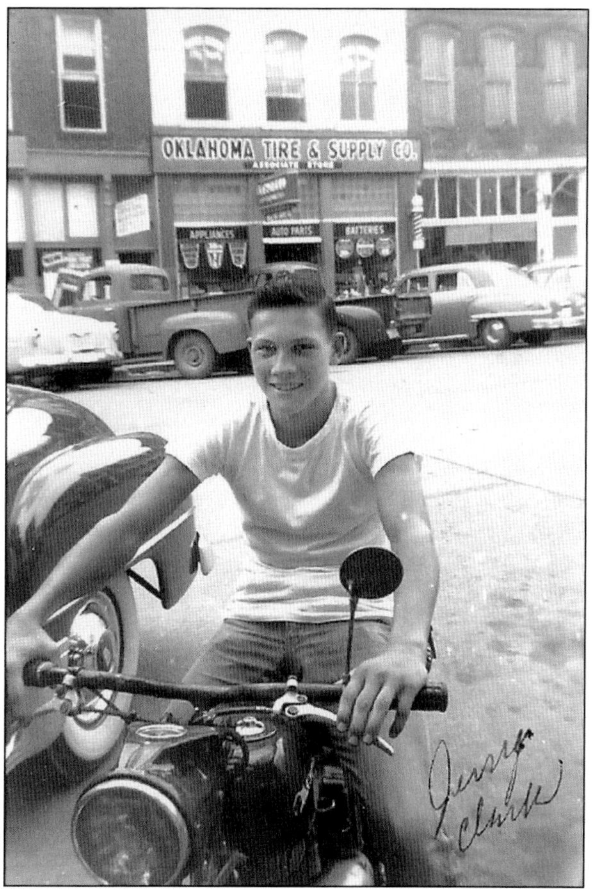

JERRY CLARK AND MOTORCYCLE. Jerry Clark parked his motorcycle across the street from the Oklahoma Tire and Supply store and the Elkhorn Barber Shop. Bentonville was a wonderful place to grow up, especially in the 1950s. (Courtesy of Tomilee Lindner Lundy.)

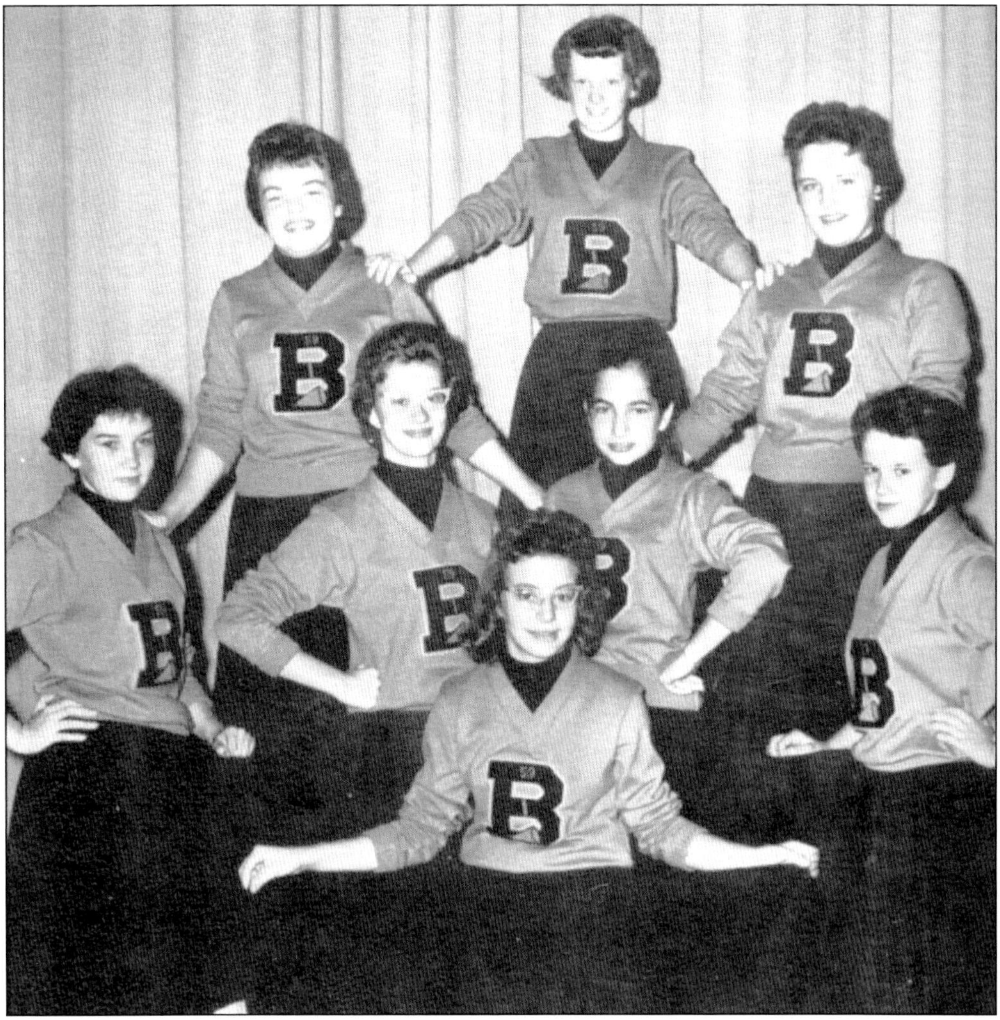

BENTONVILLE JUNIOR HIGH CHEERLEADERS, 1960. In those days, the Bentonville school was small enough for students to know just about everyone in every grade. This group posed in their gold and black Bentonville Tigers cheerleader uniforms. From left to right are (first row) Julie Howarth; (second row) Janice Cawood, Alicia Fields, Connie True, and Deanna Wade; (third row) Jill Marquess, Phyllis Black, and Gail Brock. (Courtesy of the author.)

Six

WALMART LEADS THE WAY 1951–1990

When Sam Walton and his family arrived in Bentonville in the spring of 1950, there were three variety stores, four ready-to-wear stores, six grocery stores, three drugstores, and a number of other small businesses in the immediate downtown area. Sam Walton's self-described "passion to compete" apparently was one of the reasons he chose to open a store in Bentonville where so many retail stores were already established.

Sam Walton's first Bentonville store was the Walton's 5 and 10 Variety Store at 105 North Main, which is today the site of the Walmart Visitors Center. The first newspaper advertisement for the Walton's 5 and 10 appeared in the July 29, 1950, edition of the *Benton County Democrat*. In the 1951 Bentonville Business Directory, the Walton 5 and 10 Variety Store is listed as specializing in merchandise such as candy, hosiery, housewares, lingerie, notions, stationery, toiletries, and toys.

In 1967, Sam Walton closed Walton's 5 and 10 Variety Store and opened a new store one block away in the Mid-Town Shopping Center, which had just been built and featured a free convenient parking lot. Walton's new store was named Walton's Family Center.

Wal-Mart Stores began plans in 1969 to build a general office facility and their first warehouse in Bentonville. Today, the general office remains at the same location, while there are numerous other properties in Bentonville either directly or indirectly connected to Walmart. There are also countless businesses that would not be in Bentonville at all if Walmart were not here. For example, many of Walmart's merchandise suppliers, known locally as vendors, have chosen to open satellite offices in Bentonville to constantly maintain a close business connection and ensure uninterrupted customer service.

The town of Bentonville has experienced tremendous prosperity over the years, primarily because of Walmart and its business associates. Bentonville continues to grow, and every change brings more opportunities that might never have happened if Sam Walton had not decided to move to town and open a store on the Bentonville town square.

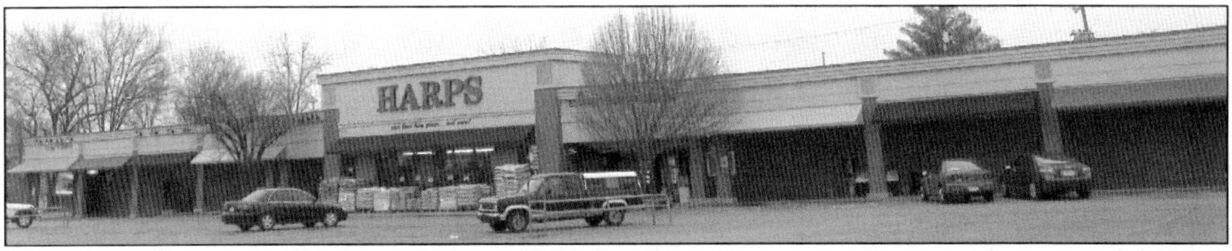

Mid-Town Shopping Center. Built in 1967, the shopping center was touted as one of the first large shopping malls in Arkansas. The Walton's Family Center opened in the Mid-Town Shopping Center in 1968, and the Walton's Family Shoe Store was also located there. While at this location, the Walton's Family Center changed its name in 1978 to Wal-Mart Store No. 75. It later included the Wal-Mart Portrait Studio No. 75 as well. After Wal-Mart moved, Phillips Food Center was located in Mid-Town for several years. Today, Harp's Food Center occupies the center of the shopping mall. (Courtesy of the author.)

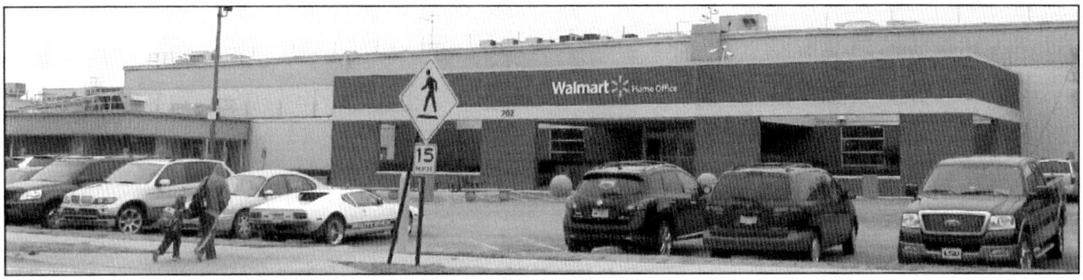

Walmart Home Office. In 1969, the corporate headquarters moved into the building now referred to by Walmart Associates as the G.O., which is located on South West Eighth Street in Bentonville. The office facility included a distribution center/warehouse that shared the same phone number. Prior to moving into the Eighth Street building, the general office and the buying office were located at 103½ South Main Street on the Bentonville square.

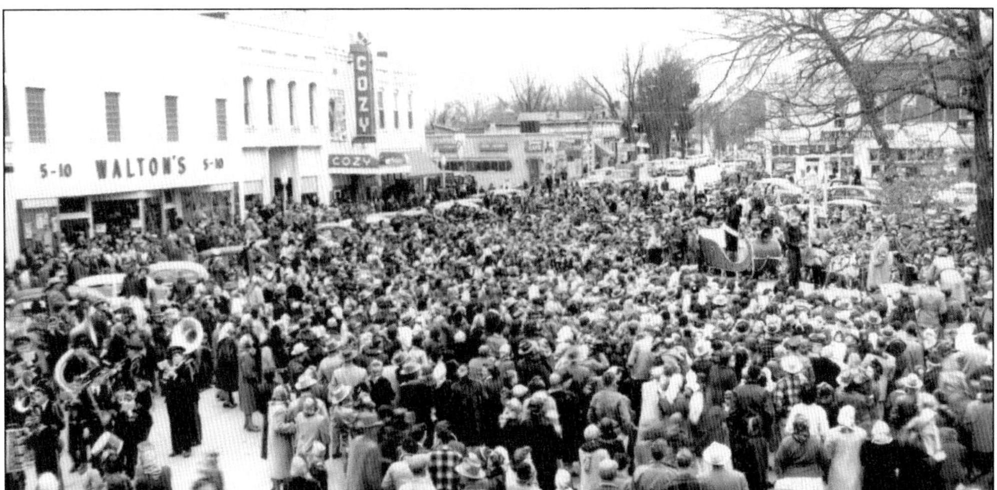

Christmas on the Square. Everyone is in the Christmas spirit when Santa Claus arrives on the Bentonville Square. In the background is the Walton's 5 and 10, next-door to the Cozy Theatre, which had a most unusual neon sign. The owner had made enough money selling strawberries to bankroll his motion picture theater business. He commissioned Raymond Jacobs to create the theater sign with a box of strawberries on top that, through the magic of neon light, appeared to fall over and spill strawberries down the side. (Courtesy of Walmart Visitor Center.)

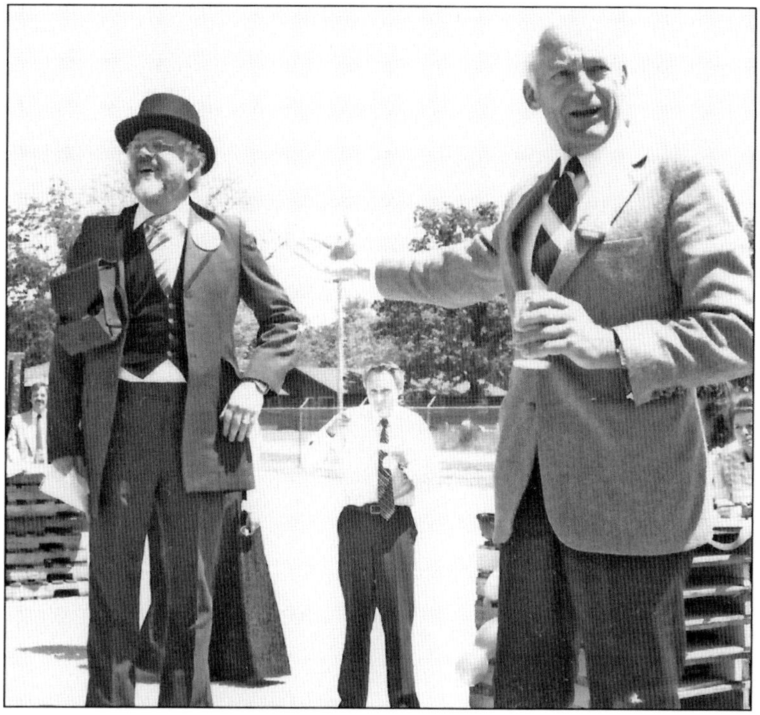

SUGAR CREEK DAYS PROMOTION. During Sugar Creek Days, Gary Black, left, dressed in vintage clothes, Bryan Banks, center, and Sam Walton have some fun with Walmart associates as they encourage support of the community celebration event that was popular in the 1980s. (Courtesy of Gary Black.)

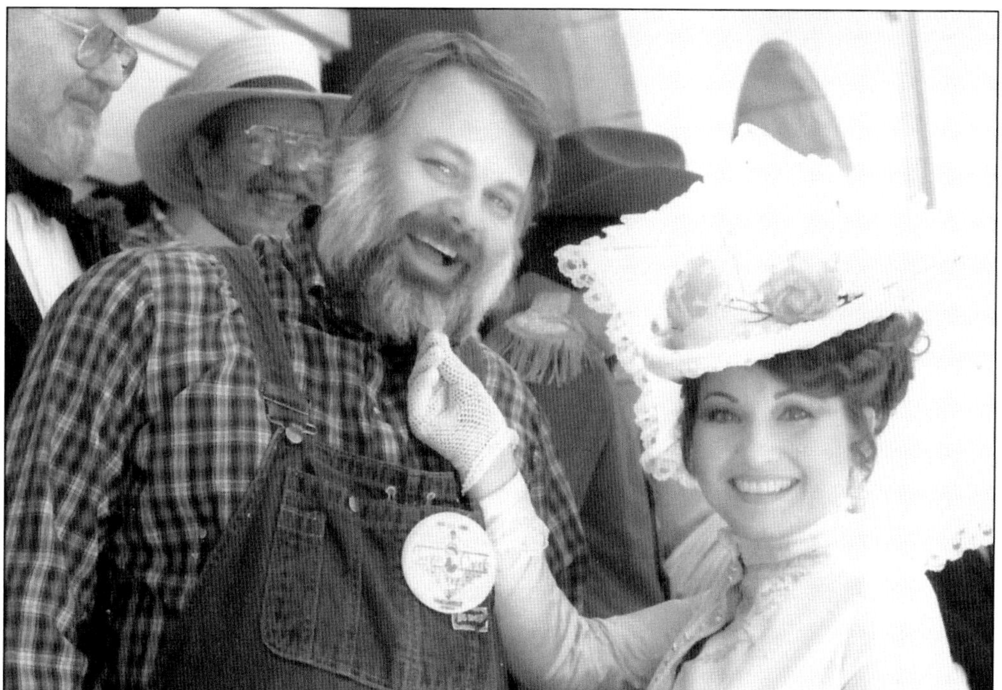

SUGAR CREEK DAYS CELEBRATION. The Sugar Creek Days annual celebration was a popular event during the 1980s. Charlie Burke shows off his beard, and Linda Hawkins models her vintage dress as they stop to pose for the photographer on the courthouse steps. Sugar Creek Days attracted many people to the town square to have fun and celebrate local history. (Courtesy of the author.)

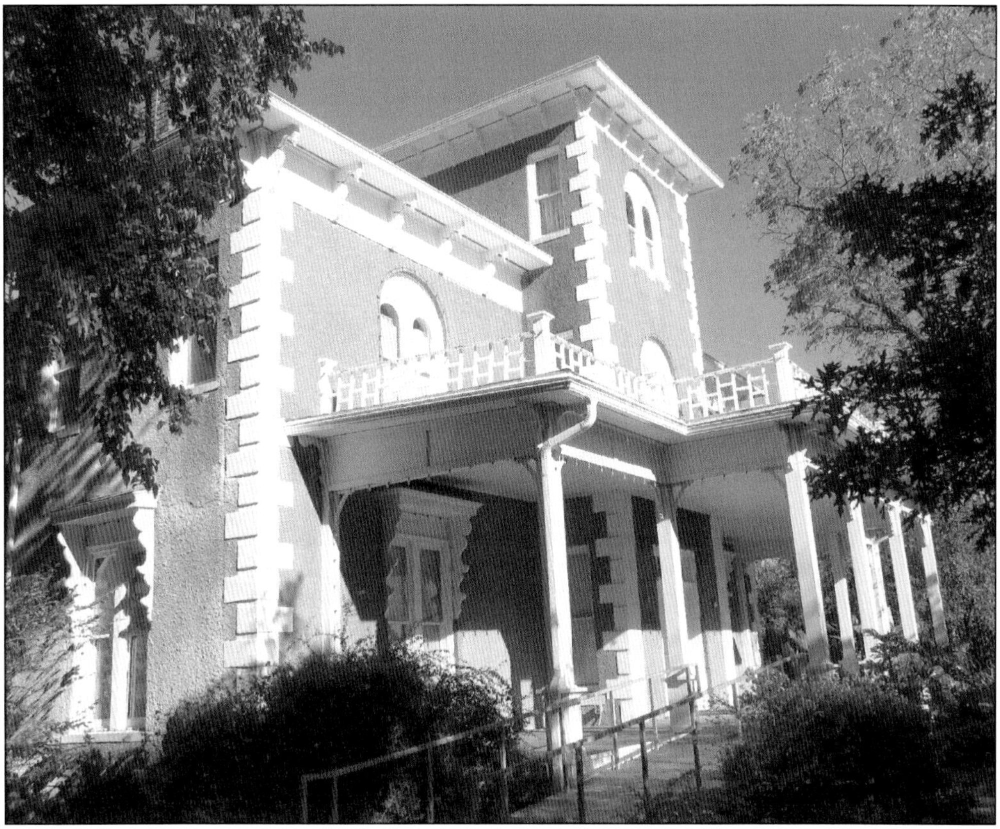

The Col. Sam Peel House. When Sam Peel built his home around 1875, most of the surrounding land was an apple orchard. The massive house was scheduled to be bulldozed to make room for a parking lot when Walmart Store No. 100 was built. The house was saved, carefully preserved, and is currently maintained by the Peel-Compton Foundation, a nonprofit organization. The house is furnished with period pieces and is often adorned by flower arrangements designed by the Bentonville Garden Club. An heirloom flower garden, vegetable garden, and apple trees add a special ambiance to the walkways around the lovely old house. (Courtesy of the author.)

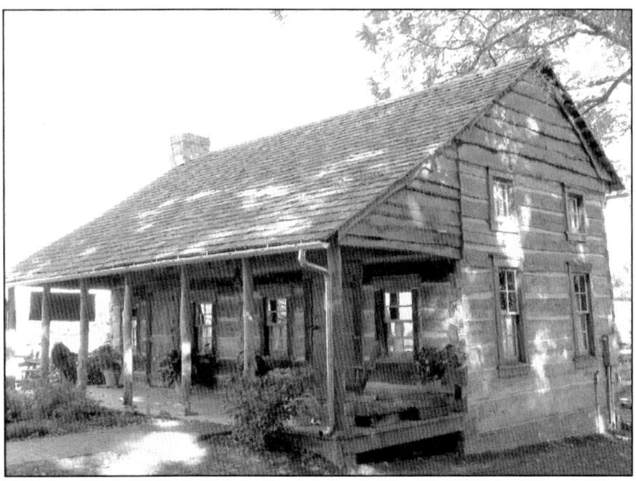

Lynch Log Cabin. This authentic Arkansas log cabin was moved to the Peel Mansion grounds from another location. It is believed to have been built before the Civil War by the Lynch family. This cabin is one of very few log structures that still exist today in Benton County. Thanks to the Peel Foundation, the Lynch log cabin has been preserved and serves as an educational exhibit for schoolchildren and visitors. (Courtesy of the author.)

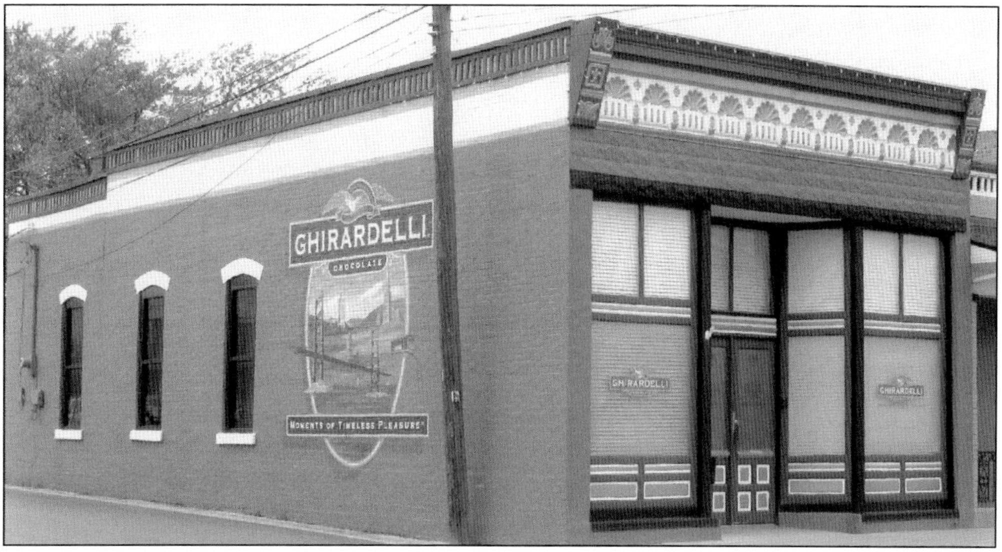

THE GHIRARDELLI CHOCOLATE BUILDING. Since Walmart, one of the largest retail businesses in the world, is located in Bentonville, it is no surprise that many retail vendors have offices located nearby. The Ghirardelli Chocolate office was located downtown in a historical building with exquisite gold-painted architectural details and a hand-painted rendition of the company's logo. The mural logo was painted by Bentonville artist Randy Townzen. (Courtesy of the author.)

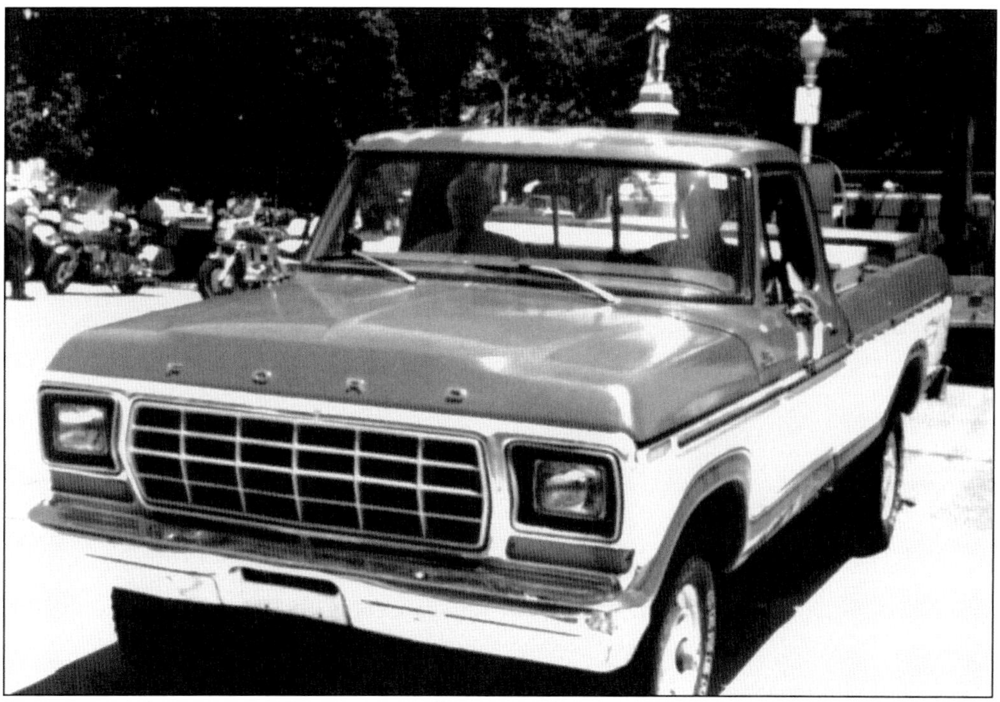

SAM WALTON'S FAVORITE TRUCK. Sam's favorite pickup truck is driven in to be on exhibit in the Walmart Visitor Center in 1993. Betty Holmes Kizziar, curator of Walmart artifacts at that time, carefully steers the irreplaceable scratched and dented truck into its new parking place. Her passenger is Gene Lauer, who also worked at the visitor center for many years. (Courtesy of Walmart Visitor Center.)

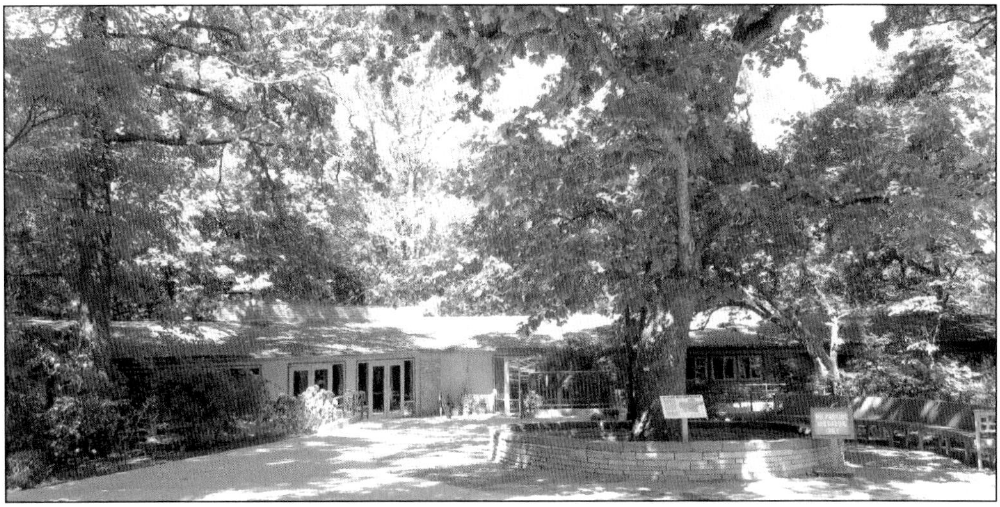

Dr. Neil Compton's House. Dr. Neil Compton was a medical doctor who saved lives, but he also provided the leadership for a project that ultimately saved the Buffalo River, which was scheduled to be dammed and would have destroyed a vast segment of Arkansas's wild outdoors. Compton's house is now a conference center at the Compton Gardens, which complements the walking trails around the Crystal Bridges Museum of American Art property. (Courtesy of the author.)

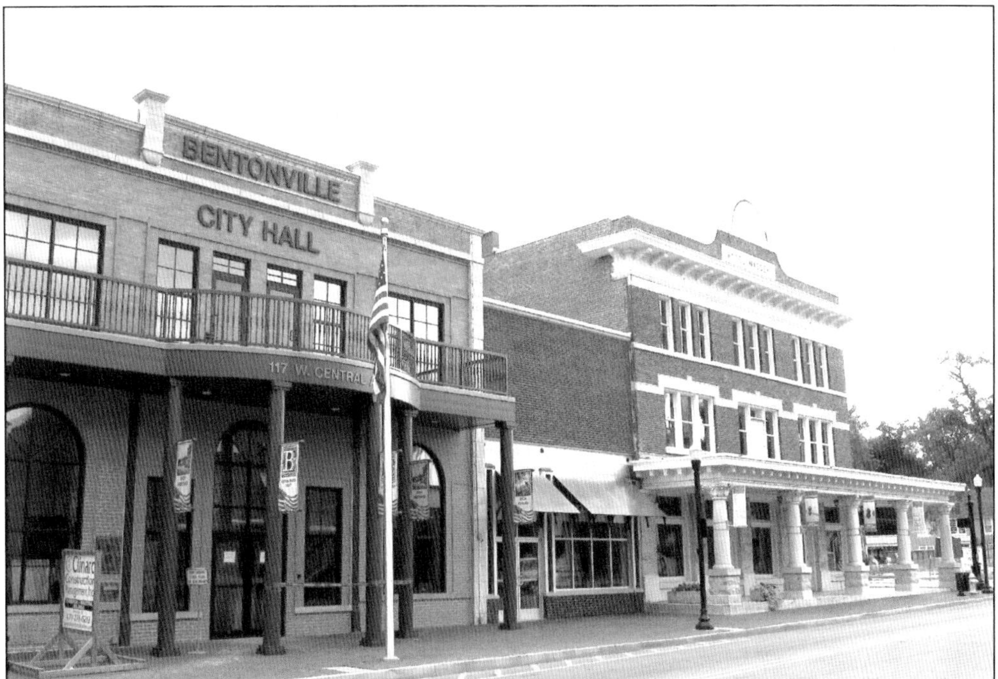

City Hall and the Massey Building. Every City of Bentonville building has been either upgraded or rebuilt in recent years, including city hall, located on West Central Avenue next-door to the Massey Building. The Massey Building was once a hotel but was refurbished into offices after a devastating fire. The old historical Eagle Hotel was at this site in 1842 but was torn down in order to build the Massey Hotel, which was designed by architect A. O. Clarke. (Courtesy of the author.)

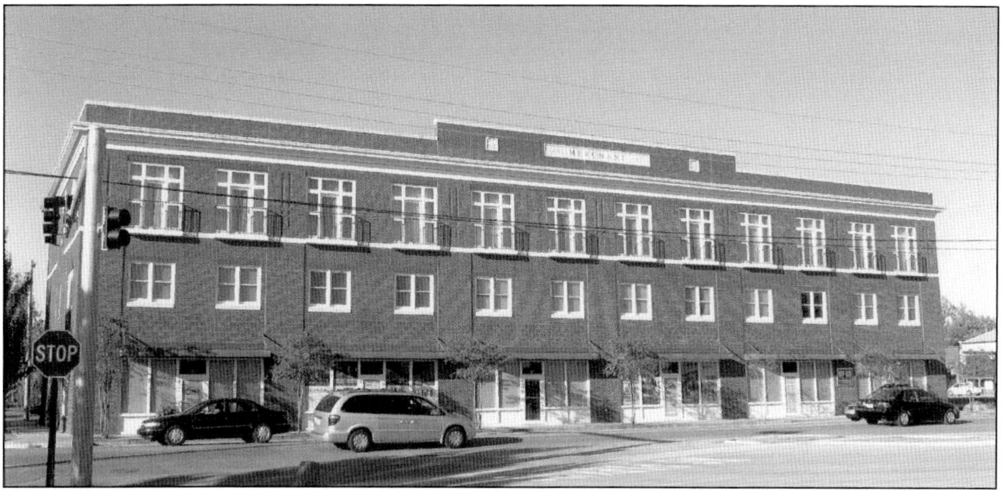

The Merchant Building. Providing office and conference space for vendors has become a successful business in northwest Arkansas. Walmart vendors selling goods to supply stores need an office nearby, so an entirely new category of real estate has been created. (Courtesy of the author.)

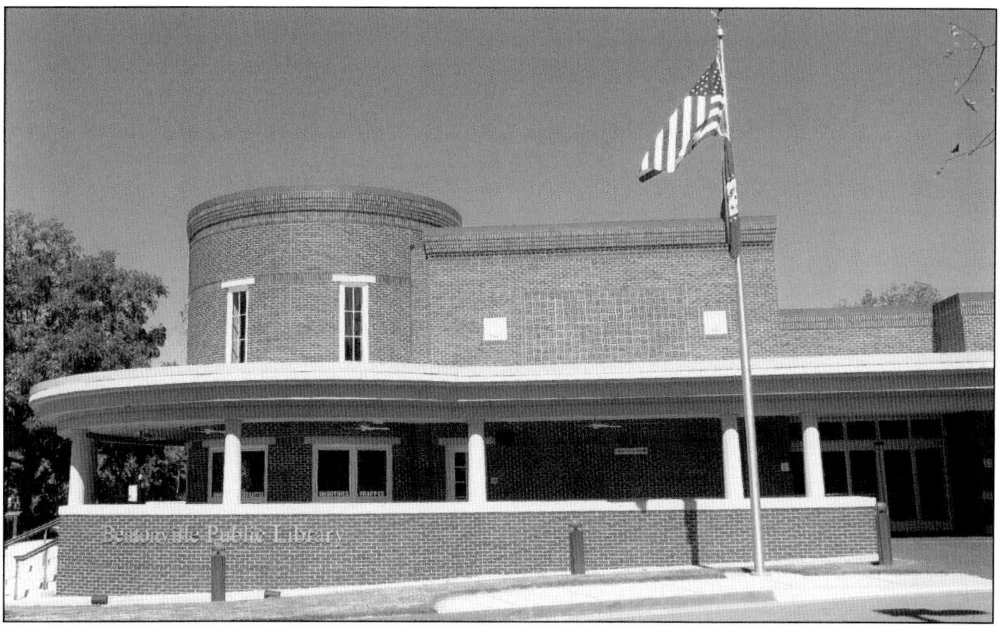

Bentonville Public Library. For years, the library shared a space in city hall in the old Benton County Bank building with the pink granite pillars. Then the library had its own space in the old Church of Christ building on A Street. Today, Bentonville has a state-of-the-art library facility, which was built under the leadership and guidance of librarian Cindy Suter. Thanks to the continued work of librarian Hadi Dudley and the Bentonville Library Foundation, the library is one of the busiest places in town. (Courtesy of the author.)

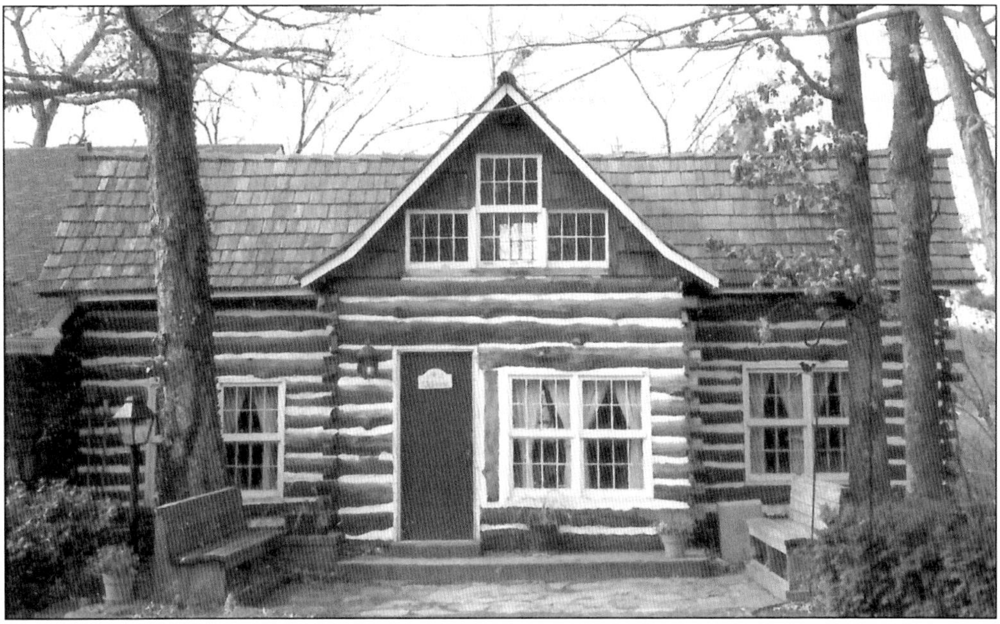

Fred's Hickory Inn. This restaurant is located at 1502 North Walton Boulevard and for many years has been a favorite gathering place for longtime Bentonville citizens as well as Walmart vendors. Fred and Lou Gaye opened the restaurant on a wooded hill where once there was a church camp known as Wildwood Camp. The charm of the rustic camp buildings provide the perfect setting for great barbecue, steaks, and Italian food. (Courtesy of the author.)

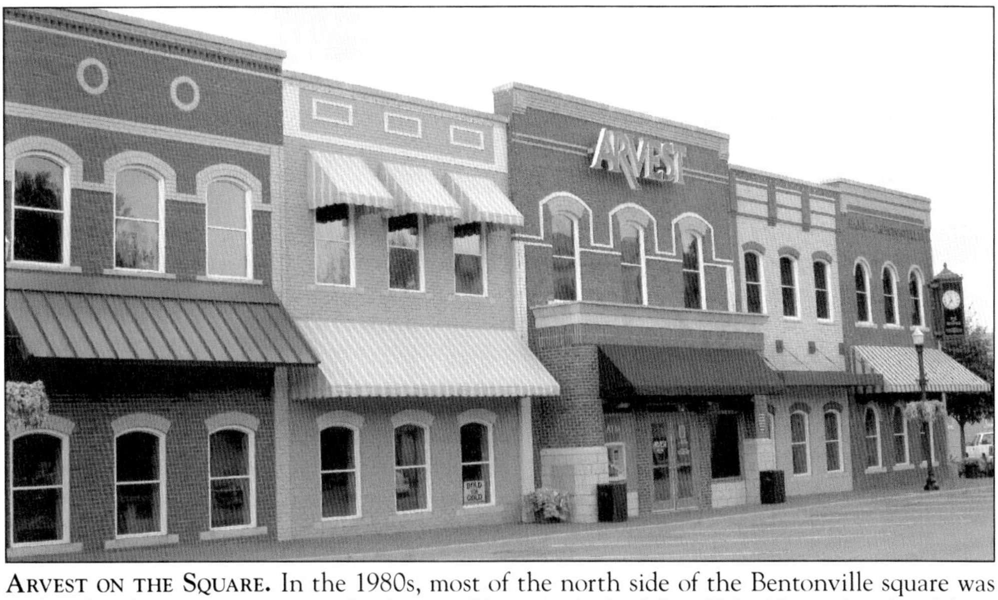

Arvest on the Square. In the 1980s, most of the north side of the Bentonville square was replaced with new construction closely resembling the look of the old buildings that dated from the 1880s and 1890s. The Bank of Bentonville was purchased by Sam Walton and associates in 1961. According to a newspaper article, Walton, at the time, had lived in Bentonville for 11 years and was a member of the Bentonville City Council. Sam and his brother, J. L. "Bud" Walton, owned 13 Ben Franklin stores in Arkansas, Kansas, and Missouri. In later years, the Bank of Bentonville was incorporated into Arvest. (Courtesy of the author.)

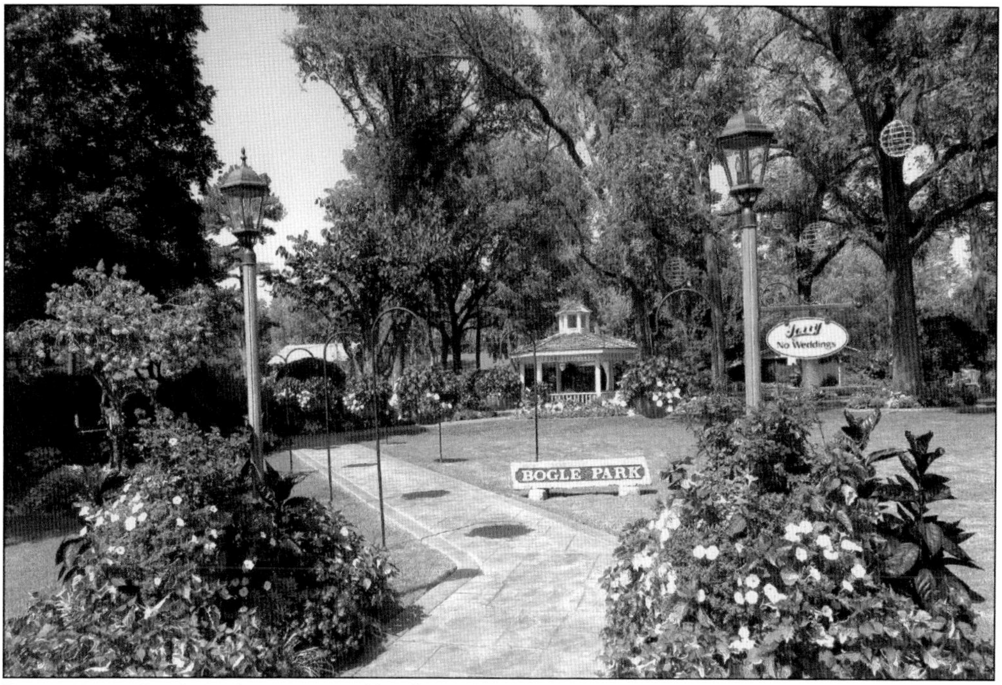

Bogle Park. Bogle Park was created by the Bob Bogle family and is a popular place for Bentonville High School students to gather for their prom pictures. Bogle was the first store manager of Walton's 5 and 10 on the town square. In 1962, Bogle was asked by Sam Walton to help with a name for a new discount store. Bogle suggested Walmart, which incorporated the Walton name with a place to shop. (Courtesy of the author.)

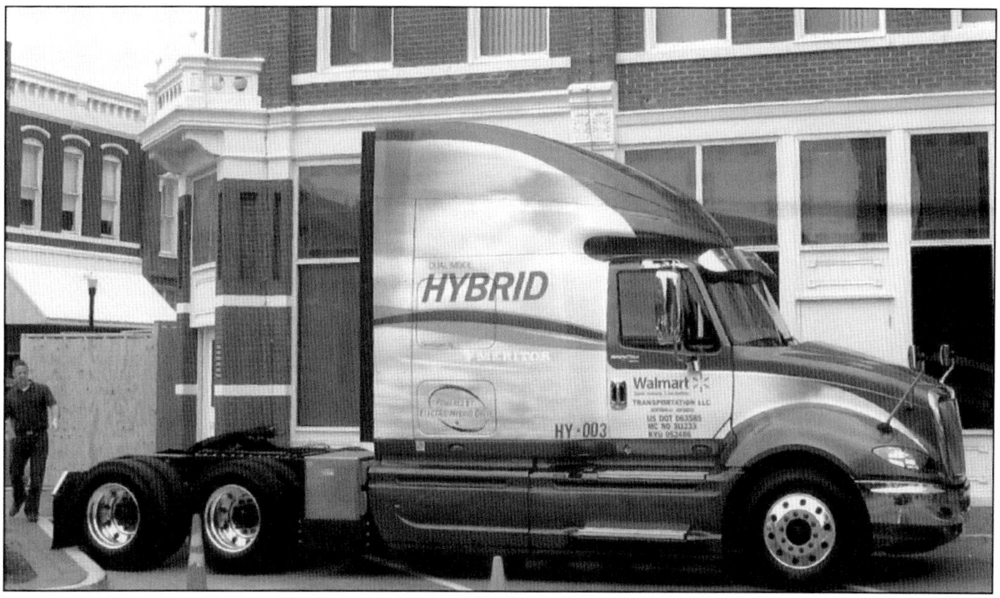

Walmart Hybrid Truck. Walmart is always looking for ways to save money, so they are testing hybrid trucks. This truck was on display in front of the Walmart Visitor Center, and the driver explained how the motor automatically shuts off while stopped at traffic lights and starts up again when the driver is ready to go. (Courtesy of the author.)

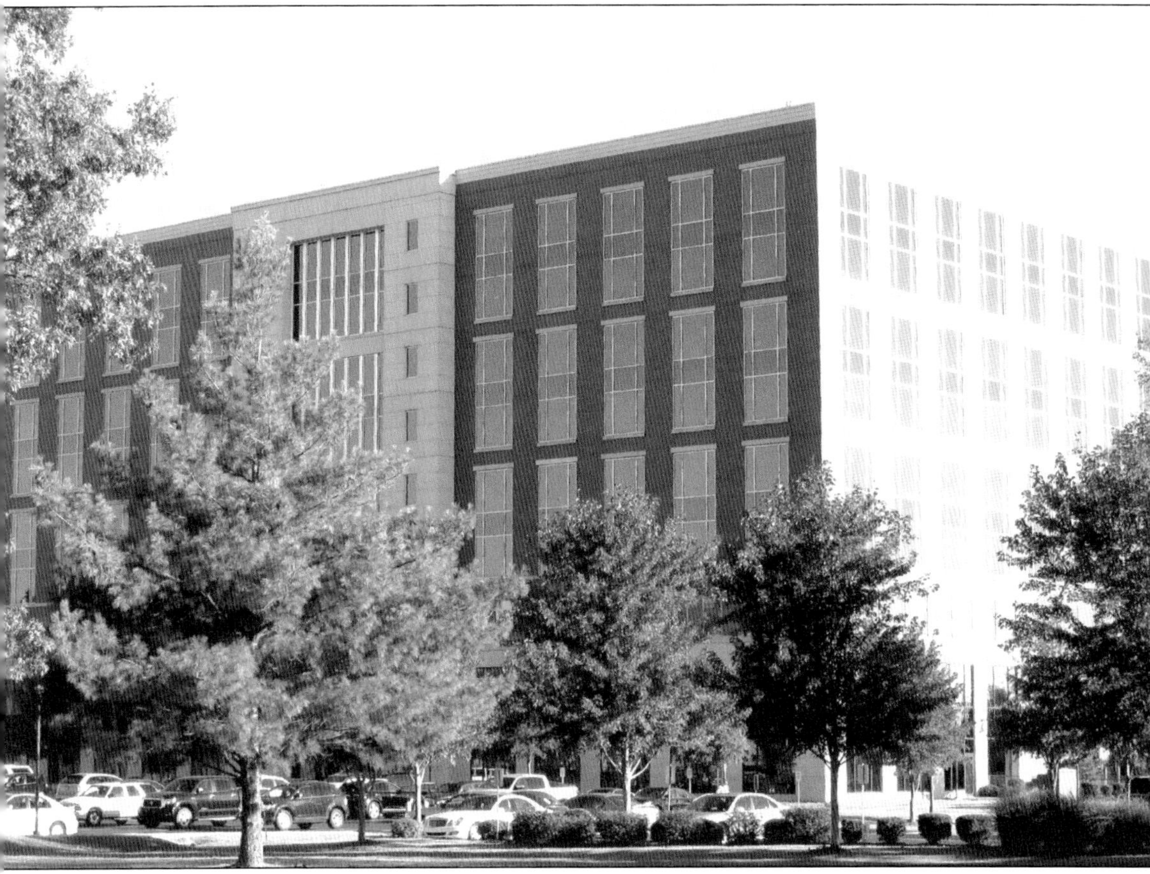

BENTONVILLE PLAZA. The largest building in town was erected across the street from the Walmart general offices. It is a convenient place for Walmart vendors to rent an office and do business close by. The top floor can be rented for social events. (Courtesy of the author.)

Seven

Today and Beyond 1991–2010

Today, Bentonville is a busy town, and it seems everyone is preparing for the opening of an extremely special place called Crystal Bridges Museum of American Art. The construction project itself has become a curious spectacle, as nothing of such large scale has ever happened before in this area. When the museum opens, Bentonville will be experiencing very large increases in tourism, and the traffic is certainly going to be more of a challenge than it already is. However, there has been much attention focused on the construction of bicycle trails and walking pathways, which should encourage locals and visitors to park their cars and enjoy the beautiful outdoors.

It is impossible to imagine what changes there will be in Bentonville in the near future, but there is much to look forward to as well. How many other small American towns could expect to have a collection of original American art, including portraits of George Washington? The exceptionally large collection of original works of art and this great facility will offer educational opportunities for schoolchildren and visitors that will rival any museum in America.

Through the years, the town of Bentonville has experienced many changes that reflect its own various chapters of American history. Today, the town is once again in a transitional phase. There is a good chance that Bentonville will be making a lot more history in the future.

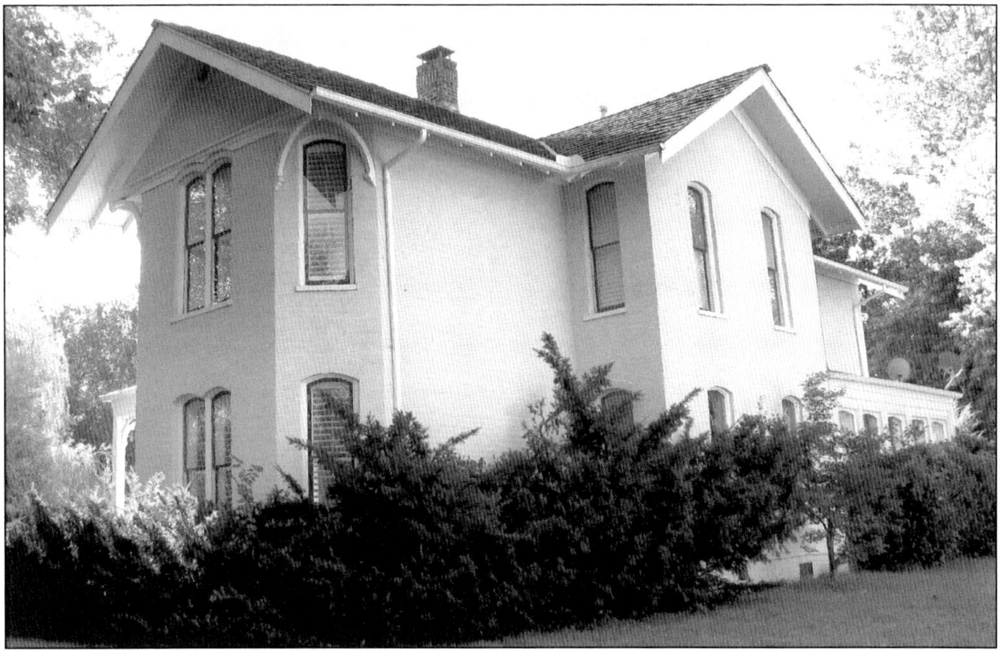

Jefferson House. This is another lovely home built with Bentonville brick, but unfortunately, the brick was painted white. This was the home of Mollie and Pearl Jefferson, who were directly related to the early Jefferson family that helped establish Bentonville. The two sisters were the daughters of Samuel Allen and Joan Neale Jefferson. (Courtesy of the author.)

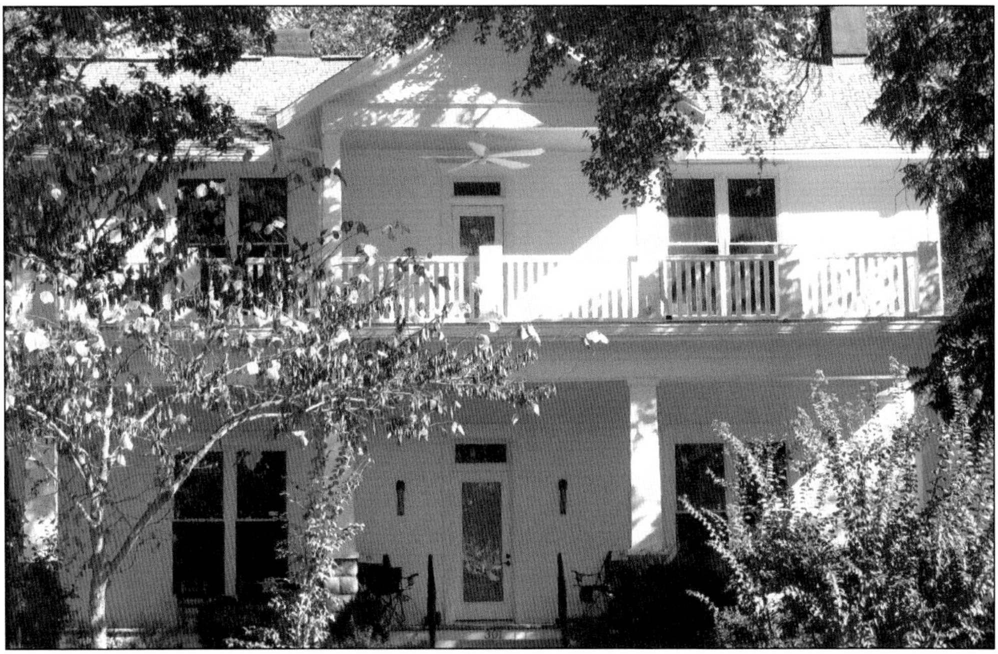

The Blake House. One of the Bentonville homes believed to have been built in 1869 and 1870, this structure has had many additions and changes over the years. It was the home of T. K. Blake, who served as jailer and Benton County sheriff and was a cousin to Betty Blake, wife of the famous Will Rogers from Oklahoma. (Courtesy of the author.)

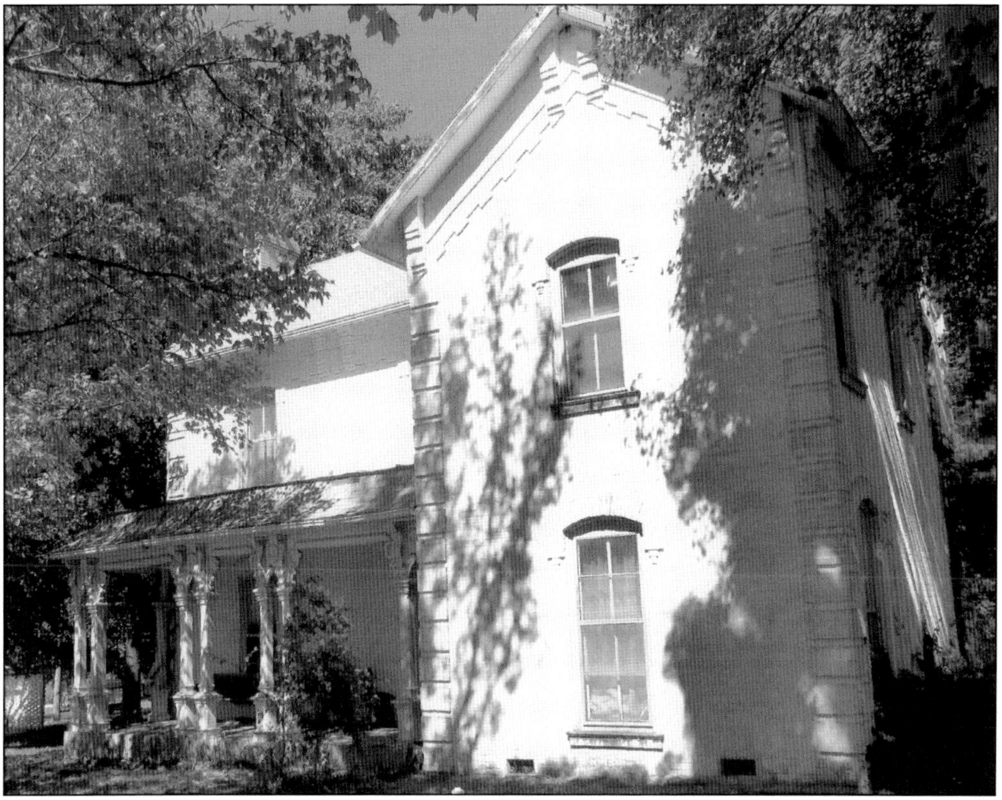

MORRISON-MAXWELL-HINMAN HOUSE. It is possible that this house was built about the same time as the Peel Mansion, since it is very similar in design and is only a short distance away. The painted brick house has a beautifully detailed decorative trim across the front porch. The home is listed on the National Register of Historic Places. (Courtesy of the author.)

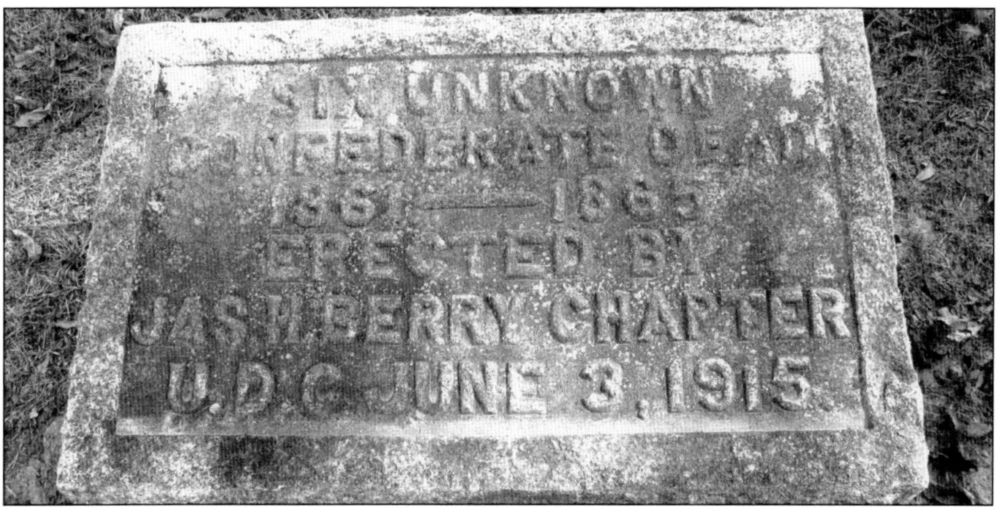

GRAVE OF THE UNKNOWN SOLDIERS. In the Bentonville cemetery, there is a grave where six unknown Confederate soldiers are buried. Nothing is known about what happened to the men, who they were, or where they were from. The United Daughters of the Confederacy purchased a marker for the soldiers many years ago. (Courtesy of the author.)

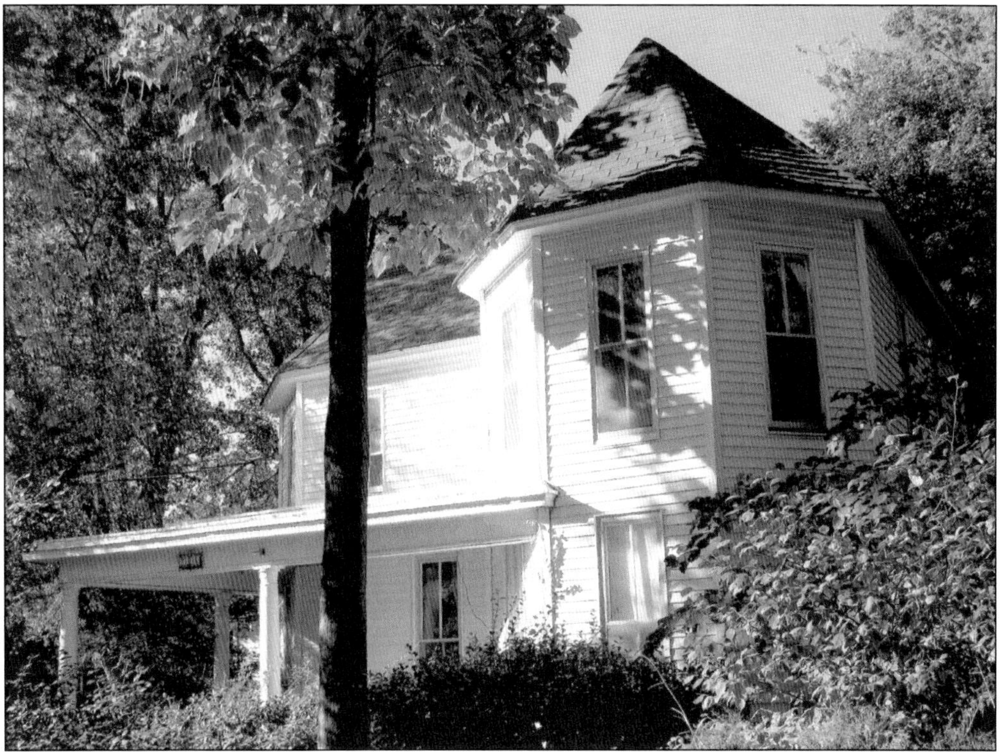

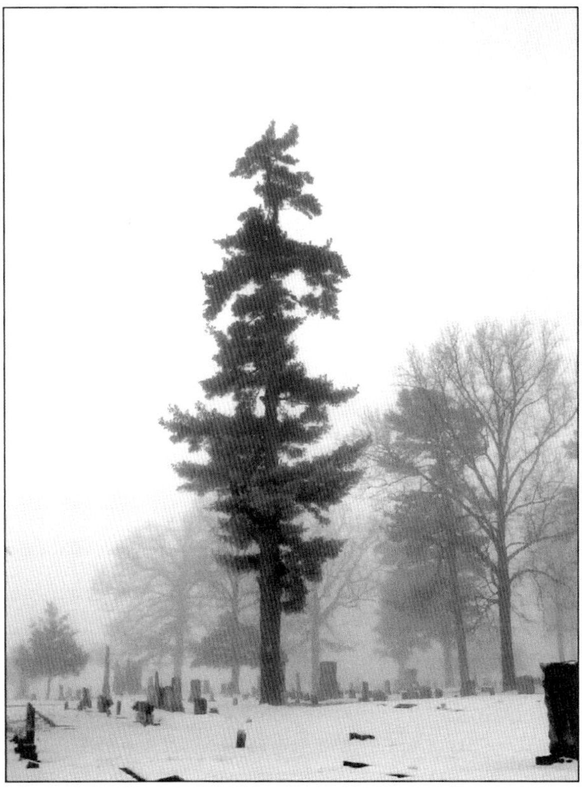

Dr. James Atkinson House. Dr. Atkinson delivered many Bentonville babies during his years of practicing medicine. This beautiful home was the residence for the doctor and his wife, Violet. The doctor's office was across the street from the Terry Block building. Dr. Atkinson also made house calls. (Courtesy of the author.)

The Last of the Old Pines. Some of the oldest and tallest trees in Bentonville are the white pines located in the city cemetery. The majestic trees are succumbing to age and are not being replaced, and unfortunately, one day, there will be no more tall pines left to mark old historical sites. (Courtesy of the author.)

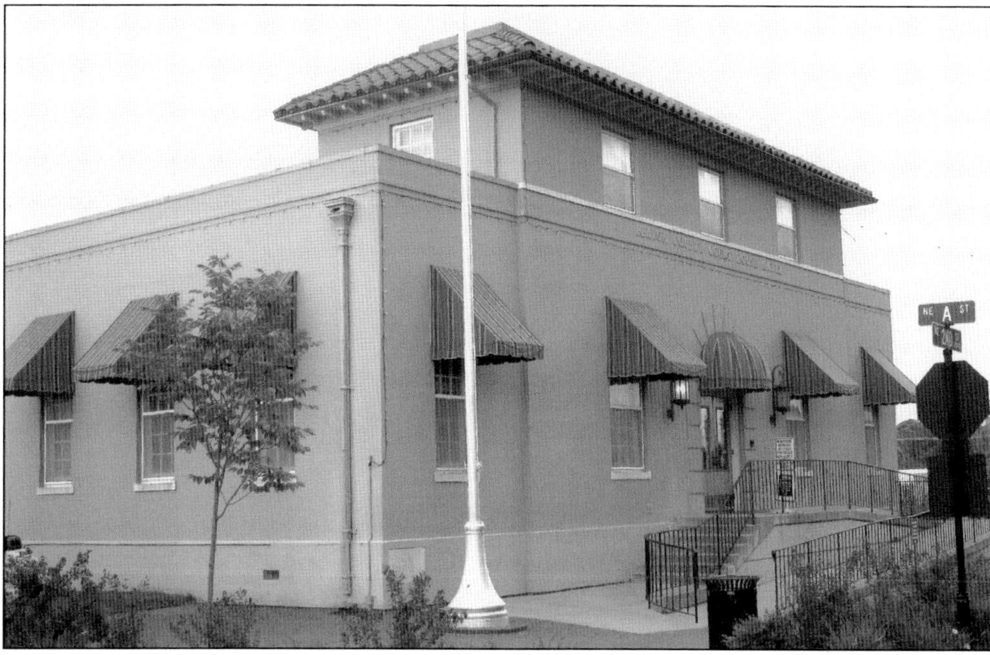

THE OLD POST OFFICE BUILDING. This building was erected in 1935 as a post office and is beautifully designed with the original tile roof. The original interior featured beautiful dark wood paneling and intricate wrought iron trim around the postal windows. (Courtesy of the author.)

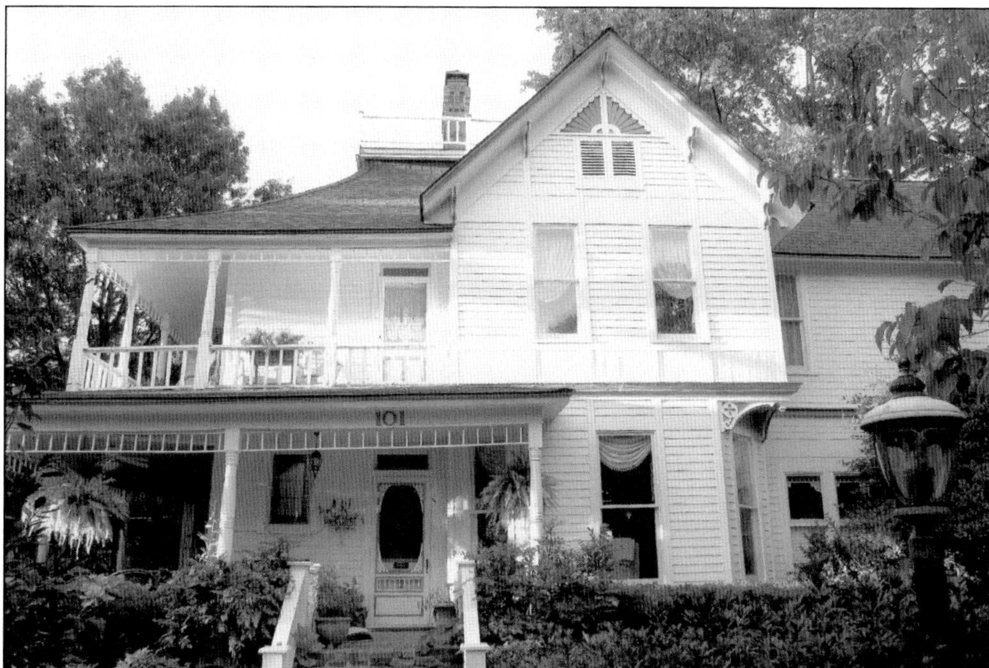

THE DEMING HOUSE. William B. Deming was born in 1849 in Ohio. He moved to Bentonville from Kansas in 1883. He purchased 152 acres in north Bentonville, and by December of that year, he had laid out 120 lots. Deming was also president of the Arkansas Tobacco Company. The structure in the picture is the home he built for his family. (Courtesy of the author.)

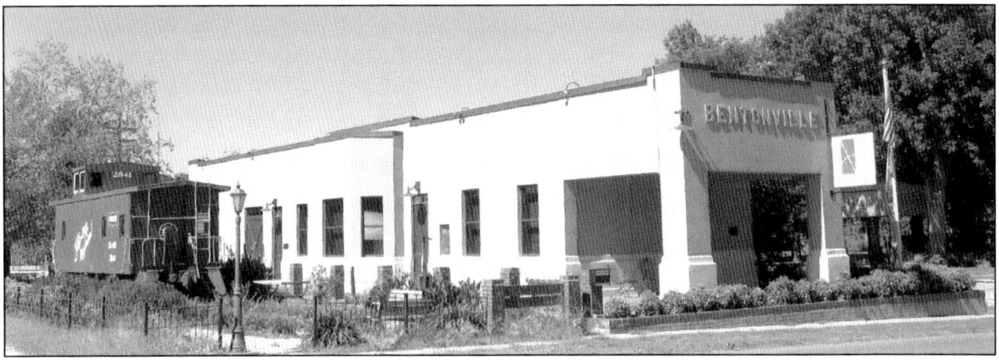

Bentonville Train Depot. Recent research has proven that the train depot structure seen in this photograph is the first floor of an earlier two-story building constructed in 1899. James Haney was the contractor hired to build the original brick depot, which was conveniently located in walking distance of the town square and the Bentonville Academy. The top story was removed when the Frisco Railroad Company purchased the depot building from the Arkansas and Oklahoma Railroad. The brick was apparently covered with cement stucco and painted gray at that time. In 1986, the building was completely renovated by an nonprofit group known as The Train Station, Inc., and for several years, the building served as offices for the Bentonville–Bella Vista Chamber of Commerce. Today, the property is owned and maintained by the Bentonville Library Foundation. (Courtesy of the author.)

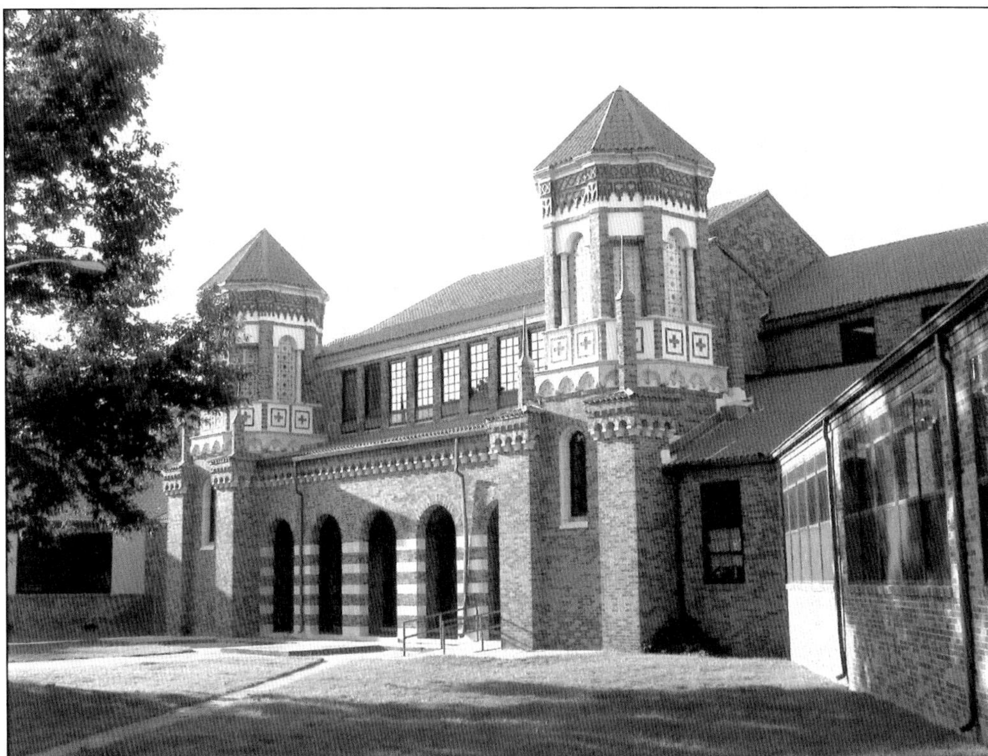

Old Bentonville High School Building. This beautiful brick school building looks more like a castle than a school. When the school was built in 1928, there was plenty of room for all of Bentonville's students, from grades 1 through 12. By the early 1950s, R. E. Baker Elementary school had to be added for the expanding population. (Courtesy of the author.)

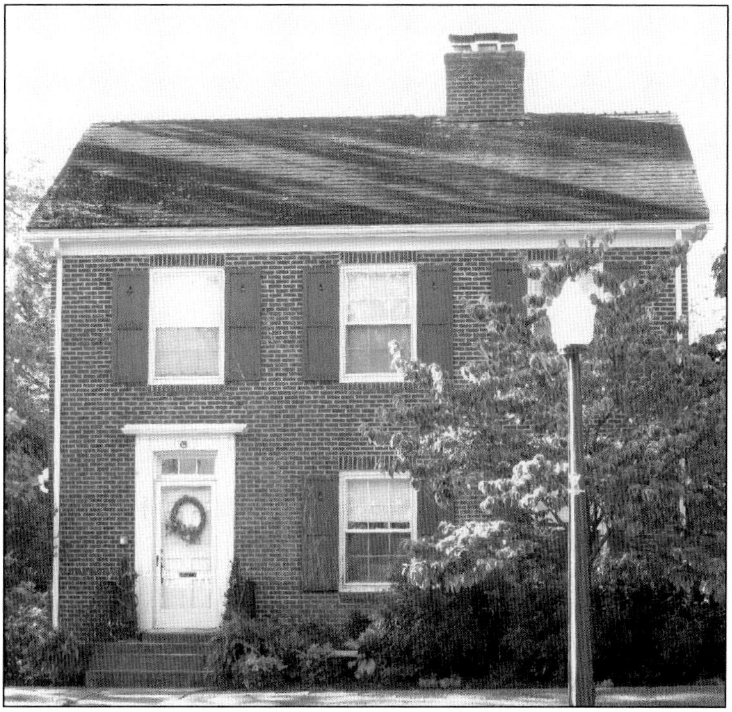

Dave and Mary Peel House. Dave Peel was the mayor of Bentonville and a banker. He and his wife, Mary, built this house in 1930 on West Central Avenue. This is one of five historical Peel family homes in Bentonville and is today the home of Steve Marquess, another Peel family descendant, and his wife, Judy. (Courtesy of the author.)

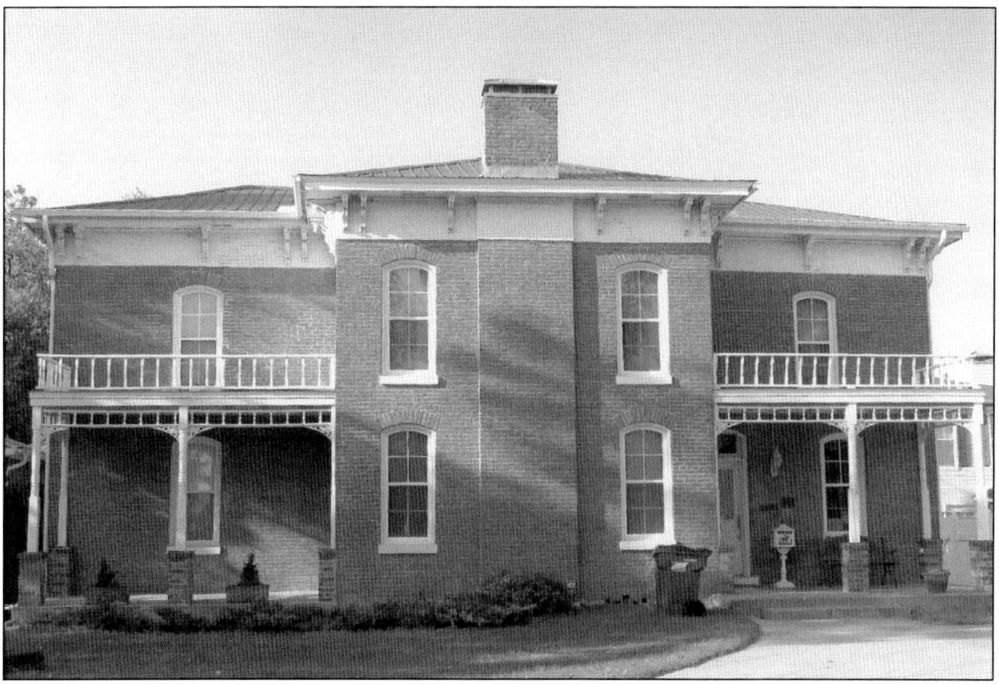

Colonel Young's House. This house is believed to have been built around 1873, as it has very early architectural features. The look of the house would be quiet different if the front porches had not been removed. The most interesting historical feature was the detached brick kitchen, which still exists but has been closed into a modern addition. The house is now part of an apartment complex. (Courtesy of the author.)

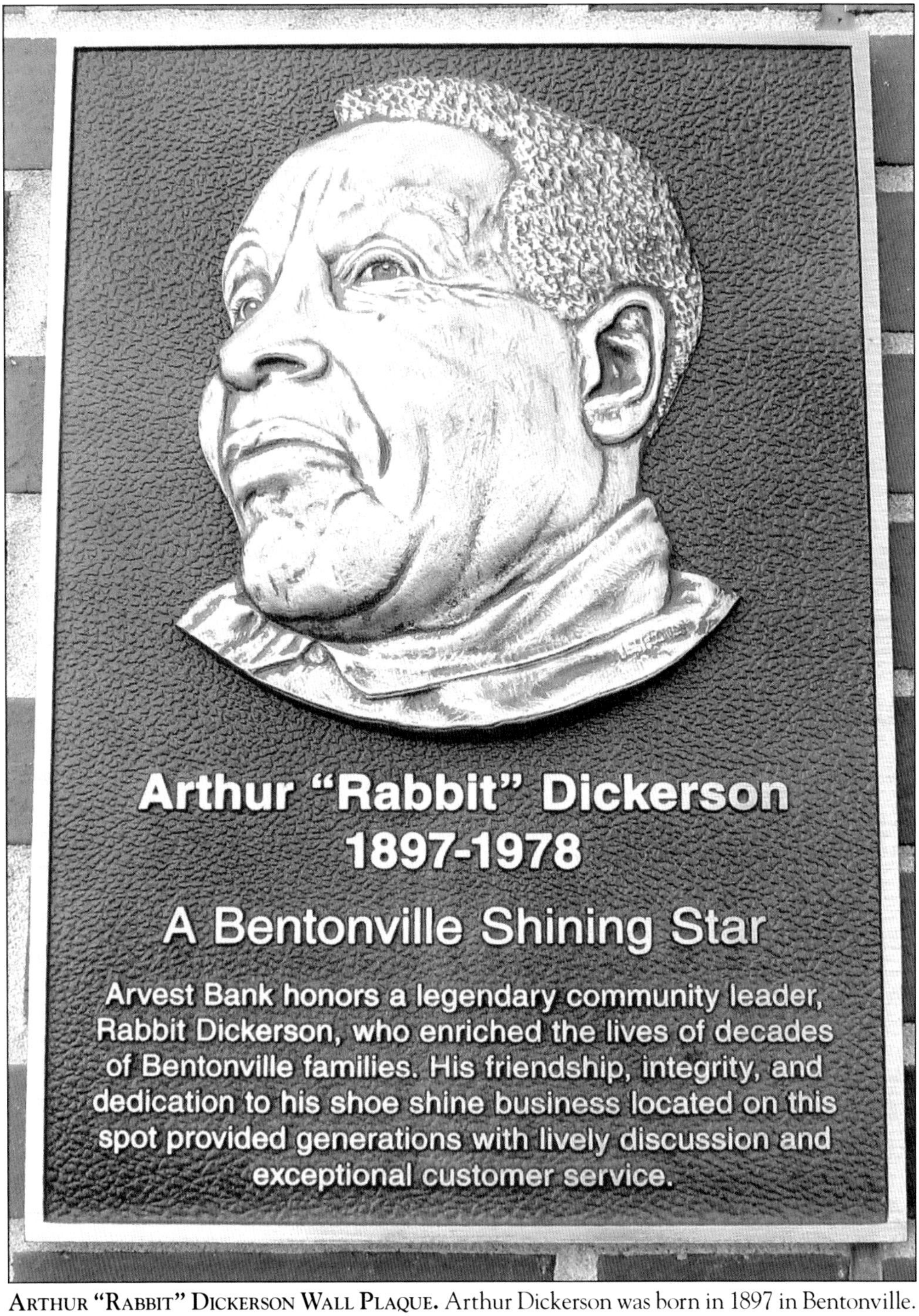

ARTHUR "RABBIT" DICKERSON WALL PLAQUE. Arthur Dickerson was born in 1897 in Bentonville. He owned and operated his shoe shine business in several different buildings in town. He did not quit working until after his 81st birthday. The wall plaque, shown above, is on display at his last business location on Main Street near the town square. Dickerson died in 1978. (Courtesy of the author.)

BENTONVILLE WATER TOWER. The water tower was built soon after R. E. Baker Elementary School was constructed in 1950. It is located near the school playground, so the elementary students watched the entire construction project from beginning to end. Since the kids had never seen anything like this before, many of the children came to the conclusion that it looked a lot more like a giant spider than a water tower. (Courtesy of the author.)

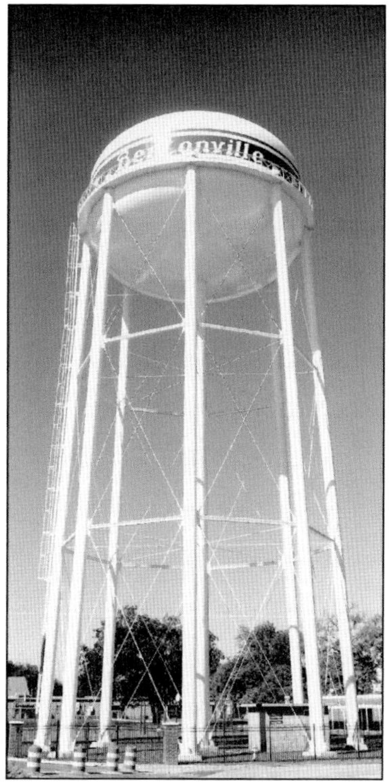

A VICTORIAN COTTAGE. Today, this little cottage is divided into apartments, but the building has retained its Victorian charm with plenty of gingerbread trim along the eaves. (Courtesy of the author.)

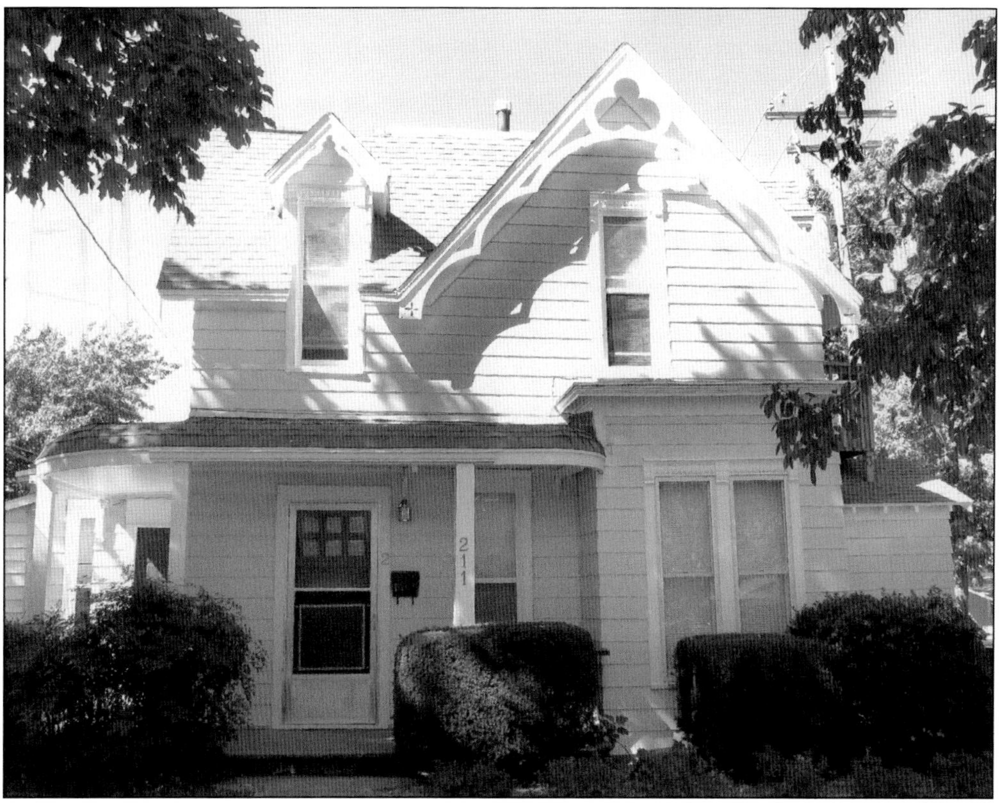

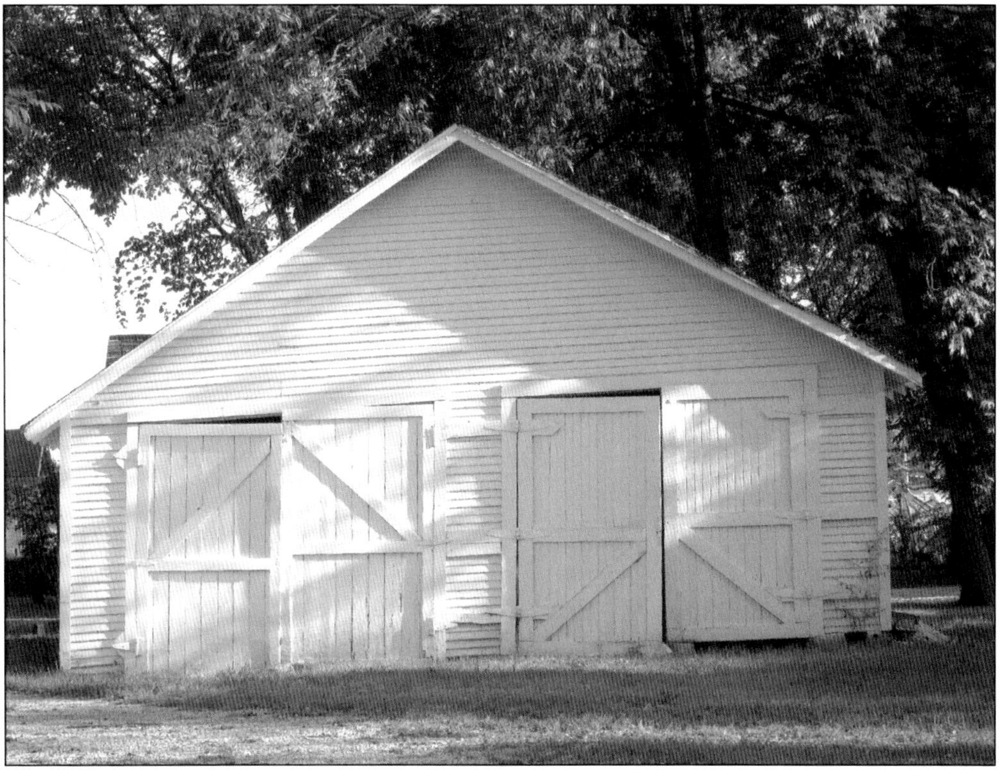

Wilkes Garage. Some people may not think of an old garage as anything to appreciate, but there are not many left. This particular garage has barn-size doors, which would have been big enough to store a buggy or two. (Courtesy of the author.)

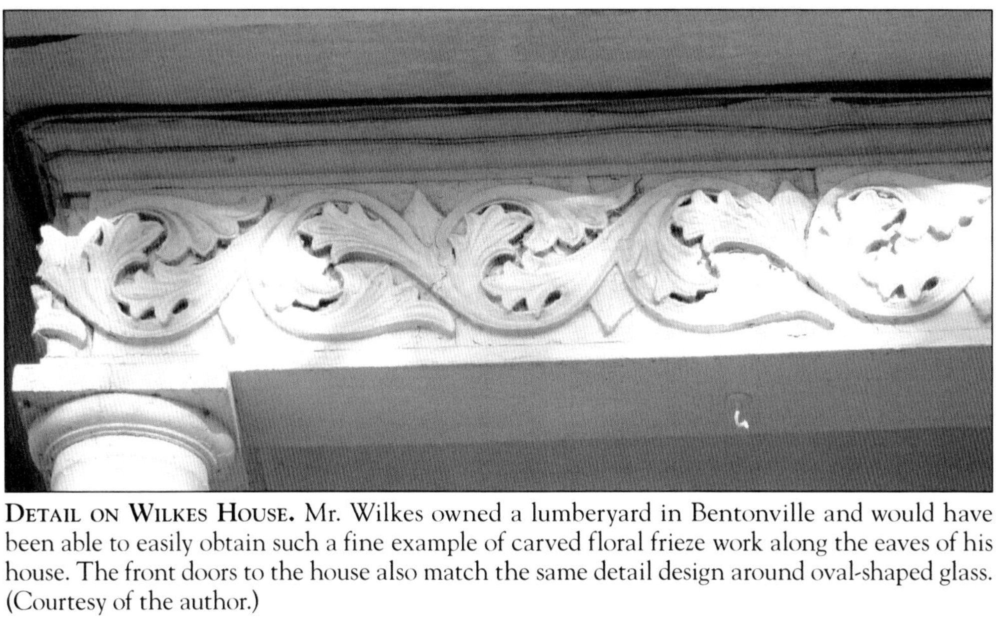

Detail on Wilkes House. Mr. Wilkes owned a lumberyard in Bentonville and would have been able to easily obtain such a fine example of carved floral frieze work along the eaves of his house. The front doors to the house also match the same detail design around oval-shaped glass. (Courtesy of the author.)

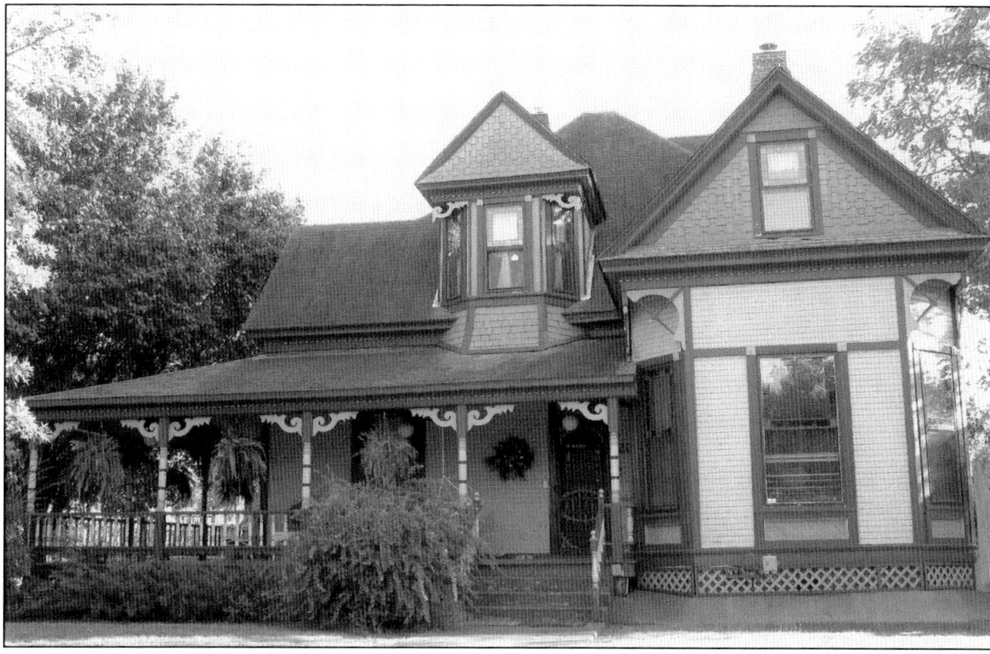

Lon Pace House. One of the fanciest Victorian houses in Bentonville, this home was built by master carpenter Lon Pace for his family. Pace built several of the largest business buildings in downtown. Some of the projects were done with architect A. O. Clarke. (Courtesy of the author.)

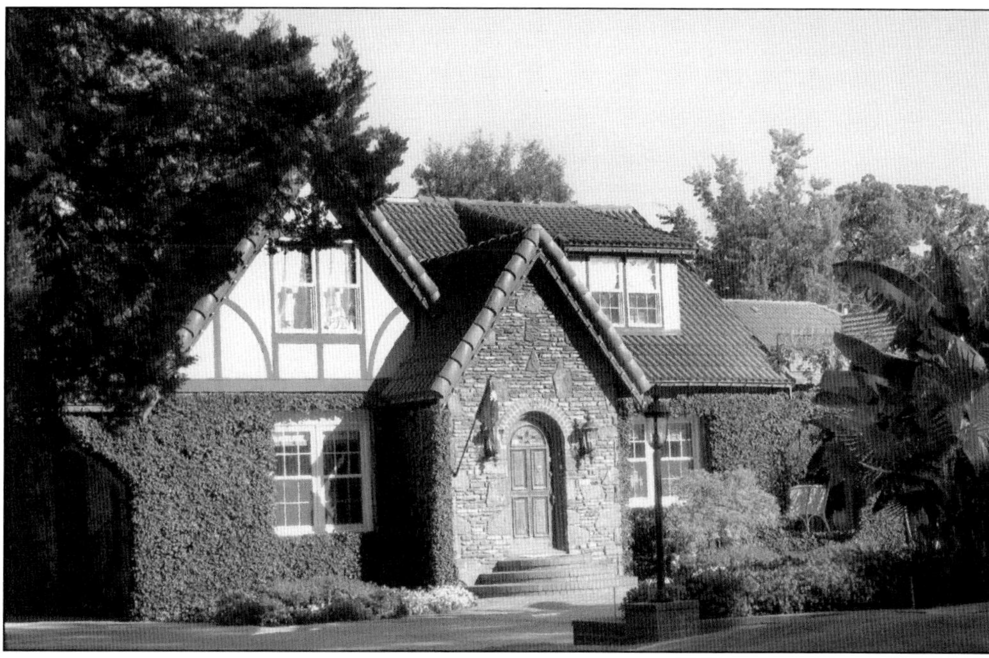

The John Wright House. Located on North Main Street, this house was once the home of Bentonville banker John Wright and his family. Wright was also the administrator for the Benton County Fair for many years. Today, the house is perfectly preserved and surrounded with beautiful, lush landscaping. (Courtesy of the author.)

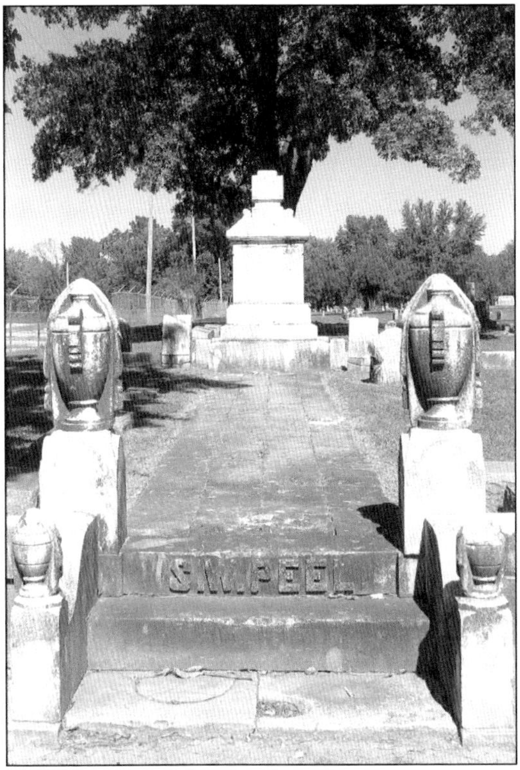

The Peel Family Grave Plot. The Sam Peel family grave plot is located in the Bentonville Cemetery, which is bordered on one side by the Walmart general office. The grave plot is anchored on all four corners with elegant half-draped urn monument that depict traditional Victorian expressions of grief. (Courtesy of the author.)

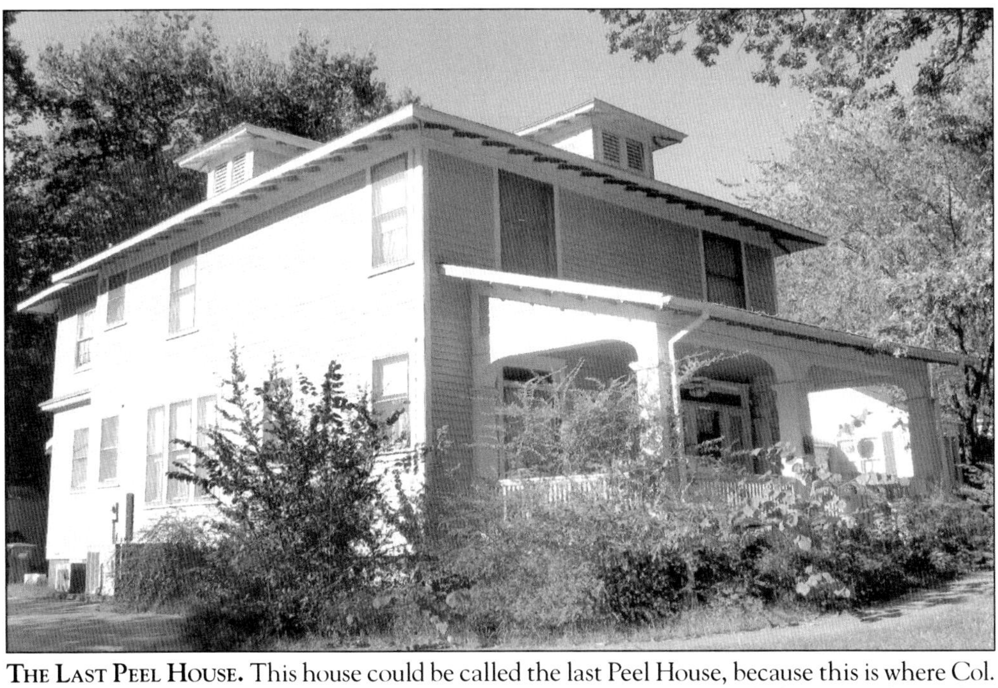

The Last Peel House. This house could be called the last Peel House, because this is where Col. Sam Peel was living when he died. However, at the time of Peel's death, the house was located on the other end of West Central Avenue. The house was moved in the 1980s to make room for a parking lot at the corner of A Street and West Central Avenue. (Courtesy of the author.)

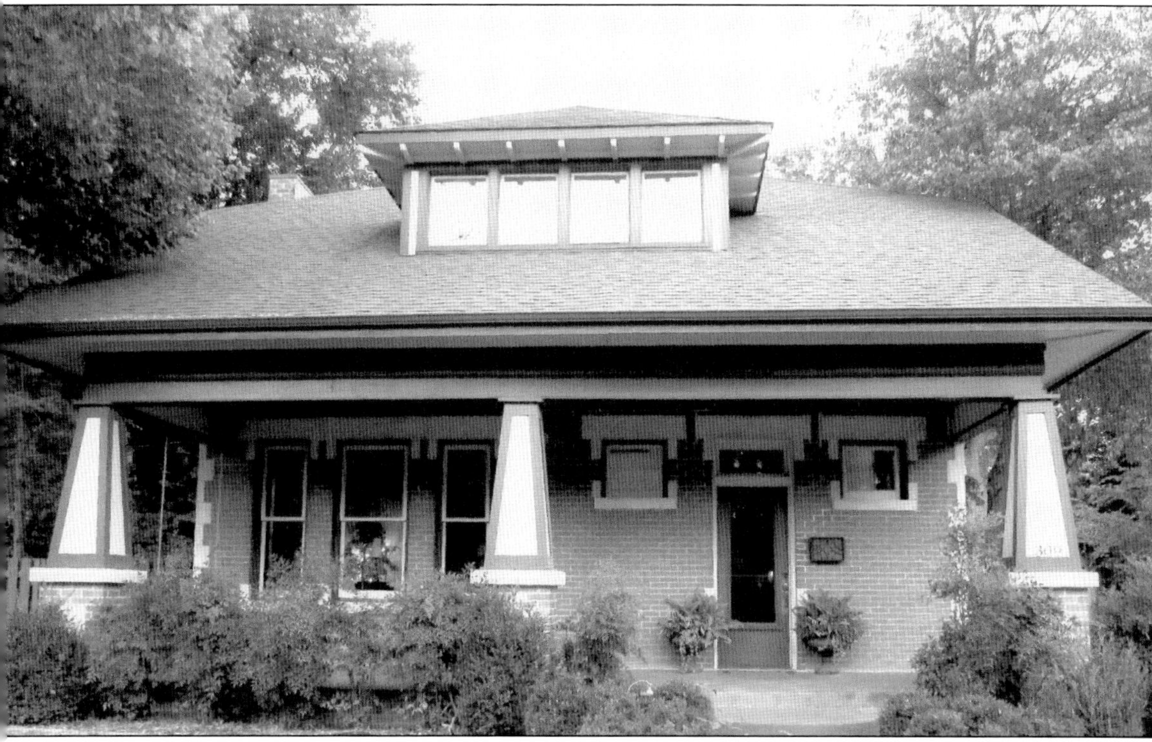

THE JACKSON HOUSE. This house is remembered by some older citizens as the residence of Dr. J. L. Jackson, who practiced medicine in Bentonville. The present owners, Mike and Kathleen Spivey, have carefully preserved the lovely home that was built by Lon Andrew Pace, a contractor who also built the Old Benton County Jail, the Massey Hotel, and the Benton County Bank building. (Courtesy of the author.)

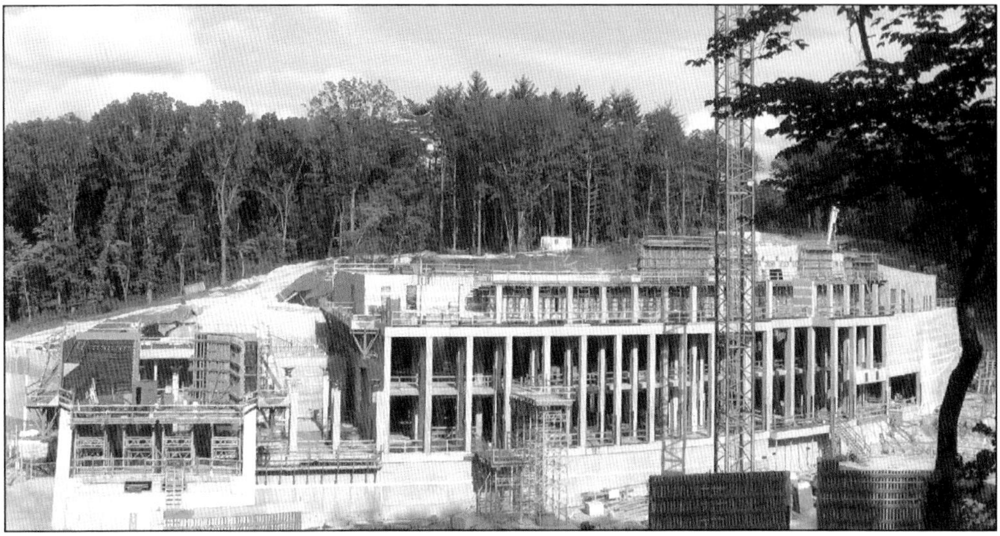

Crystal Bridges Museum of American Art. The most exciting building project in the history of Bentonville began in October 2006. The construction of Crystal Bridges Museum of American Art is underway on property surrounded by walkways and bike trails that connect it to the town square. An observation deck provides visitors with a unique perspective of the project as well as a great place to meet friends and neighbors during morning and evening walks. When completed, this beautiful facility will house a collection of American art and will offer a vast array of educational and entertainment opportunities for everyone. The project is a gift from Alice Walton and the Walton family. (Courtesy of the author.)

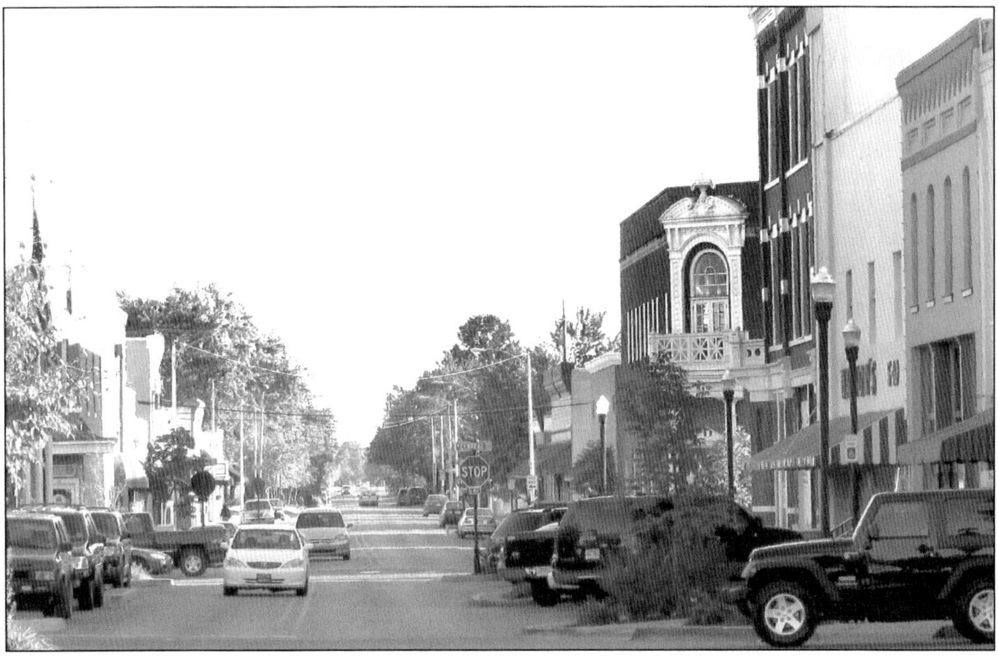

Downtown Bentonville Today. This view is looking south down Main Street, where it intersects with Central Avenue, on a quiet Sunday afternoon; however, a high number of cars and pedestrians can generally be expected during business hours. Main Street and Central Avenue are two of the oldest roadways in northwest Arkansas. (Courtesy of the author.)

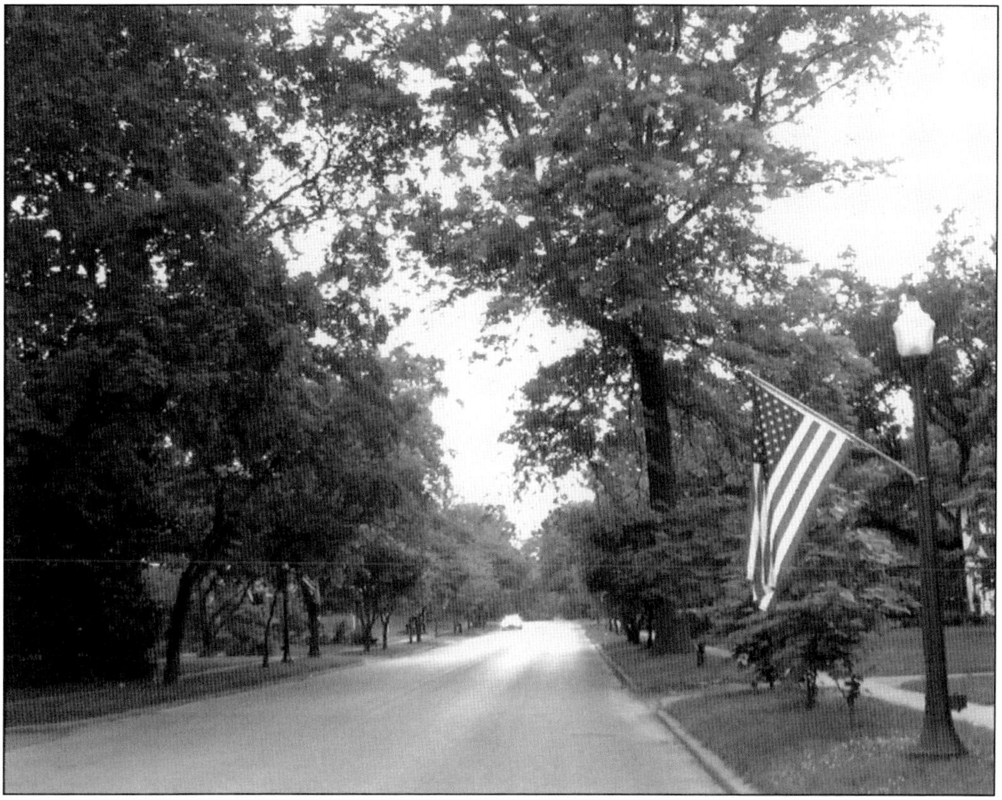

West Central Avenue. A beautiful tree-lined street through one of the oldest affluent Bentonville neighborhoods was once known as "Silk Stocking Row," because only the wealthy could afford to wear expensive silk hose. In the spring, the redbud trees bloom, and in the fall, the oak and maple trees turn color up and down the avenue. (Courtesy of the author.)

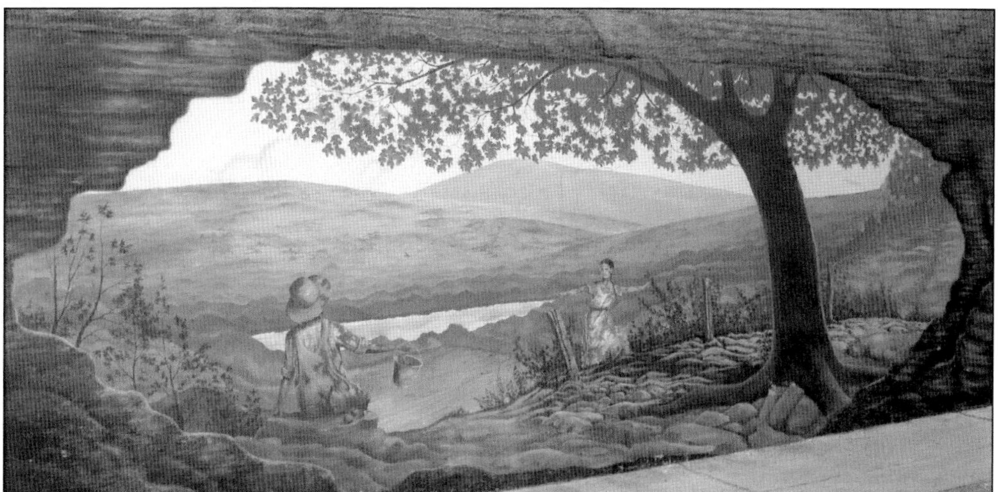

Townzen Mural of History. Bentonville artist Randy Townzen painted this mural for the Arkansas sesquicentennial in 1986. Townzen included many hidden objects that symbolize history and add a fun interactive element to the public mural. Many schoolchildren and teachers visit the mural each year during their study of Arkansas history. (Courtesy of the author.)

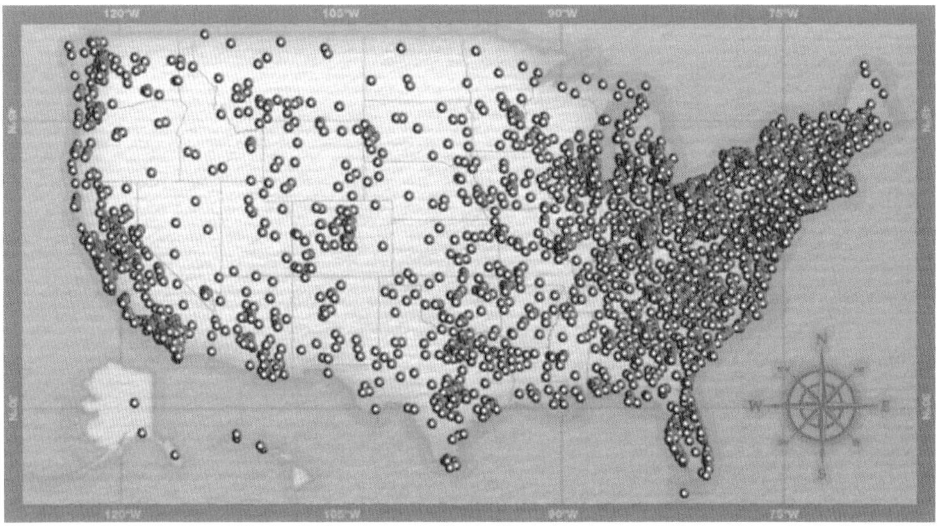